Praise f

FLOWING
ZEN

"Anthony is by far the best teacher for beginners."

—Dr. Claire Holland, MD

"I love Anthony's approach to self-healing,
and I refer all of my patients to him."

—Dr. Craig Brown, MD

"Anthony has a no-nonsense approach to teaching
the art of qigong. He gets results. Period."

—Dr. Russel Kennedy, MD

FLOWING
ZEN

ANTHONY KORAHAIS

FLOWING ZEN

FINDING TRUE HEALING WITH
QIGONG

Paperback ISBN: 9781737447009
eBook ISBN: 9781737447016

OCC011010 BODY, MIND & SPIRIT / Healing / Energy (Qigong, Reiki, Polarity)
HEA052000 HEALTH & FITNESS / Tai Chi
OCC010000 BODY, MIND & SPIRIT / Mindfulness & Meditation

Cover design by Jennifer Stimson
Edited by Melissa Miller
Typeset by Kaitlin Barwick

www.flowingzen.com

CONTENTS

FOREWORD
By Eric B. Robins, MD

Eric, you are getting by on 3 percent." These words came from Dr. C., a prominent bioenergetics psychologist. I went to see him in 1997, having completely collapsed after twenty years of severe chronic fatigue syndrome and brain fog. I felt stuck in every single area of my life. Bioenergetics is the study of the interface between emotions and energy in the body, and in this way Dr. C. was uniquely qualified to make that assessment. In other words, 97 percent of my life force was being bound up in my musculature, physiology, and energetic pathways, and it wasn't readily available in any way that would provide an optimal quality of life.

After getting little relief by following the suggestions of my physician, I started to look outside the box for answers. At one point early on, I studied with a renowned energy teacher. He was very well intentioned, kind, and powerful, but his techniques forced open too many energetic pathways too quickly, which worsened my physical condition and caused emotional and mental upheaval. Thus began a decades-long exploration to understand and remedy those factors that were making me sick, including the study of hypnosis, energy healing, neuro-linguistic programming (NLP), meridian tapping, sitting meditation, binaural beat technology, somatic psychology, and Tension & Trauma Releasing Exercises (TRE). Along the way, I was able to achieve substantial healing in terms of energy levels, cognitive function, emotional landscape and my ability to enjoy life.

Motivated and inspired by my success, I began accepting referrals involving chronic pelvic pain and functional illnesses. All of this was covered by my health care organization. Many of the patients had already been through the gamut of treatments offered by conventional allopathic medicine but were still sick and suffering. Often, patients like this require a different healing model, ideally one that activates their own innate healing resources.

Treating these types of patients requires one to make some distinctions about health and healing which are pertinent to the book you now hold in your hands. The first is that when we experience events in our lives that are stressful, terrifying, or too overwhelming to deal with at the time, we will lock these memories and emotions into our muscles and fascia. This happens automatically as a protective mechanism in order to keep these memories and emotions from coming up to conscious awareness and causing us terrible pain and anxiety. Wilhelm Reich referred to this as muscular "armoring," and it is one major way that memories are repressed. The process uses up a tremendous amount of our bandwidth (even though we may not be aware of it).

The second distinction is that chronically constricted and armored myofascia causes blockage of energy pathways and meridians in the body and can leave us exhausted and depleted.

Third, serious stressors, particularly those that occur in early childhood, can substantially disrupt our physiology for years or decades. As a result of stressful life events, we can essentially be put into a chronic fight-flight-freeze stress physiology that either stays on autopilot or is easily triggered. And even though we say in common parlance, "The body tends to heal itself," it doesn't heal particularly well when locked in a chronic stress state.

In fact, over 80 percent of patients who go to a primary care physician have some sort of functional disorder. These are medical conditions in which symptoms are caused by impaired *functioning* of bodily processes, but where nothing obvious or pathologic is picked up on physical examination, labs, or X-rays. Examples of this include hypertension, fatigue, irritable bowel syndrome, headaches, asthma, insomnia, overactive bladder, and many cases of chronic pain. In my experience, most functional disorders occur in folks whose physiology is out of whack due to the above factors.

With all of this as a backdrop, a few years ago I was doing an internet search and came across a blog post entitled "The Real Truth about the Small Universe Qigong," written by Sifu Anthony Korahais. It was one of the most brilliant things I have ever read because it explained what had been going on with me for decades. No one else had been able to fully explain this to me.

Here was someone who understood the intricate interplay of energy and emotion, not just intellectually, but at a rare experiential level. I was intrigued enough to read more of his blogs, and eventually signed up to participate in several of his online classes, including a couple of year-long courses. Sifu Anthony is a man of integrity, intelligence, clarity, and love. He cares deeply for his students and their wellbeing. He has a wealth of knowledge and experience, having taught qigong to thousands of students since 2005. When you look at him, you can appreciate an unmistakable light in his eyes and a healthy glow from his body demonstrating that he is an embodiment of that which he teaches.

This book starts with an intimate memoir of Sifu Anthony's struggles with depression and back pain, and his search for healing that was eventually achieved with qigong. The writing throughout is superb with a touch of satire, an homage to his Ivy League pedigree. He gives a captivating overview of the history of qigong to put things into context, and also provides a solid yet simplified understanding of Classical Chinese Medicine with regard to how it relates to qigong.

Sifu Anthony understands healing at profound depths and is able to integrate and synthesize information across multiple fields of study in this book. He understands suffering from the perspective of one who struggled with it (physically and emotionally) for years, and this makes him exceptionally compassionate. He explains energetic and kundalini deviations and how to address them. He grasps the role of constricted myofascia and stress physiology in blocking energy flow, impeding bodily function, and impairing healing; and he explains how qigong can address all of these facets. He is eminently capable of sifting through the qigong knowledge base in order to show students what things are truly important in advancing their practice. He does this by examining ancient secrets through the lens of modern scientific advances, and then tosses unnecessary dogma and doctrine out the window.

The teaching stories and information in this book, if taken to heart, are priceless, and can save you years or decades of work. You will have access to some bonuses that include several qigong exercises and guided meditations. These meditations, according to many of his students, contain a transformative vibrational quality that simply must be experienced.

Qigong is a powerful modality that empowers people and gives them hope. Through its regular practice, it shifts both your body and mind to a state where they can begin to heal. For this reason, qigong is one of those things I'd encourage you to be doing to either prevent the need for doctor's visits or to require far fewer of them. Godspeed!

ERIC B. ROBINS, MD
Urologist and Chronic Pelvic Pain Specialist
Coauthor, *Your Hands Can Heal You* and *The Power of Prana*

INTRODUCTION

I never set out to become an expert in an ancient Chinese self-healing art. I was young and fit when I discovered qigong, but I was also drowning in pain and suffering. Back then, my only goal was to heal myself. Qigong was simply a lifeline, a way for me to keep my head above water.

We all want to heal. Almost everyone today is dealing with some sort of pain. That pain might be physical, like chronic low back pain, or it might be mental-emotional pain, like depression or anxiety. Either way, it's a form of suffering.

In my case, I had both kinds of pain, physical and emotional. I had severe low back pain—and I also had severe depression. I was suffering, and I was desperate for a way out.

In the West, we like to separate the mind from the body. We like to distinguish physical pain from other forms of pain. We like to put things in neat little boxes.

On the other hand, Eastern thought doesn't separate mind and body into tidy categories. It mixes and swirls the two, like pouring milk into black coffee. Mind and body are unified and inseparable. There are no neat little boxes.

I fell in love with qigong because it promised a comprehensive solution to my suffering, whether it was physical or mental. And qigong delivered on that promise.

In fact, it did more than just help me to relieve back pain and depression. It brought healing on levels I didn't even know existed.

Of course, qigong is not the only solution to suffering. Many wonderful healing arts are out there. Maybe you've tried a few. If so, I hope they brought you some relief.

However, there's a reason why you're reading this book. If you're like me, then you want to take charge of your own healing destiny. Healing modalities like acupuncture and chiropractic are wonderful, but they still leave you in someone else's hands. When it comes to healing yourself, qigong is hard to beat, and that's precisely why we are drawn to it.

For me and so many of my students, finding qigong was like coming home. I feel like I was born to practice this art—not because I have some innate talent for it (I don't), but because the shoe just fits. Maybe the qigong shoe will fit you too. Maybe you'll also feel like you're coming home. This book is my sincere attempt to help you to fall in love with this art the way that I and many of my students have.

Or maybe you've been practicing qigong for years. That's wonderful! In that case, my goal is to help you to fall in love all over again, and perhaps deeper than you ever thought possible.

This book is half memoir and half manifesto.

First, I share my healing story so that you can see qigong through my eyes. I want you to understand how much qigong healed me, and also thousands of my students. That's why I've written much of this book as a memoir.

You also need to know the nitty-gritty secrets to healing with qigong. That's why some of this book is written as a manifesto. Whether you are new to qigong or you already have bunches of experience, this book will show you what really matters when it comes to self-healing.

Are you ready to fall in love with qigong?

What This Book Is Not

I want to be clear, right from the beginning, what this book is not.

When I was buying qigong books by the bushel back in the 1990s, the internet was still in its infancy. Back then, qigong books had lots of pictures and drawings because that's what people wanted. After all, you couldn't just google qigong or go on YouTube. (Fun facts: Google was created in 1998, and YouTube was created in 2005.)

I still have a qigong book with tiny images in the lower right corner. The idea is to flip the pages with your thumb and watch the images move, like an old motion picture.

Today, there are better ways to teach qigong. The internet has matured, and online learning is taking the world by storm.

I began teaching online in 2013. By 2016, I saw the writing on the wall and closed my brick-and-mortar qigong studio. I now teach 95 percent online (though I still do an annual qigong retreat in the mountains of Costa Rica). Instead of having hundreds of students in a small college town in Florida, I now have thousands of online students from forty-eight different countries.

Rather than put a bunch of pictures or drawings in this book, I will refer you to my website where you can learn lots of qigong— totally for free. Throughout this book, I will encourage you to stop reading, go to the website, and grab your free book bonuses. This is a big improvement over asking you to flip images with your thumb.

Qigong can change your life, but only if you act. Even if there were lots of pictures in this book, you would still need to get up and do the exercises. If you're going to get up, then you might as well go to my website where you can learn from the videos. While you're there, you can also take advantage of some guided meditations, which people absolutely love.

You will need to enter your email address so that I can send you the videos and other bonuses. If you like, I'll also send you my newest blog posts, a monthly newsletter with the latest qigong news (including the latest research), as well as information about my paid programs. All of this is free. We have a vibrant online community, and I hope you'll join us.

If you want a book with endless pictures of various qigong postures, then this ain't it. But if you want to really get your healing juices flowing, if you want to know what truly matters in qigong, or if you've tried qigong before but didn't get the results you desired—then this book is for you.

Obviously, this book is also for you if you are one of the twenty-thousand-plus people who have learned from me online. Hi, everyone!

CHAPTER 1
Saving Lives, Starting with My Own

People say that my enthusiasm for qigong is contagious. I love this compliment, and I also love infecting people with a passion for qigong. I hope that you catch it as you read this book!

But my enthusiasm for qigong is not all rainbows and unicorns. My passion comes from deep suffering and struggle. Before we dive into the practice and philosophy of qigong, I'd like to tell you about how qigong saved my life.

I want to tell you this story because you need to know that everything I do—my writing, teaching, and daily qigong practice—is my way of showing gratitude for the art that was my salvation. If you're going to learn from me, whether it's from a book, at a retreat, or online, then you need to understand where I'm coming from.

You also need to know, right from the beginning, that I'm not some guru on a mountain top. I'm perfectly human, not perfectly enlightened.

And this is critical for you to understand, not only because it will help you to avoid the pitfalls of the "guru trap" but also because it will show you that anyone can achieve remarkable results with qigong. If I can do it, then you can too.

Here's how my journey began.

From Ivy League to Utter Darkness

I was a sophomore at Columbia University when I began my descent into darkness. On paper, I was living the dream. I was attending an Ivy League college, I was on the dean's list, and my future was bright.

I mention Columbia here for a reason, and it's not to brag. Okay, maybe I'm also a teensy bit proud of my Alma Mater, but as you'll see in a moment, Columbia plays an important role in the story.

I'm working up the courage to tell you the intimate details about my life-or-death battle against a terrible illness. But before I do that, before I share these deep and personal details, I'd like you to understand something. If I don't set the record straight right from the beginning, I'm afraid you'll get the wrong message from this book.

Maybe you already know my story. Maybe you know that the illness I battled was called major depressive disorder (MDD), also known simply as "depression." But did you know that many people still believe that clinical depression is a character flaw rather than an illness?

And you know what? I believed the same thing for years. I thought I really *was* weak. It's bad enough to suffer from a devastating, life-threatening illness. It's worse when friends and family think you're just a weakling. And it's worse still when you start to believe them! That's how depression works. It tunnels into your mind like a termite and then weakens your foundation.

I want you to know that, before the darkness of MDD engulfed me, I was a talented young man with a bright future. I want you to know that I worked my ass off to get accepted into Columbia. In high school, I studied hard, played soccer and tennis, was an editor for the school newspaper, took AP classes, and even played violin in the Kennedy Center with the All-National Orchestra.

I want you to know this now, right at the beginning of our journey together: I am not weak. Remember this as you listen to my story.

Depression Kills, Qigong Saves

Let's jump ahead in time for a minute. Once, early in my career as a qigong teacher, I was at a local health fair in a small college town in Florida. I was in my thirties, and I was excited to be sharing the art that had transformed my life in so many ways. At my little booth, I was chatting with a woman who was in her fifties. We'll call her Ruth.

I was telling Ruth how qigong had saved my life.

"Was it cancer?" she interrupted.

"No," I said. "My battle was with major depressive disorder and—"

She rolled her eyes and then interrupted again. "Oh, I thought it was something serious." Then she put down my brochure and walked away.

Ouch! This woman literally rolled her eyes at my illness! Luckily, I was used to it by then. Depressives deal with this stuff all the time, so it didn't really faze me. Over the years, I've learned to just smile at comments like these. As a wise man once said: forgive them, for they know not what they do.

I wasn't angry at Ruth because I recognized that her statement came from ignorance and misunderstanding. Unfortunately, when it comes to MDD, there's a lot of that going around. Here's the first thing you need to know about MDD: It kills.

MDD is a specific type of depression. It's also called major depression, clinical depression, unipolar depression, or most commonly, just depression. Suicide is a top ten killer in the US and 60 percent of those deaths are related to depression.[1] In other words, depression kills more Americans every year than AIDS or leukemia.[2] And this is not just limited to the United States. The World Health

Organization (WHO) says that more than 264 million people are battling depression worldwide, contributing greatly to "the global burden of disease."[3]

Some of you may be surprised by these stats. You don't hear much about depression being a fatal disease, and this is part of the problem. When someone dies from depression, we just call it suicide—but that ignores the actual underlying illness that led to their death. The result of this is a profound lack of empathy for depressives. Ruth, the woman who rolled her eyes, is just one of millions who think this way.

We don't treat other illnesses like this. For example, we automatically give empathy to someone battling cancer. We bring her casseroles, hold her hand, and listen to her with empathy and care.

But with depression, it's the opposite. There are no casseroles. There is little to no empathy. If anything, people say terrible things to depressives. Here are some of the things that people have said over the years:

"Pull yourself together!"
"You just need a good kick in the ass."
"It's all in your head. Think positive thoughts!"
"Grow up and stop feeling sorry for yourself."
"You've got so many things to be thankful for!"
"Take [insert holistic remedy]. That's what I always do when I'm sad."

If you've battled depression before, then these statements will be familiar to you. I know you've heard terrible things too. I'm sorry that happened to you.

But why is this problem so pervasive? If you said any of those statements to someone battling cancer, we would call you a heartless monster. Cancer is all in the head? What the hell?!? Screw you!!

Let me be clear. I'm not saying that MDD is the same as cancer, because it's not. I am, however, saying that the way we treat depressives is awful. If we understood this fact, and if we changed how we treated them, then we could save thousands, perhaps even millions of lives.

And, by the way, asking people to be more empathetic toward depressives doesn't mean we need to be less empathetic toward cancer survivors, or folks with other painful or debilitating illnesses. Empathy is not a zero-sum game.

Here's one final statistic before I go on with my story. Depression is the second leading cause of death for fifteen-to-twenty-nine-year-olds.[4] The first leading cause of death is motor vehicle accidents. In other words, depression is the leading medical cause of death for fifteen-to-twenty-nine-year-olds.

I was twenty-two when I graduated from Columbia. In other words, I was right in the danger zone. Other than a motor vehicle accident, depression was statistically the most likely way for me to die young.

I didn't know this at the time, of course. I thought everyone had suicidal thoughts and that it was normal to think about filling your backpack with dumbbell plates and then jumping off the George Washington Bridge. I thought everyone my age googled (actually, it was Altavista back then) the correct way to slit your wrists with a razor blade.

It's also worth mentioning that the rate of suicide at Ivy League universities is significantly higher than normal. For example, at Harvard, the incidence is twice the national rate.[5] And at Princeton, 35 percent of students say that they developed a mental health issue while there.[6] This makes sense because the pressure at Columbia was intense.

Here's the point: It's not melodramatic to say that qigong saved my life. I was truly in mortal danger in my twenties. I was at a college that has statistically higher rates of suicide and I was battling an illness that kills more twenty-somethings than anything else. It was only years later that I recognized the real danger that I was in. I was metaphorically walking along the edge of a cliff in utter darkness, and I easily could have fallen. And if

I'm being brutally honest, I think I would have fallen—if not for qigong.

More Than Depression

So far, we've talked in depth about depression, but that's not what this book is really about. If you don't relate to depression, that's okay. In the end, we're really talking about the art of self-healing.

I'm forever grateful for how qigong helped me with depression. Not only that, it also helped me overcome chronic fatigue, anxiety, a weak immune system, a congenital heart murmur, and severe low-back pain. And that's just my own personal success with qigong. My students have seen benefits with an amazing variety of stubborn health problems: digestive disorders, auto-immune issues, fibromyalgia, and multiple sclerosis, to name just a few.

Sometimes, qigong helps with complex and confusing problems. For example, here's William's story.

Success Story: William

William is a veteran of Operation Iraqi Freedom (2007–2008). He came to me because of issues related to toxic exposure from burn pits in Iraq. Using jet fuel, they would toss everything from generic trash to medical waste into the pits for burning. As a result of that exposure, William required six different biopsies and developed chronic obstructive pulmonary disease (COPD). On top of that, because of a long career as a Cavalry Scout hauling heavy rucksacks on difficult terrain all over the world, he developed significant bone spurs on both heels.

In 2015 and 2017, William had surgeries to correct the bone spurs, a process that involved detaching his Achilles tendons, shaving down the heel bones, and then reattaching the tendons. The surgeries took a toll on William, and he couldn't bounce back quickly. As a result, he gained weight, developed sleep apnea, and had a list of several other health problems.

William started learning from me in June 2020. Within six months, he saw tremendous progress. His range of motion in both Achilles tendons improved, and he can now go up and down stairs like he used to. He can also walk for extended periods and distances. As a result of increased mobility, William dropped twenty pounds and is on course to continue improving his health.

Here's what William had to say about qigong:

> "Qigong gave me the tools to take back control of my own situation when nothing else was working for me. I am on the board of directors for a nonprofit veteran organization that helps other veterans dealing with issues of military related toxic exposure illnesses and we want to make this amazing healing modality available to our constituents as well. We're spinning up a new program of holistic health practices and qigong has a place front and center of this effort."

We'll talk more later about the benefits of qigong, including those that have been proven scientifically. For now, just know that the benefits are broad.

When Pain Is a Blessing

Whether or not you identify with depression, I'm betting that the topic of pain is of interest to you. Often, we just learn to accept our pain as part of normal life. The back pain in the morning, the neck pain at work, the knee pain when it rains—we think all of this is normal. But it's not. Normal means that you are free from chronic pain.

In the twenty-first century, few people are normal. Only a tiny percentage of people are 100 percent pain free. In my studio, there were students as young as eighteen who were in chronic pain. Age doesn't matter as much as you might think.

We'll talk more about chronic pain later and discuss why qigong is such a good solution, but for now I want to ask you to do something strange: I want you to be grateful for your chronic pain. Yes, you read that right. I want you to be grateful that you have chronic pain in your body. One day, you'll look back at your chronic pain and say, "Thank you!"

That's exactly what happened to me. Pain was a blessing in disguise. It is what originally led me to qigong.

I love books. I loved them in high school and loved them in college. And if it's possible, I love them even more today.

In New York City back in the 1990s, Barnes & Noble started opening superstores. Normally, bookstores in Manhattan were small because of the high real estate prices. But these Barnes & Noble superstores were mind-blowing in size.

I remember the first time I went to a Barnes & Noble super-store. It was on the Upper West Side, and the store took up almost an entire city block. Imagine walking into a cathedral for the first time after only ever seeing small, local churches. That's what this felt like.

At this particular store, they even let you sit and browse the books while sipping coffee in the Barnes & Noble cafe! Zillions of books *and* coffee? Yes, please!

This bookstore was four subway stops away from my dorm room at Columbia, and it was my favorite hangout. I spent count-less hours there, browsing the aisles, grabbing a few interesting books, and then reading them while sipping coffee in the cafe. As a poor college student, I couldn't buy all the books that I wanted! I did, however, buy a lot of books from them—especially martial arts books.

Remember, this was in the early days of the internet. You couldn't just go to YouTube and watch endless videos about various martial arts. If you wanted to learn more about, say, Wing Chun

Kung Fu, then books were the way to go. And this Barnes & Noble had one of the largest martial arts selections I had ever seen. There were books on every martial art you could imagine, from Aikido to Zulu Stick Fighting.

I devoured these books. I mainly read about karate because that was my background. I was proud of my black belt and my art! But I also read about things like aikido, the martial art of nonviolence. I read about Krav Maga, a brutal self-defense system created by Israeli special forces. And I read about Bruce Lee and how he mixed ideas from kung fu with Western boxing.

And one day, I started to read about tai chi. I had heard about tai chi, of course. I had seen elderly Chinese people practicing it at dawn in Central Park. Tai chi is a style of kung fu and is considered one of the "soft" martial arts from China. These "soft" arts rely not on physical strength but rather on internal strength.

Like most New Yorkers, I thought that tai chi was just calisthenics for old people. I actually remember looking over my shoulder as I pulled a tai chi book from the shelf, afraid that one of my karate buddies would catch me reading it. But I had a good reason to be browsing tai chi books.

You see, my back was killing me. I was twenty-four and had recently earned a black belt in karate. I was training hard, averaging about two or three hours per day, but wanted to train harder. I was hardcore! Bring it on!

But my back pain wouldn't let me be hardcore, and the more I practiced, the worse it got. I tried resting, but that didn't really help. Besides, I'm no good at resting. I also tried yoga, but that seemed to make it worse.

Maybe a little tai chi would help my back, I thought. Tai chi had a reputation for being a healing art, so I figured I could give it a try. A little reading certainly couldn't hurt.

And so I started looking for tai chi books to help with my back pain. And thank God, because I probably wouldn't have gone looking for solutions to depression until it was too late. I just wasn't ready to admit that I was depressed.

It's not easy to learn tai chi from a book. Honestly, I don't recommend it. However, because of my experience with karate, I was able to make sense of the pictures. A few months later, I found a tai chi video at a friend's house. Once I saw the moves in action, I was able to mimic them.

So that's how I began tai chi. But what about qigong? As is often the case in the West, tai chi was the gateway to qigong.

The Monk in the Cave

I was reading one of my new tai chi books, and it kept mentioning something called "chi kung." In the 1990s, that was the most common spelling. We'll talk more about the different spellings later, but for now just know that all of them refer to the same art, i.e., qigong.

I had never heard about qigong (or chi kung) before and was instantly fascinated. Or maybe infatuated is a better word. Do you believe in love at first sight? Well, that's what happened. I fell in love with qigong after reading just a few paragraphs.

In the history section of that tai chi book (*Tai Chi: The Supreme Ultimate* by Lawrence Galante, if you're curious), there's a story about a man named Bodhidharma. This Buddhist monk left his home in India, crossed the highest mountain range in the world on foot, and then settled down at a small temple in China called Shaolin.

I already knew about the Shaolin Temple having grown up watching Saturday-morning kung fu shows. In those shows, the Shaolin Temple was a popular theme. I had also heard about Bodhidharma, but I knew him as the founder of Zen. I had no idea that Bodhidharma was connected to the Shaolin Temple, or even that the temple was connected to Zen.

The book explained how Bodhidharma arrived at the Shaolin Temple in the sixth century AD. His mission was to teach the monks his new, more modern form of Buddhism, what would later be called Zen (Chan or 禪 in Chinese). But legend has it that he found the monks too weak and sickly for the rigors of seated Zen meditation.[7]

Bodhidharma believed that the body and mind were united, much like the ancient Roman philosophy of a healthy mind in a healthy body (*mens sana in corpore sano*). He recognized that the monks were unbalanced, and that they needed something to make their minds and bodies stronger and healthier.

As the story goes, Bodhidharma retreated to a cave, which incidentally is now a tourist attraction. He stayed there, meditating and practicing in order to find a solution. Nine years later, he emerged with a solution in the form of three sets of exercises.

1. The Eighteen Hands of the Luohans (十八羅漢手, shiba luohan shou)
2. The Sinew Changing Classic (易筋經, yi jin jing)
3. The Bone Marrow Washing Exercises (洗髓经, xi sui jing)

These three sets are now famous forms of Shaolin Qigong. In fact, I still practice and teach all three today.

(By the way, the qigong that I teach is 100 percent nonreligious. We'll discuss the differences between Buddhist and Taoist Qigong later, and why anyone can practice these arts regardless of their religious background, or lack thereof.)

Today, Bodhidharma is recognized as the founder of Zen Buddhism, the founder of Shaolin Qigong, and also the founder of Shaolin Kung Fu! He was a busy guy![8] In retrospect, I'm lucky to have found all this information in a tai chi book. Although it's likely that tai chi traces back to the Shaolin Temple one way or another, most tai chi books don't talk about Bodhidharma. It's good that this one did because I'm a sucker for a good story, and after reading it, I was hooked. This put me on a mission to find out more about this qigong thing and that Bodhidharma dude.

My Trek to China(town)

Have you ever noticed that when you're getting ready to buy a new car, you suddenly start seeing Honda Civics everywhere on the street? There's a good explanation for this, and it has to do with the Reticular Activating System (RAS). The RAS is an interesting quirk of the brain. Once you put your attention onto a subject, your brain starts to home in. As a result, you start to notice the topic of interest (i.e., Honda Civics) everywhere.

Reading about Bodhidharma and qigong activated my RAS. Suddenly, I started seeing qigong everywhere. Well, not quite everywhere, but definitely in bookstores!

After reading all the books I could find on tai chi, I still wasn't satisfied. Most of the tai chi books hardly even mentioned qigong. As you'll learn later, tai chi and qigong are inseparable, but back then, tai chi authors either didn't know about qigong or didn't want to talk about it. I wasn't going to find my answers in tai chi books, so I started searching for books on qigong. I located a few in Barnes & Nobles, but not many.

One thing I love about New York City is that, for the price of a subway token, you can go anywhere in the city. So I bought a token (yes, we still had metal tokens back then) and journeyed down to Chinatown. This was a trek because I lived on the opposite end of Manhattan; with transfers and stops, it probably took ninety minutes to get there. But it was worth it because New York's Chinatown had several specialty bookstores.

It was at one of these bookstores that I found my holy grail—three books entirely devoted to the subject of qigong. I bought all three of them and probably finished reading two on the subway ride back home. In one of these books was a qigong exercise called Lifting the Sky. As soon as I got home, I started practicing it. I view this as one of the best qigong exercises ever created, and that's why you'll learn it in the book bonuses.

At first, I didn't know the history of this exercise. It just looked cool, and I wanted to try it. I later learned that this exercise is the first of the Eighteen Luohan Hands, one of the three qigong sets taught by Bodhidharma. Through fifteen hundred years of history, somehow this amazing exercise had come all the way from the Shaolin Temple to my apartment in New York City.

Unlike the more complex tai chi exercises I had learned from books and videos, Lifting the Sky was, and still is, a simple technique. More importantly, it felt good. *Really* good. You'll get to experience this yourself when you try it. (Maybe you should take a break and go check out the bonuses now!)

The book recommended twenty to thirty repetitions of Lifting the Sky without worrying too much about the form. It suggested that I focus on my breathing instead of my body, so that's what I did. And it was a revelation.

This was my first real experience with moving meditation, and I was smitten. Instead of moving from one complicated tai chi move to the next, I just did Lifting the Sky over and over. I enjoyed my breathing, and I enjoyed the meditative flow. It was a powerful experience for me. I had found my way home.

Spending My Last Dime

After experiencing qigong and tai chi for myself, I knew it was time to find a teacher. I went to a few classes in the NY area, but felt underwhelmed. My experience in those classes was not what I had read about, and so I started contacting the authors of those books.

In the United States, we generally don't show our teachers enough respect. So when these Asian authors received a respectful, well-edited email from a thoughtful young American, they took notice. Within weeks, I received encouraging replies from several teachers. I was thrilled.

One reply in particular gave me a burst of hope. Grandmaster Liu, the author of one of my favorite qigong books, not only replied to my email but also invited me to a qigong conference in San Francisco that he would be attending.

The problem was, I had almost no money. I was living at my parents' house on Long Island and I was barely functional because of my depressive episodes. But after his encouraging email, I decided then and there that I would find a way to go meet him in San Francisco.

And so I got a job at the local Starbucks. I still remember the manager's confused expression as she interviewed me. "You graduated from Columbia but you want to work here?" she said. I probably should have left that detail off my application, but I'm honest to a fault.

"I'm going through a rough patch," I said to her, and I saw a flash of understanding in her eyes. Perhaps she was a fellow depressive because she asked no further questions and hired me on the spot. I started mixing coffee drinks the very next day.

Within a few months, I had saved enough money for a flight to San Francisco plus the cost of the qigong conference. But that was it. I barely had enough money for food, let alone a hotel.

Luckily, I had a good friend living in San Francisco, so I did some couch surfing. As a result, I was able to attend the qigong conference in November 1997. I attended Grandmaster Liu's qigong class, as well as a few classes by other well-known qigong teachers. It was an amazing weekend.

Grandmaster Liu also gave me private Shaolin Kung Fu lessons in the evenings. Why kung fu? As I'll explain later, kung fu masters have been the stewards of qigong for centuries, and Grandmaster Liu was one of these stewards.

In addition to his book on qigong, Grandmaster Liu had written a book on kung fu. Before traveling to San Francisco to meet him, I learned the Shaolin Five Animal Kung Fu form from this book, partially for fun, but also because I wanted to impress him.

This wasn't easy. All I had were line drawings and descriptions from the book. With painstaking effort, I pieced together a complex kung fu form. Grandmaster Liu was so impressed when he saw it that he offered to teach me kung fu for free.

So every evening I had private kung fu lessons with Grandmaster Liu. But there was qigong hidden in the kung fu lessons too. As I'll explain, it's often hard to separate the qigong from the kung fu (and vice versa). For example, he taught me all four sequences of One Finger Shooting Zen, a form of qigong typically reserved for kung fu disciples.

I had learned One Finger Zen from his books, but only the first sequence, and even that was a mess. In fact, I didn't even know there were more sequences! We'll talk more later about the tradition of secrecy in Chinese culture, but this is one of many examples. As a reward for my dedication, Grandmaster Liu taught me the additional secrets of One Finger Zen.

By the end of my time with Grandmaster Liu, I had learned many powerful qigong secrets, along with many kung fu secrets. Also, I could barely walk. I remember moaning for days on my friend's couch after the conference. The kung fu training was intense! I was in pretty good shape, but I could barely keep up with the fifty-three-year-old Grandmaster Liu!

Holy SH!T, I'm Depressed!

After learning all these qigong secrets, I practiced daily and lived happily ever after . . . right? That might make for a better story, but unfortunately, while I was discovering qigong, I was also descending into a spiral of depression. As a result, I made the most common mistake when it comes to getting results with qigong: I stopped practicing.

One of my greatest strengths as a teacher is that I've made all the mistakes that you are likely to make with qigong, and then some. This means that I know what you're going through, and I can give you the support and empathy you need. It also means that your excuses won't work! Ha!

My students also have something I didn't have—a teacher who can relate. Most of my teachers did not understand my struggle simply because they didn't struggle the way that I did. In the Asian tradition, students who struggle to practice simply get left behind. The ones who eventually become teachers are often the ones who didn't struggle. For people battling depression, this can be downright dangerous. Qigong works wonders for mental health challenges, but only if the teacher understands the struggle. Otherwise, qigong can actually make mental health issues worse by causing the student to feel ashamed. For example, in my first qigong class with Grandmaster Liu, he told another student that his depression would be gone in six weeks. I didn't mention my depression to him because I still hadn't fully acknowledged it myself. But I heard what he said to this student and quietly took note.

I practiced diligently for two months after meeting Grandmaster Liu, and although I definitely made progress during that time, I was nowhere near cured. This made me feel like a failure. In retrospect, I now know that Grandmaster Liu's expectations were unreasonable. He just didn't understand depression. It was irresponsible of him to offer a cure in just six weeks. Qigong is powerful, but it is not a panacea. Healing takes time, even with qigong.

I'm also to blame, of course. Part of the problem was that, at the time, I hadn't acknowledged my depression. The truth is that I was depressive for nearly a decade before I acknowledged it for what it was. Since the age of sixteen, I've kept a journal of my thoughts and ideas. I call it my little book of philosophy, a title likely influenced by my Greek DNA.

In those journal entries, there are countless references to "my dark demon." Years later, when I mentioned some of these passages to a clinical psychologist, she said that they were pretty clear signs of adolescent depression.

By the time I was in my mid-twenties, I could no longer deny that the "dark demon" mentioned in my journals was simply a poetic description of major depression. But admitting this fact wasn't easy, despite the signs. I remember doing an online search for "depression." At the time, I couldn't even afford a computer, so I arranged some time alone at a friend's computer to do some research.

I found plenty of information about depression, and I read it with both interest and trepidation. I also found several links to online assessments for depression. I remember clicking one of those links and thinking that it would prove that I'm not depressive. *I'm just a failure,* I thought. *I'm not really depressed.*

The first assessment told me that I was likely in a depressive episode and that I should seek immediate medical attention.

Meh, I thought. *It's just a stupid online test. I'm not depressed.*

So I logged off and swept the idea under the carpet. But over the next few days, that test result nagged at my mind. A few days later, I went back to my friend's house, logged on, and searched again. I found a different site with a different assessment.

I'll answer it more honestly this time, I told myself. What that really meant was, "I'll sway the results by being more optimistic."

For example, I remember a question like this:

Q: Over the last two weeks, how often have you felt down, depressed, or hopeless?
   a) not at all
   b) a few times
   c) more than half the days
   d) nearly every day

I didn't get into Columbia without good test-taking skills. I knew perfectly well which answers would garner a higher score, but those answers were so far from the truth that I just couldn't choose them. I literally tried to click on option A but couldn't bring myself to do it.

The honest answer was option D, and I felt it in my heart. I was depressed every day. I remember waking up in the morning and waiting for a few seconds to see if "it" was still there, or if maybe the fog had lifted. But day after day, for hundreds of days, it was the same. The demon was there as soon as I woke up.

Nevertheless, in an effort to be more positive, I chose option C. I did the same thing for maybe twenty questions total. At the end, I clicked "get results," expecting to have a much better score than the previous day. But I was shocked that the site gave me basically the same advice: "It's likely that you are experiencing a depressive episode and need medical help."

"Holy shit," I said out loud. "I think I might be depressed!"

You may be thinking, "Duh, of course this guy is depressed." And you're right. It's obvious in retrospect. But at the time, this was an absolute revelation. In fact, it was a profound identity shift. For the first time in my life, I was ready to admit that I was unwell.

Of course, I told exactly zero people. *I'll just practice qigong*, I thought. *Grandmaster Liu said that depression can be cured in six weeks. I must have been practicing wrong. I can fix that!*

Let's pause for a moment so that I can sound a warning. Please, please, please don't do this. Don't ignore the underlying issue like I did. I got lucky, but this approach could have easily killed me. What I should have done was go get help. At the time, I hated the idea of seeing a psychiatrist and I was against the idea of antidepressants, although for the life of me I can't remember why. Of course, I was also feeling deep shame, and I didn't want anyone to know.

Antidepressants are a hot issue, and there's no question that they can be highly problematic. But they also help a lot of people. Maybe they've helped you, and maybe they would've helped me. In the end, I think the most important thing is to get help.

What kind of help you get is up to you. Personally, I prefer acupuncture to antidepressants, but that's me. You do you.

For me, acupuncture was a godsend because I was failing miserably with qigong!

Dr. Wong to the Rescue

It had been a year since I learned qigong from Grandmaster Liu, but I wasn't practicing. It was as if I had the correct medicine but just couldn't swallow the pills.

This is a common struggle with depression. It's hard to be disciplined when you wake up in a fog of pain and despair every morning. Doing something as simple as practicing qigong for fifteen minutes a day can seem like a herculean task.

I was caught in a death spiral. The less I practiced, the more I beat myself up for not practicing. But that only made my depression work overtime, which made it even harder to practice qigong. Eventually, I felt powerless to help myself.

Sometimes in life you just need a helping hand—another human, or a group of humans, to help you where you cannot help yourself.

My mother, who is a tennis fanatic, had fallen and broken her wrist about a year earlier. This injury had threatened not only her tennis hobby but also her career as a professional pianist. In addition to getting a regular cast, she also received acupuncture. Afterward, she swore that the acupuncture helped her to heal faster. Today, all these decades later, she still plays both the piano and tennis with no hint of that injury.

My mother probably didn't understand depression back then, but mothers know their sons, and she knew that I was suffering. It must have been obvious to both of my parents because I was living in their house at the time. We didn't talk about things like depression, but I'm sure they recognized that I was not healthy.

They must have discussed it because one day they suggested that I get acupuncture. And it was more than just a suggestion. They offered to pay for some sessions, and even gave me a post-it-note with the phone number for a man named Dr. Wong. Apparently, they had asked around and gotten a referral from a friend.

My parents made it easy for me. When you are dealing with a depressive person, it's important to understand that even seemingly trivial tasks can be overwhelming. This is now known as the "impossible task," a phrase coined by M. Molly Backes on Twitter[9] in 2018.

An impossible task seems easy but still feels overwhelming to the depressive. For example, something as simple as finding an acupuncturist in the Yellow Pages would have been an impossible task for me back then. Not only would I have failed the test, but I would have felt shame for not being able to accomplish something so simple. This would have made the problem snowball. Since my parents had already done the legwork, I was able to call and make an appointment.

For six weeks, Dr. Wong kicked my ass with powerful acupuncture sessions as well as herbal remedies. I say "kicked my ass" because he didn't just insert the needles into various spots. Instead, he seemed to linger there, playing with the needles in a way that caused all sorts of intense sensations in my body.

I now know that this was a traditional form of acupuncture where the doctor purposely stimulates a strong qi reaction. And Dr. Wong got that strong reaction! I remember feeling the qi moving all the way up my leg! It wasn't painful per se, but it was intense and uncomfortable.

"Strong treatment for strong young man," Dr. Wong said when I moaned from one of the needles. I felt anything but strong, but was grateful that he didn't baby me. He was correct in the sense that even though was in a weakened mental-emotional state, my system was physically strong enough to handle the treatment. And since I could only afford six sessions, I wanted to make the most of it.

On a side note, please don't let this scare you away from acupuncture. Most acupuncturists aren't as nearly aggressive as Dr. Wong was with me. Many of them will use hair-thin needles and you will hardly be able to feel them at all. Acupuncture is a wonderful healing modality, and it makes a perfect complement to qigong.

In addition to getting acupuncture each week, I also left Dr. Wong's office with a paper bag full of strange, alien-looking ingredients. Dr. Wong gave explicit instructions for brewing and taking the medicine and warned me not to cheat. Every week he would ask, "Cheat on herbs?" I took pride in telling him, "Nope."

Each week, I would brew the herbs in a strangely shaped clay vessel. The decoction smelled absolutely awful while I was brewing it. Imagine stale, bitter coffee mixed with dirt and old socks—that's about how the herbs smelled. And it tasted worse than it smelled! The first time I tried to drink my medicine, I just couldn't finish it. I took half the dosage and felt like I was going to puke. But then I remembered Dr. Wong's admonishment not to cheat, so I came up with a solution. I held my nose while drinking the god-awful potion, and then quickly ate a piece of fruit immediately after.

Again, please don't let this deter you from taking Chinese herbal medicine. Dr. Wong preferred the traditional method, but today most herbalists prescribe powdered remedies that make brewing easier. And not all prescriptions taste as bad as mine did. Everything depends on your unique diagnosis. Your herbal remedy may even taste good to you!

It was hard, but I managed to take my medicine every day. For some strange reason, I found it easier to drink my herbal medicine than to practice qigong. In retrospect, I think it's because our culture values oral medicine more than something like qigong, which is a totally foreign kind of medicine. These cultural paradigms run deep in our subconscious, and we should never underestimate them.

Over time, as I took the medicine, I found it easier to drive to subsequent healing sessions with Dr. Wong. The first session took heroic effort because I could hardly get out of bed let alone drive myself to the doctor's office. But over the next few weeks, the effects of the treatment were obvious. I slowly came out of my months-long depressive episode, and my energy began to return.

"You know qigong?" Dr. Wong asked me one day. His English was basic, but it didn't seem to stop him from knowing exactly what was wrong with me.

"I know a little," I said, feeling embarrassed, as if being caught cutting class.

"You practice every day!" he admonished. It was a command, not a question. "You need!"

His implication was clear. With just a few words, he was telling me that I had to participate in my own healing. This is a philosophy that most acupuncture physicians embrace. Acupuncturists are likely to send you home with lifestyle tips, simple qigong exercises, or breathing exercises. True healing comes from within, and you must participate in your own transformation.

Taking responsibility for one's own healing process involves a profound paradigm shift. In a world that tells us that healing involves taking pills or getting surgery, the idea that we can heal ourselves is revolutionary. You will struggle with this. I certainly did. Practicing qigong was difficult. Or rather, I should say that *starting* each session was difficult. Once I was a few minutes into my fifteen-minute session, the struggle was gone, and I actually enjoyed the flow.

Back then, I didn't understand the power of ritual. For example, if you develop the habit of practicing qigong every morning at 7:00 a.m. while your coffee is brewing, then you won't struggle the way that I did. It will take effort to develop the habit initially, but once established, it will have a momentum of its own. And that momentum will carry you through the difficult times. We'll talk more about the power of ritual in chapter 7.

For me, acupuncture was crucial. It got me back on my feet to the point where I *could* struggle with habits, willpower, and ritual! It's better to struggle with practicing than to simply not practice at all.

Today, I encourage students to get whatever help they need to pull out of their tailspin. This might include the following:

- Orthodox medical treatments
- Massage therapy
- Acupuncture
- Mental health therapy
- Chiropractic
- A heart-to-heart with your qigong teacher
- Dietary changes
- Supplements and/or herbal medicine

In the twenty-first century, we must use an "any means necessary" approach to developing a daily and enjoyable qigong routine. I've even seen students benefit from getting a dog! This makes sense because dogs have been proven to help with depression. If rescuing a dog and getting weekly massages is what you need to get on track with your qigong, then do it!

To Be or Not To Be

Dr. Wong helped to get me back on my feet. Thanks to his acupuncture and herbs, I felt strong enough to resume my daily fifteen-minute qigong routine again. Practicing qigong always made me feel better, and I started to build momentum. With that momentum, I began to put the pieces of my life back together.

I got a job and started working nine to five. I got an apartment in NYC and moved out of my parents' attic. I reconnected with old friends and even started dating.

For what feels like the fiftieth time, I'd love to tell you that I lived happily ever after and that I kept up my daily habit of qigong. It's not easy to recount all my failures like this. But I'm not going to bullshit you because that's not who I am, and it's not going to help you. Obviously, this story does have a happy ending—otherwise, you wouldn't be reading this book. Eventually, I did manage to develop a strong, daily qigong routine, and as a result, I was finally able to heal.

But not quite yet. On the way to that success, I failed over and over again. I'm sharing this so that you know the truth about what it takes to succeed with an art like qigong. The path is messy and challenging, and yet it's still worth it. So when you fail, remember that I failed too. If I can succeed with qigong, you can too. It won't be pretty. My path certainly wasn't. But it can be done.

Back to the story.

Things were going pretty well, certainly much better than before. I was functioning, and by all outward appearances, I seemed normal. And yet, I felt incredibly fragile, like a delicate coffee mug that might break if you accidentally set it down too hard.

I wish I could tell you that there was a major event in my life that triggered another bout of depression. In truth, it was nothing major. It was just a series of minor things, one right after another, combined with a harsh New York winter. Without knowing how I got there, I found myself back in a depressive episode.

Depression often comes in waves. We call these waves "episodes," and they typically last anywhere from three weeks to three months. In severe cases, they can last for years without abating. My first episode lasted roughly eight months.

As I entered this new depressive episode, things quickly fell apart. I was downsized from my job and had to go on unemployment. Then my girlfriend broke up with me. But perhaps worst of all, I lost my daily qigong habit.

At the time, practicing qigong meant doing about fifteen minutes per day. A fifteen-minute session certainly sounds easy, and in many ways, it is. It's not rigorous, it's enjoyable, and it leaves you feeling great. So why on earth did I stop practicing?

The best way I can explain this is to compare qigong to sitting meditation. In theory, practicing sitting meditation for fifteen minutes every day should be easy, right? You just sit on a cushion and do nothing! Easy peasy!

Anyone who has ever attempted a sitting meditation practice knows that this is not, in fact, easy peasy. Meditative arts may look easy, but they require a level of courage that is rare in our modern world.

I would manage to do three or four qigong sessions one week, but then only one session the following week. I was inconsistent, and that was a problem, because consistency is critical with qigong. To get results, you need to practice more days than you miss. Ideally, you should be practicing every day, even if it's just for two minutes (more on that soon).

The only thing I managed to consistently do every day was beat myself up for not practicing qigong. "You're a piece of shit," I told myself hundreds of times per day. Thanks to Brené Brown's books (highly recommended), I now know that I was caught in something called a "shame storm." The more shame I felt, the more I shamed myself.

As you can imagine, the combination of a depressive episode, a shame storm, and an inconsistent qigong practice was not healthy. Once again, I should have gotten help but didn't. Live and learn I guess—except that I barely lived to learn more.

During this particular depressive episode, I was crossing 110th Street one day when a taxi bumped me gently. New Yorkers jaywalk all the time, and near-misses like this are surprisingly common. I say "miss" because, despite the little bump, he didn't hurt me. In many ways, it was no big deal. It was probably my fault. I was in a depressive daze and wasn't paying attention.

As I walked away, I ignored the cab driver, who was, of course, cursing at me and gesticulating aggressively with his hand. Instead, I heard the voice in my head say this: "A bus would be better than a taxi."

This voice was not giving me friendly advice about the quickest way to get home. No, this voice was giving me advice about how to quickly end my suffering. I now know that this is called suicidal ideation, and that it's a risk factor for depression. But back then, I only knew this as the voice of my demon.

I had heard this voice many times. It had told me to put weights in my backpack and jump off the George Washington Bridge. It had told me that a beer, a bathtub, and a razor blade would be a relatively painless, albeit messy, exit. And now it was telling me that a bus would be a quick way to go.

For years, this voice had told me that I didn't deserve to live, that I wasn't welcome here, that I should just give up and get off this spinning rock. During this particular depressive episode, I started to believe the voice, and that was new to me.

A chill ran down my spine when I realized the implications of what the demon was whispering in my ear. Suddenly, I had a Zen-like clarity, a moment of pure lucidity. "I'm going to die if I don't do something," I said to myself. Imagine standing on a twentieth floor balcony. Even with a protective railing, you would sense the danger, right there, just a few feet away. Every cell in your body would wake up and pay attention. That's how I felt at that moment. I felt alert, awake, and alive. But I also felt death nearby.

When I got home, I sat on my bed to think. Unlike Hamlet, I didn't launch into an eloquent soliloquy about the comparative merits of living versus dying. But the same basic question was on my mind: To be, or not to be? If your Shakespeare is a little rusty, remember that Hamlet's famous soliloquy is basically a debate on the merits of suicide. The soliloquy is a profound and poetic description of what we now call suicidal ideation.

Explaining suicidal ideation to a person who's never experienced it is not easy, but I'll try anyway. Imagine that you had a dog that you loved very much. Now imagine that, because of a freak accident, your dog was destined to be in terrible pain for the rest of her life. However many years she had left, she would suffer daily and deeply.

I'm not saying that putting your dog to sleep would definitely be the right thing to do. Philosophers have debated ethical topics like this for centuries. Who am I to say what's right? But what I *am* saying is you would *think* about putting your dog to sleep. You would definitely consider it.

Suicidal ideation works in a similar way, except that you're the dog. After years of deep and daily suffering, we think about putting ourselves down. It's a logical and practical solution to a horizon full of nothing but suffering.

And it's not just our own suffering! We also imagine the suffering that we're causing to those around us. This is a key point to remember when dealing with suicidal ideation: we convince ourselves that our friends and family would be better off without us. This is rarely true, but it's what we feel.

That night in my apartment, I was like Hamlet, minus all the poetry and talking out loud stuff. On my bed, I deeply contemplated the nature of life and death. And it was more than an intellectual pursuit. Alone in my apartment in Washington Heights, I fought an epic battle of the spirit.

Here's where we finally start to move toward a happy ending. You'll be glad to know that I won that battle. Years later, having worked through much of my shame, I can honestly say that I'm proud of myself. I mean, I was like Gandalf fighting the Balrog. I kicked a demon's ass and didn't even have a magical staff!

During that battle, I felt death nearby. It was visceral, not just in my mind. I felt its presence deep in my bones, and it was alluring. Like Hamlet, I felt the calling of a sleep that would end the suffering once and for all.

Normally, there's resistance when facing death, a primal "no!" that runs through your body. But this time, there was no fear. For whatever reason, I was able to look calmly at death. I was able to stare at it, without running or looking away. I craved the nothingness from before I was born.

I think modern humans spend much of our lives looking away from death. Two hundred years ago, death was a common sight. You saw the bodies of relatives who had died, even young children. You saw the animals in the yard and knew they would be food one day soon. Perhaps you even slaughtered the animals yourself. (My mother actually did this growing up on a farm in Indiana.)

Today, we are sheltered from death. We rarely see dead bodies. Our meat, if we eat it, comes in packages at a supermarket. Infant mortality has dropped to miraculously low levels. And the closest most of us come to death is when our pets pass on.

Up until that moment on the bed, I had never really looked at death. Suddenly, it was no longer far off or imaginary. It was there in my bedroom with me. This might sound odd, but I looked right into Death's eyes. To my surprise, what I saw was life itself.

Like most epiphanies, this probably won't sound profound as I retell it, but I assure you that it was a revelation at the time. While looking at death, I saw that I was not yet fully alive. For years I had lived in a slumber—not dead, but not really alive either. I was trapped in a purgatory of suffering.

I saw that suicide was one way out of the suffering, but I also saw another path. I decided that I would keep death open as a last resort, but I would not choose that option until I had given life a fair shot. I decided that, at least for a little while longer, I would live.

Two Minutes a Day

I had decided to live. I emerged victorious from my "to be or not to be" battle. And yet, I didn't know *how* to live. I knew that qigong could help heal me, and I truly felt that it was my path. But I had failed time and again with qigong, and I was scared to try again. It was a conundrum.

I needed a solution, and fast. I was desperate to make qigong work for me. Feeling cornered, I decided to take a vow.

It feels weird writing that. I was not a monk. Why would I even think to take a vow? I can't answer that question even after all these years. But I did it. I took a vow—not to God, not to a Buddhist order of monks, nor to a church. Instead, I took a vow to my higher self, the self that was still mostly asleep but starting to wake up.

This happened on December 31, 1999. While the world was in the throes of Y2K panic, I was alone in my NYC apartment, ringing in the new year with solitude and existentialism.

"I vow to do fifteen repetitions of Lifting the Sky every day in 2000, no matter what," I said aloud. I intentionally didn't say fifteen minutes per day because I had failed with that so many times already. So I chose fifteen repetitions instead. It felt like a goal that was so easy I couldn't possibly fail.

And yet it wasn't easy. I remember lying in bed one night a few weeks later, exhausted from a long day of work. I was already dozing off when I realized with a shudder that I hadn't done my fifteen repetitions!

So I got my ass out of bed and did my stupid qigong, dammit.

Was it good qigong? Nope. Was it the way I had been taught? Nope. Did I keep my vow? Yep.

Today, there's a name for what I was doing. I call it The Two-Minute Drill, and it's something that I teach all my students.

For me, at the time, fifteen reps of Lifting the Sky took roughly two minutes. But other people might do ten or twenty reps in two minutes. It depends on the pace of your breathing.

It turns out that two minutes is a better goal than fifteen reps. Try it for yourself and you'll see that it works like magic. Whereas saying, "I should practice for fifteen minutes" will often result in a bunch of negative self-talk, saying, "I'm going to do two minutes" doesn't.

I'm living proof that this method works. I'm proud to say that I kept my original vow for over four thousand consecutive days. That's eleven years without missing a single day of qigong!

In the beginning, it was mostly just the Two-Minute Drill. But gradually, I started doing longer sessions. Soon, I found myself doing five minutes a day, then ten, then fifteen, and before I knew it, I was doing fifteen minutes twice a day!

So why did I stop? Why only four thousand days? After eleven years of practice, I decided that I had fulfilled my vow, and that it was okay to miss a day now and then. But I rarely do. I typically practice at least 360 days per year. (And yes, I keep track. More on that later.)

And we're not talking about two minutes anymore! For nearly two decades now, I've averaged about two *hours* of quality practice per day. That's on *average*.

Slow and steady wins the qigong race. And you know what? I'm winning.

My Worst Day

One day, about a year into my vow, a qigong classmate gave me some advice that I'd like to pass on to you. Her advice was simple: compare your current worst day to your best day from a year ago.

This was actually quite easy because I journal so much. So I dug out an old journal from a year prior and started reading. In there, I found a veritable catalogue of depression, anxiety, and hopelessness.

Wow, I thought as I read. *I was a hot mess!*

I continued reading and found one depressive entry after another. I had to read through two months' worth of entries before I found a single positive one. And even that entry, which described a rare good day in the life of Anthony, sounded pretty bad in retrospect. My expectations for health and happiness had been so incredibly low back then!

It suddenly became clear that my standards had risen. I expected—and often received—so much more out of life! And that's when it really sunk in. I remember I was sitting on the couch in my apartment on 157th Street. Milo, my roommate's cat, was sitting next to me. He was a huge and beautiful Russian Blue, and we often had good conversations. Thank God for Milo. He helped me through some rough times.

"Holy shit, Milo," I said. "My best day from a year ago would be my worst day today!" Milo purred. I'd like to think he was happy about my progress.

Here's a chart that shows what I suddenly saw in my mind that day:

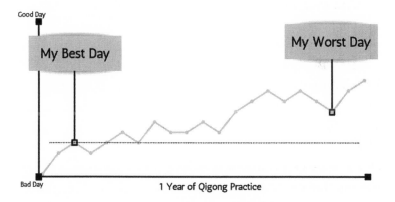

As you can see, the high crest of my best day from 1999 was actually lower than the low crest of my worst day in 2000.

Imagine your best day this year. Now imagine that, next year, every single day will be at *least* as good! That's what I experienced from 1999 to 2000.

With this new perspective, I could see that twelve months of daily qigong had indeed transformed my life. I wasn't free from depression yet (more on that later), and my back pain wasn't completely gone, but I was making solid progress.

One important thing to remember is that you may not notice your progress. It's exactly like a child growing up. Parents don't necessarily notice the growth because they see their child every day, but relatives who only see the child once or twice a year are amazed at the difference.

This was a wake-up call. My former best day was now my current worst day—and I hadn't even noticed! What else was I failing to notice?

Doctor, Heal Thyself

Qigong is a lifestyle. I tell my students that I want them to fall in love with the art and practice it for the rest of their lives—which will be longer and happier as a result. When you successfully implement the daily habit of qigong, the trajectory of your path changes.

They say that people who are lost in the desert, or even a forest, tend to walk in circles unless they have a compass. They may only be off by a few degrees on the compass, but that's enough to go in circles. They literally end up right back where they started after walking for hours.

I like to think of qigong as a sort of compass. It helps us to course-correct on a daily basis. It keeps us on the right path and prevents us from going in circles.

Three years after my vow, my path had changed dramatically. I was a different person. I had a good job, and life was getting better all the time. My energy levels had grown steadily, and I was able to plan ahead rather than just struggling through the day.

When I thought about my future, all I could think about was qigong. Something was beckoning. Although I was doing well, I was not yet on my true path.

I don't know exactly when it happened. There was no specific "aha" moment. I just gradually came to accept that my life would be dedicated not just to practicing qigong, but also to sharing it with others.

I had been telling people about qigong for years, but you know how it is. Friends and family don't really listen to you. They were happy to see me doing better, but honestly, most of them didn't even know that I was suicidal. They never asked, and I wasn't ready to tell them. So the huge importance of qigong in my life was lost on them.

At the time, I was working at Columbia. I had landed an awesome gig as a network administrator, and it came with a lot of benefits: health insurance, unlimited sick days, thirty paid vacation days, and reasonable hours. I not only made enough money to get my own apartment, but I got to take Chinese language classes for free. My boss even played video games with me and my coworkers!

I look back on that job with fondness. It was cushy, predictable, interesting, and I could have stayed there for years. It would have led to a perfectly normal and respectable life. And I came close to choosing that life.

A few years into this amazing gig, our super-cool boss decided to leave for greener pastures. Unfortunately, he was replaced by an incompetent oaf. That oaf lasted for about nine months, during which time half his team quit. Eventually, he was fired.

I was the most senior person left, so they offered me his job. It was a huge step up in responsibility, and also in salary. Plus, I would get a chance to become the cool boss who plays video games with his team!

It should not have been a difficult decision, but it was. The ancient Greek parable of Hercules comes to mind. When offered a choice between a pleasant and easy life or a challenging but virtuous life, Hercules chose the harder path.

I stood at a crossroads just like Hercules. Should I take the promotion? Logic told me to take the job and stay at Columbia. But my heart told me otherwise. I wanted to do more with qigong, and more with my life.

Rather than accept the job, I gave three months' notice. Then, in February 2004, just over four years after taking the vow, I sold all my stuff, hopped on a plane with two bags, and moved to Florida in pursuit of something bigger.

Why Florida? My parents had moved to Florida a few years earlier and my brother had followed with his own family. I come from a close-knit family, so it was a natural choice to be near them. But the real reason I chose to move to Florida was to attend acupuncture college. This was the grand plan. This was my new path.

Qigong College

Why acupuncture college? Quite simply because there's no such thing as qigong college! I decided to attend acupuncture college to deepen my understanding of Classical Chinese Medicine, which is woven into qigong.

In 2004, I enrolled at Dragon Rises College of Oriental Medicine. If that name makes you cringe a little, I get it. The term "oriental" is outdated and arguably even racist. Despite this, acupuncture colleges and diplomas all over the country use the term "Oriental Medicine."

Racism aside, that term makes no sense because what we're really talking about here is the oldest form of continuously practiced medicine on earth: Chinese Medicine. This form of medicine later spread all over Asia. For example, Japan has a tradition called *Kampo,* which literally means "Chinese Medicine in Japan." Japanese-style acupuncture is popular, and I suppose this is why some colleges chose the term Oriental Medicine rather than Chinese Medicine, but it's not accurate.

The accurate term is Chinese Medicine. Even in Chinese, the term is simply "Chinese Medicine." However, in the twentieth century the term "Traditional Chinese Medicine" was popularized by Chairman Mao. This is ironic because Mao did his best to remove everything traditional from the medicine. Remember: Mao believed that religion was poison, and he killed millions of people in support of this belief.

Traditional Chinese Medicine sounds nice, and it has a catchy acronym too (TCM). But TCM is really just watered-down Chinese Medicine. What I studied was not Oriental Medicine, not Kampo, and not TCM. I studied what was once called Chinese Medicine and is now being called Classical Chinese Medicine.

I was specifically looking for this kind of medicine. I had done my research and found a well-respected acupuncture college in Gainesville, Florida. This was another reason why I moved to Florida—the college was only a ninety-minute commute from my parents' house.

My plan was to finish acupuncture college and *then* start teaching qigong professionally. But as you know, life rarely goes as planned. Finishing acupuncture college wasn't in the cards for me; teaching was.

My qigong master had already asked me to start teaching in 2003, but I respectfully declined. I was a star student, and at the time he didn't have any active teachers in the US. But I just didn't feel ready to teach. Unlike most new teachers, my hesitation wasn't with the art of teaching. My parents are both music teachers and by the time I enrolled in acupuncture college, I had already taught tennis, violin, and karate.

When I taught tennis, I either taught young kids or older adults. In both cases, I could easily beat any of my students without breaking a sweat. My skill was obvious to them and also to me. With the violin, I taught young kids. Again, the gap in skill was obvious to them and their parents. And when I taught karate, two minutes of sparring with a student was enough to show them that I was qualified to be their teacher.

But with qigong, the skill is invisible. Even today, after decades of practice, it's tricky (but not impossible) to demonstrate my skill in qigong. In my opinion, the best way to demonstrate skill in qigong is by successfully healing yourself. I had done a tremendous amount of healing in just a few years but still didn't feel completely healed. I didn't feel like I was a shining example of the benefits of qigong—not yet.

Then something unexpected happened. Most acupuncture colleges include some sort of qigong or tai chi in the curriculum.

Despite seven to eight years of prior qigong training, I had no choice but to take a mandatory qigong class when I enrolled. And I'm glad I did. It was fun to learn a new style of qigong!

But it turned out that many of the acupuncture students were dissatisfied with the qigong that was being taught at the college. One of the teachers taught more tai chi than qigong, and the other taught endless, complex forms. It was common to hear complaints about these issues in the student lounge.

"So I found your name in the back of a qigong book," a fellow classmate said to me one day, out of the blue. It was true. I was listed in the back of my teacher's book as a qigong instructor. As I mentioned, he really wanted me to teach, so he listed me (and several other international instructors) in the back of his newest book.

Word got around, and soon several students were pestering me to teach. I taught them a few simple techniques, but then word spread even faster. Soon several of my acupuncture professors became interested.

One thing led to another, and in December 2005, I taught my first official group qigong class. It was a twelve-week class and fourteen students signed up. Half of them were from my acupuncture college, and the other half were their friends and family.

I put my heart into that twelve-week class, but my skill as a teacher was low compared to today. On top of that, I had zero blog posts for students to get additional information. (For comparison, I have over 160 blog posts as of this writing.)

Despite all this, the students did remarkably well. Several of them had done qigong for years, so they learned quickly. But that class opened a totally new experience for them. The big difference for them was learning what I now call the Five-Phase Routine. (Back then, I just called it the fifteen-minute routine.)

After that twelve-week course, word spread like wildfire in my small college town. It didn't take long for me to have enough students for another twelve-week course. And then another. And then another.

The Flowing Zen Studio

Over the next few years, I taught in martial arts studios, churches, yoga rooms, and the University of Florida gym. Gradually, acupuncturists, chiropractors, massage therapists, and MDs heard about my classes. They either attended on their own, or simply referred their patients. My student base grew, and I kept adding more qigong classes to meet the demand.

In 2008, two acupuncturists and a chiropractor, all of whom had taken my qigong classes, approached me with a business idea. They wanted to open a multi-disciplinary wellness center combining acupuncture, chiropractic, massage, and of course, qigong. I liked the idea but wasn't sure how I could possibly open a business while also finishing acupuncture college. My parents ran a music school for over twenty years, so I had a good idea what was involved in opening a new business.

For fun, we started scouting locations for the wellness center. One day, a realtor showed us a stand-alone building that was, quite simply, perfect for us. As I stepped into a big open area with a huge bay window, I instantly knew that this would be my future qigong studio.

I also knew that I was at a crossroads. I would have to choose between the studio and acupuncture college. I wouldn't be able to do both. I had been in college for four years, but I was only 70 percent of the way through because I had dropped down to part time to teach qigong. I would need another two years going part-time to graduate.

By this time, it had also become clear that my talents were better utilized as a qigong teacher than an acupuncturist. There were plenty of skilled acupuncturists in the world, including my classmates. But I learned that good qigong teachers were extremely rare. Furthermore, the remaining time I had in acupuncture college was mostly clinical. In other words, I already knew all the theory and physiology of Chinese Medicine, and that's all I really needed for qigong.

When you say yes to one path, you say no to another. Had I said yes to finishing acupuncture college, I would have had to say no to my qigong studio. I decided to say yes to qigong because I recognized that I was meant to be a qigong teacher, not an acupuncturist.

In August 2008, I opened the doors to the Flowing Zen Studio in Gainesville, Florida. The studio was a gorgeous, 750-square-foot room with tons of natural light. This room was attached to a wellness center with a waiting area and fitness treatment rooms.

Over the next eight years, I would go on to teach over five thousand live classes to two thousand different people in that room. With little more than a dream, and with very little business experience, I somehow built one of the more successful full-time qigong studios in the country. Anyone who spent time in the studio knows that it had a palpable healing energy as well as an uncanny ability to connect people to each other through the art of qigong.

So why did I close my doors in 2016? In a nutshell, because I was being called to teach globally rather than just locally. The studio, like all brick-and-mortar businesses, demanded a ton of my time and energy. I loved my job, but the sixty-hour weeks prevented me from starting other projects (like this book).

Closing the studio was one of the hardest things I've ever done. When I returned the keys to the landlord, my eyes were not dry. I know for a fact that I'm not the only one who shed tears when the studio closed. It was a qi-filled haven for many of us, and it was heartbreaking to say goodbye.

And yet, I don't regret my decision. It was the right move. Today, many students live in areas where online instruction is the only option. For example, one student lives in a remote part of Norway. She is twenty miles from the nearest small town, let alone a qigong studio! For her, my online classes were a lifesaver.

The whole world is my classroom now. If you have an internet connection, and if you can understand enough English to make sense of my New York accent, then you can get quality qigong instruction. You don't need to travel to Asia like I did. You don't even need to leave your house.

Seeking What They Sought

Unfortunately, I didn't have the benefit of online learning. I traveled extensively to learn from Asian masters, whether it was a one-hour subway ride in NYC or a twenty-three-hour flight to Malaysia. Because I'm first generation from a more traditional approach to qigong, I had to suffer through outdated and inefficient teaching methods. All of my teachers were skillful at qigong, but this doesn't mean they were also skillful at teaching. You could say that I learned the hard way so that my students don't have to.

My discipleship with Grandmaster Liu was less traditional than one hundred years ago, but still much more traditional than the way that I now teach. The training was often grueling. For example, we would train qigong and kung fu for six to eight hours a day outside in the Malaysian heat and humidity. The philosophy of "respecting the master" was also strong in his school, and there was a ton of archaic Chinese etiquette that went along with it. Often, the dynamic felt cultish.

All told I was his disciple for seventeen years. As one of his star students, I was also chosen as his chief instructor for the United States. In chapter 8, I'll explain why I finally left him in late 2014.

I first met Grandmaster Liu in California in 1997, as I explained earlier. Over the years, I went to Malaysia many times to learn from him, staying for about a month each time. I also chased him around the world since he gave workshops in the US, Canada, Europe, and Central America. I even hosted him at my studio in Florida, where he taught workshops nearly every year.

During my time with Grandmaster Liu, learning from other teachers was frowned upon. Despite this, I still took classes and workshops from several well-known Sifus, including Yang Jwing

Ming, Park Bok Nam, Bruce Frantzis, William C. C. Chen, Bingkun Hu, Yap Soon-Yeong, and Zhang Yun. In some of these cases, I only learned from these Sifus for eight to twelve hours, but it was enough to leave an indelible mark on me. I still practice what they taught me all these years later.

I was also heavily influenced by several teachers before I met Grandmaster Liu, notably my first karate teacher, Sensei Bonnie Baker, who I mentioned earlier. Sensei Teruo Chinen, an Okinawan karate grandmaster, also had a lasting influence. In many ways, he was my first qigong teacher. While living in New York City, I also learned Northern Shaolin Kung Fu from Sifu Hui Cambrelen, and Nei Gong from Sifu C. K. Chu.

From 1995 to 1996, I lived in San Francisco near Golden Gate Park. Early in the morning, you would find dozens of people practicing qigong, tai chi, and even ballroom dancing there! During this time, I didn't really understand qigong but I met a kung fu teacher in the park. I called him Sifu, and his surname was Fung, but I never got his full name or learned anything about his history. In retrospect, that was a mistake on my part because Sifu Fung definitely opened my eyes to new possibilities.

It was during this time that I was formally introduced to seated Zen Meditation (called zazen) at the Sonoma Mountain Zen Center in Santa Rosa, California. I only went a few times, but I learned the basics and continued to practice on my own. Unfortunately, zazen exacerbated my depression, an experience that I now know is fairly common. But this was a mixed blessing because it also primed me to learn moving meditation, which is a much better fit for depressives. By the time I found qigong, I was ready!

So that's my training in a nutshell. Instruction is only half the equation, however. Except for those periods when my depression was at its peak, I averaged at least two hours of daily practice, whether it was karate, neigong, qigong, kung fu, or tai chi. More importantly, my previous years of violin training helped me to practice more efficiently. I often zoomed past my classmates in skill, not because of raw talent, but because I had already mastered the art of practicing.

I'm grateful for all of my teachers, and also my grand-teachers, and great-grand-teachers. I stand on the shoulders of giants, and so do you. Thanks to the deep work of these past masters, we inherit an amazingly rich and powerful tradition!

However, I need to be clear about something: Honoring our teachers and the past masters does not mean that we need to follow in their footsteps. There's an old Zen saying that sums up this point:

Seek not to follow in the footsteps of the masters of old.
Seek what they sought.

I'm about to wrap up the memoir portion of this book because I want to shift the focus away from me and onto you and your bright future with qigong. More importantly, I hope that, as you learn more about qigong, you won't try to follow in my footsteps. Instead, I hope you will seek what I sought. And what I sought was true healing—first and foremost in myself, and then later by helping others. Here's a quotation that I love:

"If you want to awaken all of humanity, then awaken all of yourself. If you want to eliminate the suffering in the world, then eliminate all that is dark and negative in yourself. Truly, the greatest gift you have to give is that of your own self-transformation."

—Wang Fu[10]

The quotation is spot on. You could use it as your one and only compass for the rest of your life, and it would never fail you. And I hope that's exactly what you'll do. I hope that you will embrace this fundamental truth—that focusing on your own self-healing is the best way to heal the world.

Do you know what it's like for someone like me—someone who was once so sickly that he could barely help himself—to now be helping other people to heal themselves? Do you have any idea what it feels like to hear a student say that I helped to save their life? It feels indescribably wonderful. My life has meaning where it once had only darkness and suffering. I found healing not only in myself, but in my livelihood.

You need not become a qigong teacher in order to do great things. You can help to heal our sick world through the work that you're already doing. Or you can help by sharing your positive energy with the world, by becoming a beacon of health in a world filled with sickness. We'll talk more about this in chapter 8.

Of course, if you want to become a qigong teacher, that's also wonderful. I believe that when qigong explodes in popularity, we'll need lots of good instructors. But either way, you must start with yourself. Start with your own self transformation by seeking what the past masters sought!

Shall we begin that transformation?

[Try It Now] Lifting the Sky

It's time for some action. It's time to do some qigong.

As I mentioned earlier, the days of learning qigong from static pictures are long gone. Instead, you can watch a video of the exercise from several different angles. Simple.

Perhaps even more important than a video, and something that most people don't appreciate until they try it, is a guided meditation. This will give you the same experience as if you were in a live class.

If you're reading this on your Kindle, then just click this link here.

If you're reading the print version, then remember this: flowingzen.com/bookbonus.

Or you can use the QR code below. Just open the camera on your mobile phone and point it at the shape. Once you do that, a link will pop up. Click the link, and it will take you to the book bonuses. Magic!

Show that you are committed to your own transformation by doing some qigong right now. Or if you can't do it now, then schedule a time when you can. It will take you ten to fifteen minutes to learn Lifting the Sky. After that, you can practice in as little as two minutes. Do it now!

Notes

1. "Suicide," World Health Organization, September 2, 2019, https://www.who.int/news-room/fact-sheets/detail/suicide.
2. "Cancer Statistics at a Glance," Centers for Disease Control and Prevention, https://gis.cdc.gov/Cancer/USCS/DataViz.html.
3. "Depression," World Health Organization, January 30, 2020, https://www.who.int/news-room/fact-sheets/detail/depression.
4. "Depression," World Health Organization, January 30, 2020, https://www.who.int/news-room/fact-sheets/detail/depression.
5. Quinn D. Hatoff, "Donning a Mask: Suicide at Harvard," *The Harvard Crimson*, December 12, 2012, http://www.thecrimson.com/article/2012/12/10/suicide-harvard-mental-health/?page=2.
6. Angela Wang and Anna Mazarakis, "The COMBO Series: Survey Finds Almost Half of Students Report Feeling Depressed," *The Daily Princetonian*, April 23, 2013, http://www.dailyprincetonian.com/article/2013/04/the-combo-series-survey-finds-almost-half-of-students-report-feeling-depressed.
7. If you've never practiced classical Zen meditation, then you may be wondering how it can possibly be rigorous. Trust me. Sitting still and confronting your mind for hours every day is one of the most demanding things you'll ever do.
8. It's unlikely that Bodhidharma practiced or taught Shaolin Kung Fu. It's more likely that the qigong exercises he taught mixed with local martial arts and gradually morphed into Shaolin Kung Fu. But he was such an important figure at the Shaolin Temple that they gave him credit anyway!
9. M. Molly Backes (@mollybackes), "Depressive commercials always talk about sadness but they never mention that sneaky symptom that everyone with depression knows all too well: the Impossible Task," Twitter, August 27, 2018, 6:43 p.m., https://twitter.com/mollybackes/status/1034239973392871426?lang=en.
10. This quote is often attributed to Lao Tzu, but it's more likely from Wang Fu (王浮), a Taoist master. from the fourth century CE.

CHAPTER 2
What Qigong Is (and Isn't)

When someone asks what I do for a living, I typically say the following: "I teach people how to get their self-healing juices flowing using an ancient Chinese art called qigong. Have you heard of it?" Ending with a question often sparks a conversation, which is probably the best way to get people interested in qigong.

When it comes to explaining qigong, words will always fall short, especially for people who have no reference point. By the time you finish this book, you'll probably be pretty excited about qigong. You'll want to tell friends and family, and that's great! But what will you tell them?

That's a great question. I'll tell you what isn't very helpful for fresh beginners—a long definition like this one:

Qigong is an ancient Chinese mind-body practice that restores wellness, builds mental and emotional strength, reduces stress, increases vitality, promotes longevity, and builds resiliency. Sometimes called the grandmother of tai chi, qigong is a major branch of Classical Chinese Medicine, making it a cousin of acupuncture. Because qigong incorporates a variety of gentle breathing methods, flowing movements, and mindfulness meditation, it can be practiced by absolutely anyone, regardless of their age, health, religion, or fitness level.

Don't get me wrong, this is about as good as we can do with one hundred words or less. Nevertheless, it's not particularly helpful for people who know nothing about qigong. Their eyes will glaze over before you finish.

I'm guessing that the definition is helpful for you though. That's because you're in a different category. Even if you know very little about the word "qigong," you still know more than billions of people! And soon you'll know more than 99 percent of the humans on the planet, including many qigong teachers! Are you ready to learn more about this amazing art?

How to Pronounce Qigong

Let's start with the word itself. Chances are you're saying it wrong in your head. Let's correct that now so you don't keep doing it all the way through this book! Many people pronounce "qigong" wrong, and it's easy to understand why. That pesky "q" at the beginning is pretty confusing!

You're probably reading it and pronouncing it like this:

KEE (like the English word "key")
GONG (like the English word "gong")

That's wrong, but don't worry! You're not the only one. In fact, I've encountered my share of qigong instructors who pronounce it wrong! The correct pronunciation is hard to describe in a book, so all we can do is approximate the sounds. Here's my best shot at describing two Chinese sounds that don't really exist in English:

Qi is pronounced like "chee." It sounds a bit like the word "cheese" without the "s" ending.

Gong sounds a bit like the word "gunk," but with a "g" at the end instead of a "k."

Ugh. This is hard! I'm so glad I'm writing this book in the twenty-first century! If you want to hear the real pronunciation of "qigong", then go grab your book bonuses (flowingzen.com /bookbonus). There's an audio file in there with me pronouncing it correctly.

Transcribing Chinese words into our Roman alphabet is a problem, and it's not a new one. In the nineteenth century, Thomas Wade and Herbert Giles created a system of transliterating Chinese, now called the Wade-Giles system. I'm sure that Mr. Wade and Mr. Giles meant well, but what they created is a truly awful system that is unnecessarily complex, defies common sense, and barely gets the job done. The Wade-Giles system is an abomination. It should be loaded onto a rocket and sent to the deepest, coldest part of space.

Don't take my word for it. Here's what Alan Watts, the famous Eastern philosopher, had to say about the Wade-Giles system:

> "No uninitiated English-speaking person could guess how to pronounce it, and I have even thought, in a jocularly malicious state of mind, that Professors Wade and Giles invented it so as to erect a barrier between profane and illiterate people and true scholars."

Unfortunately, Wade-Giles was the most popular transliteration system until the 1970s. It has since been replaced by a newer and better system called Pinyin, which is the official system used by over a billion Chinese. But old habits die hard, and a lot of people still use the Wade-Giles system. Hell, even I still use Wade-Giles for "tai chi" because taijiquan is unrecognizable in the West.

The Pinyin system of transliteration was developed in the 1950s, and it is vastly superior to Wade-Giles. A transliteration system needs to spell not just the characters 氣功 (qigong), but thousands of other Chinese characters as well. Pinyin does this in a simple and efficient way. Wade-Giles does not.

If you only know a few words in Chinese, then it's hard to fully grasp why Pinyin is so much better. Trust me when I say that there is little-to-no disagreement among modern scholars. This is why Pinyin is taught in virtually every university in the US.

Arguments against Pinyin typically come from people who know neither Pinyin nor Wade-Giles. Usually, these are people who learned a few Wade-Giles words in the 1970s or 1980s, and are stuck in their ways. Of course, anyone who previously published a book with chi kung or chi gong in the title will probably put up an argument as well. I empathize with their copyright headaches, but arguments like this can be ignored.

I agree that "chi kung" looks better than "qigong," but that's just one word out of thousands. The creators of Pinyin had to find ways to represent a variety of different Chinese "ch" sounds that don't exist in English, so they chose "q" to represent one of them.

The Meaning of the Word

Now let's look at the meaning of the word. Here's a poetic translation of the Chinese word:

Qigong: the art of cultivating life-force energy.

That's a great working definition, and it's probably all you'll ever need. But it'll be fun to dig a little deeper.

The Chinese word is composed of two characters:

氣 功

Remember that in the Chinese language there is no alphabet. Those things you see up there—those are called logograms. A logogram is simply a written character that represents a word or phrase. Chinese words contain one or more logograms, in this case, two.

The first logogram in qigong is *qi*:

氣

vital energy, or life-force energy

Interestingly, English is one of the few languages that doesn't have a direct translation for this word. In India, it's called *prana*. In ancient Greece, it was called *pneuma*. In Japan, it's called *ki*. In ancient Hebrew, it was called *ruach*. And in Latin, it was called *spiritus*.

What are all these words referring to? You'll find all sorts of definitions out there, including some metaphysical ones. Me, I like things simple.

The best modern translation for *qi* is energy. Whether it's the energy that moves food through your digestive tract, the energy that mobilizes your immune system, or the energy that animates your cells—all of that is qi. This energy is everywhere. Life creates it, makes it grow. Its energy surrounds us and binds us, permeating every living thing.

If that sounds a lot like the Force from *Star Wars*, it's because I stole the last three lines from the movie. Actually, George Lucas borrowed his concept of the Force from ancient kung fu legends. Just about every superpower you see in *Star Wars* can be found in the old kung fu novels—but with lightsabers instead of swords. So the connection is not coincidental. Thinking of qi like the Force, but without the supernatural powers, is not far off the mark.

Personally, I haven't yet figured out how to pull off Luke's trick from *The Empire Strikes Back*. No matter how much qigong I practice, I simply cannot levitate my iPhone to me from across the room! Nevertheless, the superpowers that I have developed with qigong—health, vitality, mental clarity, resilience, fortitude, happiness—are plenty.

Coming back to our translation, the second logogram is:

功 (gong)

achievement, merit, work, good result

In our context, this refers to the act of cultivating a skill. In other words, it refers to practicing or mastering something. For example, I'm sure that you recognize the following two Chinese words:

Kung Fu

The first word is the same 功 from qigong but spelled differently. The Pinyin spelling is gong fu, but hardly anyone uses it because, well—because of Bruce Lee. His influence in the 1970s made the words "kung fu" a household name. (Fun fact: Bruce Lee's first book was called *Chinese Gung Fu: The Philosophical Art of Self Defense*. But Hollywood later changed that spelling to Kung Fu.)

Colloquially, *kung fu* means "martial art," specifically a martial art that comes from China. But literally, it means "cultivation over time." That same idea of "cultivation" is in the word *qigong*.

When we put the two logograms together, we have "energy" and "cultivation." But the Chinese language is one of subtlety, and those two words don't really convey the deeper meaning of the word *qigong*. That's why I prefer my poetic translation from above: the art of cultivating your life-force energy.

Qigong Terms throughout the Centuries

So far, we've been talking about qigong as if it's neatly bundled up into one unified art. Actually, the word *qigong* is a modern invention and has only been in common use since 1949. Today, it has become an umbrella term for hundreds of different qigong styles and thousands of different qigong exercises.

If we went back in time and spoke with past masters, they might not even recognize the term *qigong*. They would probably get the gist of what you were talking about, but if you asked them what art they practiced, they would likely answer with a different term.

They might, for example, say that they practice *neigong*. This was a popular term during the Ming Dynasty (AD 1368–1644). *Nei* means "internal," and *gong* still means "cultivation." So a poetic translation would be "the art of internal cultivation." It's still an accurate description for what we do.

Many teachers still use the term *neigong*, me included. Some teachers insist that neigong is different from qigong, and they're not entirely wrong, but it's just semantics. For example, The Small Universe (Xiao Zhou Tian, 小周天) is an advanced technique which involves directing the energy along two specific acupuncture meridians. There is little-to-no physical movement. To an observer, it would look like sitting or standing meditation. If there's anything that qualifies as neigong, it's The Small Universe.

However, many teachers use the term qigong instead of neigong to describe The Small Universe, myself included. I like this approach because it simplifies things. I use qigong as the umbrella term for all the techniques that I teach, including The Small Universe. To me, neigong is a sub-category of qigong. Other teachers may have different classifications. Just be wary of teachers who dismiss qigong as inferior to neigong. When you drill down, they may be talking about the same thing.

Here's a list of some other terms for qigong throughout the centuries:

- neigong, 內功, inner cultivation
- neidanshu, 內丹, inner alchemy
- waidan, 外丹, outer alchemy
- daoyin, 導引, guiding and pulling
- yangsheng, 養生, nurturing life
- liangong, 練功, training skill
- lianqi, 練氣, training qi

This list isn't comprehensive, for several reasons.

1. Many skills were lost over time, either due to the secrecy of Chinese culture, due to war, or due to Mao's Cultural Revolution, which killed untold numbers of qigong masters (not to mention millions of people in general).
2. Many masters called their art by the name of the technique itself. My own grand-teacher sometimes did this with the art of One Finger Zen (Yi Zhi Chan, 一指禪).
3. Many masters were illiterate and didn't write their techniques down.

Nevertheless, there are two major themes that unify all these seemingly different arts:

1. All of these arts utilize the concept of the Three Treasures of Jing, Qi, and Shen (more on this later).
2. All these arts use the same basic theory of meridians (or channels) used in acupuncture.

In that sense, the term qigong is perfect as an umbrella term because all these arts involve the cultivation (gong) of our internal energy (qi). Personally, I think it's helpful to have a single umbrella term like qigong, especially in the age of internet searches. This art is confusing enough to beginners without dozens of different names floating around! We can always use additional terms to identify the specific types of qigong that we're practicing.

The Four Main Categories of Qigong

Because qigong is not just one art, and because there are thousands of different techniques, there's a *huge* range of possible benefits that you can cultivate. These benefits depend on which direction you want to go. It's a bit like strength and fitness. Do you want to train for a marathon or for wrestling? What are your goals?

With qigong, there are four general directions that you can go:

1. Medical Qigong (also called Health Qigong)

2.   Scholar's Qigong (also called Confucian Qigong)
3.   Martial Qigong (also called Warrior Qigong)
4.   Spiritual Qigong (also called Buddhist/Taoist Qigong)

Let's look closer at each of these four categories to help you decide which direction might be best for you personally.

Medical Qigong (also called Health Qigong)

Medical Qigong is a branch of Classical Chinese Medicine, and thus a cousin of acupuncture. It was specifically designed to help you heal from pain and illness. If you've been given some sort of medical diagnosis for what ails you, then you want Medical Qigong. Even without an official diagnosis, if you have chronic pain, depression, anxiety, or a digestive disorder, then Medical Qigong is also for you.

In the twenty-first century, however, the term Medical Qigong is sometimes used to refer to clinical sessions. I'm not sure how or when this happened, but it's historically inaccurate and it has caused confusion for students and lawmakers alike. Typically, a Clinical Qigong Therapist will diagnose the patient just like an acupuncturist. Then, instead of using needles, she will open the patient's energy points using her hand, often without any actual contact. It's like a combination of Reiki and acupressure.

To make things even more confusing, a qigong clinician will often prescribe specific qigong exercises for you to practice at home. Of course, these exercises would also fall into the category of Medical Qigong. See the confusion?

I prefer to use the term Clinical Qigong Therapy for this healing modality because it makes it clear that there are two people involved rather than one. To me, Clinical Qigong Therapy is a subcategory of Medical Qigong.

Scholar's Qigong (also called Confucian Qigong)

This category covers a lot of ground, with benefits that range from boosting intelligence and memory, to helping with decision-making, to improving your luck (yes, you read that right). These techniques were practiced by Confucian and Taoist scholars to enhance their intellectual capabilities. The techniques overlap with Spiritual Qigong and tend to involve little to no movement.

This type of qigong is not well known. That's a shame because it has huge potential for helping school kids. We now know that kids who practice sitting meditation will see a boost in their intellectual capabilities, but I believe that this boost would be even bigger with Scholar's Qigong.

Of course, this type of qigong isn't just for kids. Many adults would love to improve their memory, myself included. As we age, those neurons don't seem to fire quite as fast as they once did. Scholar's Qigong can help oil that brain machinery.

I also use Scholar's Qigong to help me focus. We live in a distracting world. In fact, much of our modern world is designed to distract us, including smartphones and social media. Scholar's Qigong helps me to focus so that I can better concentrate on the task at hand, from practicing qigong to starting a business to writing this book.

Martial Qigong (also called Warrior Qigong)

In the old days when martial arts were a matter of life and death, practitioners needed speed, agility, power, and stamina. Courage, mental clarity, and grace under pressure were also of prime importance. Warrior qigong developed to meet this important demand.

Today, Warrior Qigong is probably most useful for peak performance, whether that is for physical athletes or mental athletes. The energy cultivated in Warrior Qigong will be equally useful for running a marathon or writing a novel. Both require resiliency, stamina, and courage.

I should mention that, for many of my students, Warrior Qigong was also critical for self-healing. In theory, Medical Qigong should have fixed their pain or illness. But in reality, they needed the extra boost from Warrior Qigong to push through their more stubborn energy blockages.

Spiritual Qigong
(also called Buddhist/Taoist Qigong)

Monks and nuns were responsible for much of the development of qigong over the millennia, so it should come as no surprise that spiritual cultivation is a major category. But what does that mean exactly? What is spirituality?

The first distinction to make is that "spiritual" does not mean "religious." For example, the qigong techniques that I teach can be used by anyone, regardless of their religious background (or lack thereof). And in fact, many qigong techniques were simultaneously practiced by people of different religious backgrounds: Buddhists, Taoists, Muslims, and more.

Not all schools of qigong, however, are secular. Some teachers do infuse religion into their teachings. Falon Gong, a qigong school that has been persecuted in China, is an example. Its controversial founder, Li Hongzhi, is more of a quasi-religious leader than a qigong teacher. If you have a teacher like this and it makes you uncomfortable, then find another one.

My view of Spiritual Qigong is simple. Practicing qigong in general, and certain techniques specifically, will increase both the frequency and depth of peak experiences in your life. That sense of oneness, wholeness, and expansiveness that you felt on that perfect summer day while watching the sun reflect off the water—that's a peak experience, and it's something that can be cultivated.

Where Tai Chi Fits In

By now, you're probably wondering where tai chi fits into the qigong picture. Of the two arts, tai chi is more widely recognized in the West. In fact, whenever people ask me what I teach, it usually goes like this:

Them: "Oh, you're a teacher? What do you teach?"

Me: "I teach people how to get their self-healing juices flowing using an ancient Chinese art called qigong. Have you heard of it?"

Them: [Silence]

Me: "It's the grandmother of tai chi."

Them: "Oh! Like the old people in the park!"

This helps to frame things in their mind. Even though most people don't understand what tai chi is, they've probably heard of it and maybe even seen it. I've found that calling qigong "the grand-mother of tai chi" is an effective way to begin educating people about qigong.

And it's absolutely true. It's safe to say that, if not for qigong, tai chi would never have developed in the first place. Nevertheless, it's still useful to understand the difference between these two arts.

For starters, tai chi is a martial art. Remember earlier when I mentioned that the word *kung fu* means a Chinese martial art? Well, tai chi is a substyle of kung fu. Technically, the full name of tai chi is *taijiquan*, sometimes spelled *tai chi chuan*. The "quan" or "chuan" at the end identifies it as a martial art.

In the twenty-first century, there's a ton of overlap between tai chi and qigong. For example, tai chi is often practiced in a non-martial way, making it very similar to qigong. And qigong exercises are often incorporated into tai chi, especially for warming up and for developing flexibility.

But tai chi isn't the only martial art that incorporates qigong. Many other styles of kung fu—like Baguazhang, Xingyiquan, and Shaolinquan—also use qigong.

Why People Prefer Qigong over Tai Chi

If I had a nickel for every student who complained to me that learning the tai chi form was stressful, that it hurt their knees, and that they fell in love with qigong because of its simplicity—well, I'd probably have a few hundred nickels. Which really isn't a lot of money now that I think about it, so maybe we need to update that expression?

Anyway, if you've tried tai chi in the past and hated it, then you're not alone. Please don't get me wrong. I love tai chi and practice it regularly. But tai chi isn't for everyone, especially since there's a huge variation in how it is taught. The truth is that tai chi has been in a weird limbo for decades. Sometimes it's taught as a healing art, sometimes it's taught as a hardcore martial art, and sometimes it's taught as neither.

In the US, tai chi has most commonly been taught as a series of slow-motion calisthenics. This has brought some decent health benefits. But as you'll soon learn, those health benefits pale in comparison to what you can do with qigong.

Not only are the healing benefits of qigong greater, but the art itself is more accessible. For example, with qigong, we don't need to memorize complex routines because we typically focus on repeating a single exercise many times before moving on to the next one. This frees you from worrying about the next move. This also allows you to enjoy your breathing, to savor the flow of the exercise, and to relax into the tranquility of the session—all of which will contribute to getting better health benefits.

But with tai chi, people typically practice a series of exercises, one after the other. Instead of enjoying one exercise twenty times, you will typically do twenty exercises one time, all in a prescribed sequence. Some people love it like this, but many people don't. They find the whole process to be too intellectual and too challenging. They signed up for tai chi classes to relieve stress—but got the opposite!

The good news is that these very same people have a totally different experience with qigong. Often, students tell me that learning qigong felt like coming home after years of wandering. I know the feeling. Welcome home!

Who Practices Qigong?

For centuries, qigong was practiced by four classes of people:

- Spiritualists, including monks and nuns
- Martial artists, including the military
- Royalty, especially the emperor
- Classical Chinese physicians fortunate enough to know some qigong, and their patients

That's pretty much it though. It wasn't something that was practiced by the public. They just didn't have access to the teachings.

There were some family styles of qigong, but typically these were connected to martial arts. The typical Chinese family didn't think about learning qigong to solve their health problems. Instead, they looked to acupuncture, herbal medicine, and folk remedies.

Everything started to change in the twentieth century when qigong and tai chi masters began to teach more openly. Some of them, like the patriarch of modern tai chi, Yang Cheng Fu, specifically promoted their art as health care for the general public. And now in the twenty-first century, the qigong landscape is like nothing the world has ever seen before.

Who practices qigong today? The answer is anyone who wants to! Over the years, I've taught all kinds of amazing humans. I've taught people in wheelchairs, weekend warriors, stroke victims with limited mobility, soccer moms, and college professors. I've taught students as old as ninety-one and as young as six. I've taught professional athletes and professional mathletes. I've taught men, women, and everything in between. I've taught Blacks, Asians, Latinos, Native Americans, Christians, Muslims, Buddhists, atheists, gays, queers, lesbians, transgenders, and people from forty-eight different countries and counting.

In the twenty-first century, most people start practicing qigong because they want to address a specific health problem. Obviously, that's how I found qigong, and that's also how I teach it. I believe that healing should be the foundation.

Things are changing fast though. Not all qigong teachers approach the art in the way that I do—and I, myself, might change in the future. For example, qigong could revolutionize the sports industry. If elite athletes suddenly discovered how much qigong could boost their performance, they would be knocking down my door. In that case, they would be coming to me for something other than health.

This wouldn't be so different from what happened in the past—except with elite athletes instead of elite martial artists. Remember that, in the past, martial artists weren't hobbyists like today; they were professional warriors, generals, and soldiers. They were as disciplined as an Olympic athlete.

For example, the famous Chinese general Yue Fei (岳飛) taught a set of qigong exercises to his soldiers to keep them healthy. This set, called the Eight Pieces of Brocade (Ba Duan Jin, 八段錦), survives to this day. I still teach and practice this set.

Spiritual Qigong is another area of growing interest. Many people come to this art specifically with spirituality in mind. They want to enhance their existing meditation practice, or even enhance their existing religious practices.

As you can see, asking who practices qigong is quickly becoming a trivial question. It's like asking who practices fitness. And the answer is that lots of people do, for lots of different reasons. But if

I had to pick one thing that most modern practitioners of qigong have in common, it would be this:

> We practice because we believe that the human body has an invisible, internal healing mechanism that can be unlocked with the art of qigong.

Flowing Zen Qigong

When I first started teaching, I built a website, but I needed a name for it. I wanted to capture the essence of qigong but without using esoteric Chinese words. One morning, after a particularly good qigong session, three words popped into my head: "Zen that flows."

A few days later, while sitting in an acupuncture class, those three words morphed into two. "Flowing Zen!" I said quietly to myself. It was a eureka moment for me. I felt like a Newton after the apple fell on his head.

As soon as I got home from class, I logged into my computer and purchased the domain name flowingzen.com. That was back in 2005, and it's still my website all these years later. It has also become the name of my LLC, the name of my particular style of qigong (Flowing Zen Qigong), and now it's the name of my first book!

This name is perfect for four main reasons:

First, my teaching revolves around a rare qigong technique called Flowing Breeze Swaying Willow. As you can probably guess, this technique is all about getting the qi flowing. You'll learn about Flowing Breeze Swaying Willow in chapter 6.

Second, my teaching emphasizes the importance of entering into a meditative state before performing any qigong movements. We call this "Entering Zen" because it shifts us into a Zen state of mind. You'll learn about this skill in chapter 6 as well.

Third, masters throughout history have given unique names to their particular qigong styles. That's why there have been thousands of different qigong styles. I believe that Flowing Zen Qigong is a poetic and accurate name for what I teach.

Fourth, much of the qigong that I teach comes from the Shaolin Temple. As I mentioned earlier, this was the birthplace of Zen Meditation, Shaolin Kung Fu, as well as Shaolin Qigong. It feels good to honor this ancient tradition by using the word *Zen*.

Zen is a transliteration of the Japanese word 禪 (pronounced "zen"), which in turn was a translation of the Chinese word 禪 (pronounced "chan"), which in turn was a translation of the Sanskrit word *dhyana* (pronounced "dee-ahna"). So the word went from *dhyana* (Sanskrit) to *chan* (Chinese) to *Zen* (Japanese). Today, it's also an official English word that, according to Webster, means "a state of calm attentiveness in which one's actions are guided by intuition rather than by conscious effort."

A while ago, I was criticized for using a Japanese word (*Zen*) to describe Chinese arts. This criticism is unfounded because I began my journey with two Japanese arts: Goju-Ryu Karate and seated Zen meditation. Both of these arts heavily influenced my practice of qigong.

All of this is beside the point because the Japanese word is really 禪, not *Zen*. The famous eighteenth-century Zen Master Hakuin Ekaku wouldn't be able to read the word *Zen* because he couldn't read English. *Zen* is just our feeble attempt to spell it using our alphabet.

I'm not a huge fan of these nationalistic divisions anyway. It's true that qigong comes from ancient China, but that civilization no longer exists. So when I say that qigong is Chinese, I'm not referring to Communist China.

Qigong is a living art, I am an artist, and Flowing Zen Qigong is my masterpiece. It's amazing how well Flowing Zen Qigong works for modern practitioners. When I first started teaching in a small athletics room in Florida, I never could have imagined that it would one day turn into a global phenomenon.

In chapter 6, you'll learn the most important aspects of this style so that you can start to get benefits immediately. Many of these skills can be incorporated into other styles of qigong as well. Ultimately, I just want you to fall in love with the art of qigong. If learning some Flowing Zen Qigong contributes to that goal, then I will have accomplished my mission.

To clarify things for the modern reader, I will specifically mention Flowing Zen Qigong (uppercase) when referring to my particular style. I will also capitalize the names of other qigong styles, such as Wild Goose Qigong. When referring to qigong in general, I will just use the word "qigong" (lowercase).

Are you ready to get your zen flowing a little bit better?

SUCCESS STORY: DIANNE

Dianne had always been active, but she was unable to stick to any regimen for longer than two years. She tried ballet, aerobics, swimmercize, pilates, yoga, and meditation. All these modalities worked to a certain extent, but she still felt that something was missing. Either she wasn't making discernible progress, or she'd get injured. Flowing Zen Qigong was that missing piece for Dianne.

Prior to qigong, she was unable to stand for even fifteen minutes without her back going into spasms. Now, using qigong as a form of moving meditation, she can stand for longer and longer periods without pain. Her energy levels have improved, she's able to focus more and is finally completing old projects. She's engaging with people more than ever, and she's sleeping better. She is also better able to cope with the occasional depressive episode.

Dianne learned from me online, and she found the online Flowing Zen community to be especially helpful. "I feel like this isn't just a class I'm taking but rather a shared path of wellness with an amazing group of people."

CHAPTER 3
The Ancient Roots of Qigong

I *luvs* me some history, but I also realize that it's not everyone's cup of tea. I'll try to keep this chapter focused on the information that will be most useful to you in your twenty-first century qigong journey. We won't dive into unnecessary or uninteresting parts of qigong history. There are plenty of other books on that subject, so we'll stick to aspects of qigong history that will directly benefit the modern practitioner.

Understanding the origins of qigong will help you to appreciate the cumulative wisdom of generations of masters. It will also help you to be better informed. For example, here's an illustrative conversation I had years ago.

I met Pete in Central Park in New York City while I was still living there. We had both chosen the same spot for our morning practices. Afterward, we struck up a conversation. Naturally, we started talking about qigong and tai chi.

When he asked what kind of qigong I practiced, I said, "Shaolin Qigong." (Today, I've learned and practiced many different styles of qigong, but back then, Shaolin Qigong was my main practice.)

"Ah," he said, nodding. "I prefer the older Taoist styles, like tai chi."

"Older?" I said, honestly confused. "The qigong that I practice traces back to the sixth century CE."

"Well, tai chi is much older than that!" Pete said.

Now, the most important thing you need to know about qigong is that it works wonders for health and vitality. Don't ever forget this fact. In that sense, it really doesn't matter if qigong is 1500 years old or 4000, right? What matters is that it works. But for fun, let's look at the facts.

How Old Is Qigong?

Qigong is probably older than history. For example, we have archeological evidence (pottery) dating back to 5000 BCE showing a qigong posture that looks exactly like a famous qigong posture called "Hugging the Tree." I still practice and teach this technique today.

Here are some other bits of historical evidence:

- ca. 400 BCE—The Classic of the Way's Virtues (The Dao De Jing, 道德經) by Lao Tzu (老子) speaks about focusing on your qi through breathing, and also about cultivating softness (a hallmark of qigong practice).
- ca. 400 BCE—Chuang Tzu (莊子) talks about how past masters breathed qi down to their feet, which is an advanced qigong technique where you direct the qi down the leg meridians.
- ca. 300 BCE—The Circulating Qi Inscription (Xing Qi Ming, 行氣銘) describes the Small Universe Qigong technique, an advanced qigong method that I still practice and teach.
- ca. 200 BCE—The Yellow Emperor's Classic of Medicine (Huang Di Neijing, 黃帝內經), which is the fundamental text of Classical Chinese Medicine, speaks about breathing qi and keeping the mind tranquil to promote longevity. It also talks about Qi Circulation Theory, the Theory of Five Elements, and the Theory of Yin and Yang

As you can see, there's considerable evidence suggesting that, at the very least, qigong predates the birth of Jesus. And if you include the evidence from ancient pottery, then qigong predates the pyramids!

How Old Is Tai Chi?

Let's get back to my conversation with Pete. When I raised an eyebrow at his statement that tai chi is *much* older than qigong, Pete was undaunted.

"The *I Ching* talks about tai chi," he said. "That dates to the ninth century BCE!"

Let me be clear that I would never critique a beginner for a statement like this. An expert, however, should know better. Pete's statement was factually incorrect, but for some reason, it's an opinion that pops up more and more often in the tai chi world.

Let's bust this myth once and for all.

The *I Ching* (*The Book of Changes*, 易經) is an ancient Chinese divination text that does indeed date back to the ninth century BCE. And yes, it *does* talk about tai chi—but *not* the tai chi that Pete and I were discussing.

The *I Ching* speaks about the *philosophy* of tai chi, not the martial art of tai chi.

Tai chi, the beautiful, slow-motion martial art that is also good for the health, should actually be called tai chi chuan (太極拳). When we leave off the "chuan" at the end, we're no longer talking about a martial art. Instead, we're talking about the ancient Chinese philosophy of yin and yang. In other words, tai chi (太極) is a philosophy, but tai chi chuan (太極拳) is a martial art. Of course, tai chi chuan incorporates the philosophy of tai chi (i.e., the theory of yin and yang), which only adds to the confusion.

Most people leave off the chuan, especially in America. I'm guilty of this too. It's easier to just say "tai chi."

The term *tai chi* has become ubiquitous. It's gotten to the point where if you say "tai chi chuan" people look at you funny. After scratching their heads for a minute, they eventually say, "Oh, you mean tai chi!" If we're going to use the abbreviated term "tai chi" (and let's be honest, we are), then it's important to know what we're abbreviating from!

Pete falsely asserted that the martial art of tai chi dates to the ninth century BCE. Am I nitpicking by correcting his statement? No, I don't think so. Here's why: If someone asserted that Socrates was born one thousand years ago, you wouldn't shrug and say, "close enough for jazz!" He was born nearly 2500 years ago! You can flub the historical dates a little, but not by a couple millennia!

So how old is tai chi chuan then? There are two main theories about the origins of this art:

Theory #1—tai chi chuan was created by the Taoist monk Zhang Sanfeng in the twelfth century AD.

Theory #2—tai chi chuan was created by Chen Wang Ting in the seventh century AD.

Many modern scholars subscribe to the second theory because of the lack of evidence to support the first theory. After considering the evidence, I now subscribe to theory #2. But even if you subscribe to theory #1, that's still two thousand years later than what Pete was suggesting.

I often say that qigong is the grandmother of tai chi. Qigong is not just one generation older than tai chi, but two. And when it comes to these arts, each generation lasts a millennium!

Remember those ancient qigong texts I mentioned earlier? Even if we ignore the pottery, we've got solid evidence dating back to at least 300–400 BCE. In other words, qigong, at the absolute least, is fifteen hundred years older than tai chi chuan. And it may be as much as six thousand years older!

As I stated before, the most important thing about qigong is not how old it is, but that it confers so many benefits. Older does not always mean better. Let's be sure to avoid that kind of thinking.

No one truly knows how qigong was practiced thousands of years ago. All we can do is make an educated guess based on the evidence. Nevertheless, some of that evidence clearly describes techniques and experiences that are amazingly close to what we experience today.

For example, the idea of breathing qi (energy) down to your feet might sound crazy to you, but to me, that sounds like something called the Big Universe (大周天, Da Zhou Tian). In this technique, we breathe and direct the qi down the yang leg meridians to an acupuncture point at the bottom of the foot. Next, we direct the energy back up the yin leg meridians.

In learning about the history of qigong, I feel a timeless connection to those ancient humans—from the other side of the world, from a totally foreign culture, from a long, long time ago—who practiced something like what I practice today. And I hope that you'll feel a similar connection as you practice this beautiful art!

The Qi of Tai Chi Chuan

Pete was not only misinformed about the origins of tai chi, but he was also confused about its meaning. During our conversation, he tried to contend that the "chi" from tai chi chuan means "energy." This, too, is incorrect.

It is not the same as the chi (or qi) from qigong (or chi kung).

In Chinese, the word is made of three characters or logograms:

1. tai 太
2. ji 极
3. quan 拳

Notice the middle logogram there. It's "ji," not "chi." This is actually closer to the correct pronunciation. Check your book

bonuses (flowingzen.com/bookbonus) for the correct pronunciation of the words "qigong" and "tai chi chuan."

Regardless of how we pronounce it, however, there is no question that the second logogram is nowhere to be found in the word
qigong!

1. qi 氣
2. gong 功

In other words, the "qi" (氣) from qigong means "energy,"
but the "ji" 极 from taijiquan does not. Yes, of course taijiquan
is all about the cultivation of qi, but that doesn't mean that qi is
in the name!

For those who are curious, *ji* means "utmost." In this context,
however, it blends with tai to form *taiji*. This could be translated
as "cosmos," but it is a nod toward the philosophy of yin and yang.
We'll talk about this later.

Many people who learn tai chi are actually looking for qigong.
They just want some simple, enjoyable exercises to improve their
health. They don't want to learn long, complex routines, and they
certainly aren't interested in martial arts.

By the way, my efforts to educate people about qigong sometimes get misinterpreted as a dislike for tai chi. This couldn't be
farther from the truth! I practice tai chi regularly, and I think I'll
be practicing it for the rest of my life. It's a beautiful art.

However, I'm an educator and I want people to make informed
decisions. Whether you choose to practice qigong or tai chi or both,
it should be based on quality information. As I said, we can view tai
chi as a form of qigong. We can certainly cultivate qi with our tai
chi. And most schools of tai chi also teach some qigong exercises.

In my experience, tai chi is the perfect martial art for people
who think they're not interested in martial arts. If you've ever
been turned off by the testosterone-fueled energy of a martial arts
school, or if you believe strongly in the philosophy of nonviolence, or if you're not as strong or as big as most other folks and

you'd like to feel more confident and empowered—then tai chi might be perfect for you.

If you're thinking that tai chi sounds like the perfect martial art for women, you'd be right. What many people don't realize is that the same reasons that make tai chi a good choice for women make it a good choice for smaller-framed individuals like me!

I'm 5'7" (170 cm) on a good day and weigh 152 pounds (71 kilos). I'm fit and keep in shape (thanks to qigong and tai chi), but I am by no means big or strong. In the modern world of martial arts, I am a welterweight. That's four classes below heavyweight!

I learned this fact the hard way. I've got two black belts in karate, and I have practiced a half dozen different martial arts since 1992. And what I learned—by taking tons of punches and kicks—is that what works for the big boys doesn't work for me.

I was lucky. My very first martial arts teacher was a woman. And not just any woman, but a total badass named Sensei Bonnie Baker. (*Sensei* is the Japanese equivalent to the Chinese title *Sifu*. Both mean "teacher.")

I'll never forget first meeting Sensei Bonnie at Columbia in 1992. I'm guessing that no one forgets meeting her because her presence is striking (pun intended). She walked into the room wearing a pristine white karate uniform with a tattered and frayed black belt that screamed, "This thing is older than you!"

Silver hair, tied in a simple ponytail, ran all the way down to her low back. Her piercing baby-blue eyes seemed to look right through me, as if I were just the next victim in a line of bad guys in a kung fu movie. At the time, she was in her fifties, but she put all of us nineteen-year-old college students to shame, men and women alike. She would crank out twenty-five pushups on her knuckles and then wait for us young'uns to finish. Her look said, "If a fifty-something, 125-pound woman can do this, I don't want to hear any complaining." So we didn't complain, not anywhere near her at least.

A few years into my training, we were practicing a self-defense move to escape from a choke hold from behind. The escape involved ramming your elbows into the attacker's ribs, stomping on their toes, and if necessary, striking their groin. All these strikes were just to loosen them up for a hip throw to the ground.

Sensei Bonnie always liked to choose a big, strong young man in the room to demonstrate the technique. "Really grab me," she would say. A half second later, they would be on the ground, wincing.

But one time, she chose an absolute hulking monster for the demo. I mean, this guy was a beast, probably 6'4", 300 pounds, and strong as an ox. When Sensei Bonnie said, "Really grab me," he didn't hesitate, and it looked like he would crush her. She could hardly move, and I knew from experience that this was a problem because she wouldn't be able to deliver those loosening strikes, which were a critical part of the technique. He was also lifting her off the ground a bit, so there was no way she could stomp on his toes.

Oh shit, I thought. *He's going to make a fool of her!* Ye of little faith. I should have known better.

Next thing we knew, the hulk was on the ground. For a moment, I couldn't understand what had happened. I knew Sensei Bonnie didn't elbow him, didn't stomp his foot, and couldn't reach his groin. But somehow, she still managed to escape the hold and then throw him.

Then it all made sense. "You bit me!" the hulk said from the ground. Apparently, Sensei Bonnie had quickly tucked her chin just before the hulk had wrapped his arm around her throat. With her chin tucked, she was able to not only prevent herself from being choked, but her mouth was also pressed right against his forearm.

"I sure did," she said, and the room filled with laughter. These days, Sensei Bonnie would probably get sued for doing something like that, but I for one am grateful for that lesson, and I think many of the other small-sized men and women in the class felt the same way. What she taught us that day is that you don't need to use strength to overcome strength. You need technique, and you need presence of mind.

In the 1960s when Sensei Bonnie was a student, karate was the only art that was available to her. Today, we are lucky to have so many choices. We can choose an art like tai chi chuan that focuses not on brute strength. We can also choose an art that gives us health benefits without all that punching and kicking!

Internal vs. External

In the world of martial arts, you'll hear talk about "internal" and "external" styles. For example, many people will refer to karate as "external" and tai chi chuan as "internal." What does this all mean? There's a simple way to explain it.

External training focuses on things that you can see with your eyes, like muscles. Pushups, something that most modern martial artists do, is a basic example of external training. If you do lots of pushups, the results will show in your muscles.

Internal training focuses on things that you can't see, like qi. Lifting the Sky, one of the first exercises that I teach, is an example of internal training. If you practice Lifting the Sky, you will get health benefits.

In the end, however, there really isn't such a thing as a purely external or purely internal art. There are internal or external methods, but most martial arts end up combining both. In some cases, like with the karate that I learned, the secrets of internal training were either lost or kept not taught. If you dig deep enough, you'll find both internal and external methods in most arts, even karate.

For example, my karate training with Sensei Bonnie emphasized external methods. We did lots of pushups and we practiced our kicks endlessly. In contrast, my tai chi chuan training emphasized internal methods. I practiced qigong exercises and meditative techniques that cultivated internal power (*neijin*). The emphasis in my karate days was external, and the emphasis in my tai chi chuan days was internal. However, and this is important, I still do pushups!

Can you see how the black and white distinction between internal and external starts to fall apart? It all depends on how you train, and what you emphasize. For example, there are a lot of tai chi chuan practitioners who—ironically—do not emphasize internal training at all. In fact, they often don't even know what internal training really is!

For example, a student once told me that he practiced the Yang Style Long Form from start to finish every day. He truly believed he was doing internal training simply by going through a tai chi form. But we did the same thing in karate. Forms training doesn't magically become internal just because you do it slowly.

Another qigong student, Patrick, is a serious karate practitioner. He didn't want to learn tai chi chuan from me because he was happy with his karate. No problem! That's what qigong is for! So he learned some qigong, including some techniques for building internal power.

The irony here is that Patrick practices a martial art (karate) that is widely considered to be external, but he does more internal training (qigong) than most people who practice the so-called internal martial art of tai chi chuan!

For a few hundred years, the term *internal martial art* (neijia quan, 內家拳) has been used to refer to three specific arts:

1. Pa Kua Chang (or Baguazhang)
2. Hsing-I Chuan (or Xingyiquan)
3. Tai Chi Chuan (or Taijiquan)

All of these arts incorporate qigong exercises that build internal power. And all of these arts rely more on internal power than external strength when it comes to self-defense. But remember that qigong is older than tai chi chuan. It's also older than the other two arts of Bagzhang and Xingyiquan.

In other words, past masters took suitable qigong exercises, incorporated them into their martial arts training, and eventually ended up with a new style of kung fu. If Patrick becomes an amazing grandmaster and creates his own style of karate, then two hundred years from now, his karate might be just as internal as tai chi chuan! Qigong is truly the secret sauce in any internal martial art.

My tai chi chuan is powered by the internal strength that I develop through qigong. I also practice other martial arts. I stopped practicing karate years ago, but I still practice Shaolin Five Animal Kung Fu and also a tiny bit of Baguazhang. Qigong is the engine that powers all of them. Yes, there are different qigong exercises for each of these martial arts, but the differences are minor. Internal training always follows the same basic principles.

Because of the internal power I've developed over the years, I can handle a bigger and stronger opponent despite my small size. This isn't just about raw technique or decades of experience either; it's something different. I can hit harder than my small size suggests and can also move surprisingly fast even though much of my training is done in slow motion. And perhaps most importantly, internal power enables me to stay relaxed while engaged in sparring, self-defense drills, and even in real-life encounters. In other words—I'm more graceful under pressure because of all my internal power training.

These skills are not only useful in self-defense, but also in daily life. For example, being able to relax under pressure is something that could easily save your life on the highway. In fact, it saved mine years ago when it helped me to avoid an oncoming truck that was trying to pass a tractor trailer on a small, country road.

In the twenty-first century, we're unlikely to get into a fight with our fists. While self-defense is still important, the truth is that most scenarios boil down to grace under pressure, not technique. This is another reason to love qigong, because the benefits of this practice extend into so many different areas of modern life.

SUCCESS STORY: TATIANA

Tatiana suffered a spinal cord injury at the age of twenty-one. She has been in a wheelchair ever since. She discovered Flowing Zen Qigong in her mid-fifties.

Within a week of beginning my online programs, she noticed a big increase in her energy levels. She also got rapid relief from insomnia, which had tortured her for years. Instead of struggling to fall asleep two to three times per week, she now only struggles two to three times per month. And even on nights where she struggles, she still feels good in the morning.

"That's a four-fold increase in life quality," she told me.

Tatiana also saw a dramatic improvement with her eczema. For years, she had it on the back of her head and on her shoulders. She tried cortisone treatments, but they didn't work. Just three months into her qigong practice, the eczema vanished completely!

A birch pollen allergy, which she had had since her twenties, also disappeared within a year of taking up qigong.

Today, Tatiana faithfully practices twice per day. "I cannot imagine my life without qigong now," she told me.

Spiritual But Not Religious

"Will doing qigong turn me into a Buddhist?" she asked. Elaine's southern accent was thick and beautiful. She was the definition of elegance, an older lady with perfect hair and exquisite poise.

Being the uncouth New Yorker than I am, I almost laughed out loud. It sounded like such a strange question. But Elaine's question was sincere.

"It hasn't turned me into a Buddhist yet!" I said. She smiled and seemed pleased with this response. She ended up being a terrific student.

Let me be clear that I am neither Buddhist nor Christian. Nor am I Taoist, Hindu, Muslim, Jewish, or Sikh.

"He's an atheist. Burn him!"

Nope. Not an atheist either.

People sometimes loathe this answer, but the truth is that I've always been what people now call SBNR—spiritual, but not religious. I was not raised with any religious tradition—unless classical music counts—and yet from a young age, I have considered myself to be spiritual. In college, I studied both Eastern and Western religions and have a deep respect for all the great teachers, from Jesus to Buddha to Lao Tzu. But I simply can't say that I belong to any religion.

My friend James is the opposite. When I visited his home in Malaysia, I noticed that the family altar contained three small statues: Guan Yin Bodhisattva, the Immortal Li, and Mother Mary. Those are Buddhist, Taoist, and Catholic statues, respectively. I had seen family altars with both Buddhist and Taoist icons, but this was my first time seeing Catholicism thrown into the mix.

"James, I'm curious about your altar," I asked. "How do you reconcile Catholicism with Buddhism and Taoism?

"It's not such a big deal here," he said.

"But it's a big deal in the Vatican!" I said.

James shrugged. "We just follow the teachings of Buddha, Lao Tzu, and Jesus," he said.

"But don't these teachings conflict with one another?"

He shrugged again, and that was that. That was his answer. I was dumbstruck because, in a way, it was the most enlightened answer he could have possibly given.

James's answer really isn't that different from mine. I don't relate to one specific religion, and neither does he. Of course, he grew up with several traditions, whereas I grew up with Beethoven. But underneath it all, our views are similar.

Similarly, qigong can be spiritual without being religious. For example, over the years I've taught Catholic priests, Jewish rabbis, Buddhist monks, Hari Krishna devotees, Muslim sheikhs,

Protestant ministers, and also plenty of atheists. And they all benefited.

But we need to look at the Buddhist and Taoist schools of qigong because they are significant, historically speaking. We've already talked about Bodhidharma and the Shaolin Temple. That's the beginning of Buddhist Qigong.

Taoist Qigong traces back to the very first Taoist, Lao Tzu, who lived somewhere between the sixth and fourth centuries. Although we don't know much about him, it seems clear from his masterpiece, the Tao Te Ching, that Lao Tzu practiced some sort of qigong.

So both Buddhism and Taoism have qigong traditions tracing back millennia. But what is the difference in their approach to qigong? Not surprisingly, their approach to qigong mirrors their philosophy of life.

For example, Buddhist qigong tends to be more staccato, with distinct moves that are easy to learn. Lifting the Sky is a good example. This approach fits with the Buddhist philosophy of being simple, direct, and effective. (If you haven't learned Lifting the Sky yet, then take a break and go grab your book bonuses at flowingzen.com/bookbonus.)

Taoist qigong tends to be more flowing and circular. This fits with the concept of yin and yang and the flow of the Tao. "Double Dragons Play with Pearl" is a good example of this. (Again, you can learn this technique in your book bonuses.)

But things get more complex as we move through history. For example, the famous qigong set called the Eight Brocades is usually considered to be a Taoist form. It is attributed to Yue Fei, a famous Chinese general (1103–1142). But Yue Fei learned martial arts from Zhou Tong, who had studied at the famous Shaolin Temple, which is Buddhist.

Are the Eight Brocades Buddhist, or Taoist? To me, it's obvious that it's a mix. The Eight Brocades look extremely like the first Eight exercises from the Shaolin Eighteen Luohan Hands, but with a Taoist flavor. In other words, things don't always fit into neat little boxes.

There's a saying in Chinese that basically implies that all forms of kung fu trace back to the Shaolin Temple. Obviously, this statement upsets a few people, especially the folks at Wudang Temple. Hollywood seized on this and chose to portray the two temples as bitter rivals. But that's just movie theatrics.

A more accurate statement might be that all roads went through the Shaolin Temple. In other words, the Shaolin Temple wasn't necessarily the birthplace of all styles of kung fu, but rather it was a greenhouse. Over the centuries, the Shaolin Temple was incredibly welcoming to outsiders. We know that Catholic priests stayed there, as well as Muslim imams, Hindus, and of course, Taoists.

It seems that the Shaolin monks were exceedingly good at pirating good ideas whenever they saw them. Imitation is the sincerest form of flattery, right? When the Shaolin monks found something useful, they held onto it. In many cases, they became the stewards of these techniques for generations.

The qigong that I inherited was already a mix of both Buddhist and Taoist theories. Qigong deals with the subtleties of the human mind and energy, so it touches on some of the deepest aspects of existence. In this sense, it's no wonder that many of the theories are borrowed from spiritual traditions.

But there's nothing stopping us from continuing to borrow from other traditions as well. For example, I have always been fascinated by science. The qigong that I teach borrows heavily from this tradition. That's why I use so much modern terminology in my teachings. The art of qigong is alive and ever-changing, and although some people think that this approach is not traditional, I would beg to differ. I'm following the long tradition of adapting qigong to my world, just like the Shaolin monks did for centuries.

The Martial Stewards

Today, I mostly teach qigong that is non-martial. For example, Lifting the Sky is not a martial arts technique, nor is it a form of Martial Qigong. In other words, my students can completely bypass the martial aspects of qigong.

This is a new development, historically speaking. In the past, if you wanted to learn qigong, then you often had to learn martial arts as well. Many of these martial artists were also monks, nuns, or spiritualists. Self-defense was still integral to the training. You just couldn't avoid it.

We should be grateful to the martial artists for practicing, preserving, and perfecting the art of qigong for thousands of years. In many ways, they were the ideal candidates for steward-ship. The Shaolin monks and Wudang priests practiced qigong because, among other things, it was useful in defending against bandits on the road. But more than that, qigong was a perfect match for them. They had the discipline, the motivation, and also the perfect environment in which to practice. Thanks to their dil-igent efforts, qigong was not only preserved, but it reached greater and greater heights.

Today, we underestimate the motivation that people once had for self-defense. Remember that, before firearms, martial arts were serious business. Your life, and maybe the lives of your family or your village, depended on your skills. For example, there are countless "family" styles of kung fu. These styles developed all over China, and they were meant to protect an entire family or clan from bandits or marauders in the days before police. Without police to protect your family, you were at the mercy of the darkest aspects of human nature. People found strength in numbers and large fami-lies. But they also found strength in martial arts. And we're not just talking about fisticuffs here. We're talking about weaponry!

Family styles of kung fu always included some sort of weap-onry. It might be as simple as a seven-foot wooden staff, or as

sophisticated as a Chinese straight sword. Sometimes it was just
the men who were taught kung fu, but often the women learned as
well. (Chinese culture can be extremely sexist, but there is an interesting streak of feminism in the kung fu tradition. For example,
one of the greatest martial artists of all time was a Buddhist nun
named Ng Mui.)

I mention the weaponry here to make a point about qigong.
Martial artists, especially back then, were always looking for ways
to improve their defensive capabilities. Weaponry is an obvious way
to do that. Despite what you see in the movies, a person fighting with bare hands is no match for someone with a weapon. The
Chinese saber, for example, is relatively easy to learn and devas-
tatingly effective. In the hands of someone with even just a few
months of training, it was a great equalizer.

These no-nonsense martial artists who developed sophisticated
martial arts around a wide variety of weapons were also interested
in qigong. That tells us something important about the practical
benefits of qigong. If qigong hadn't provided them some sort of
tangible benefits, then they wouldn't have used it!

Yue Fei, the famous general I mentioned earlier, taught qigong
to his soldiers because it was useful for the business of soldiering.
Dong Haiquan, the founder of Baguazhang, taught qigong to his
kung fu students because he found it useful as an imperial body-
guard. And the monk Zhi Shan, abbot of the Shaolin Temple,
taught qigong to his kung fu disciples because it was helpful for his
political revolution.

In the end, many of the secrets of qigong were protected by
the temples, especially the Shaolin and Wudang Temples. These
two temples are the stuff of legend. There are countless movies
and books portraying martial artists from Shaolin and Wudang. A
modern-day rap group even named themselves after Wudang. Talk
about brand recognition!

Secrecy and the Twenty-First Century

The qigong world is awakening in the twenty-first century. Secrets are being revealed, and notes are being compared. I truly believe that this sharing of information is for the benefit of all humanity. Unfortunately, not all qigong teachers agree with me. For example, I once tried to sign up for a qigong workshop, but my money was refunded. I emailed the teacher to ask why.

"I know who you are," he said, "and I don't want you stealing my qigong."

Stealing? I was happy to pay, just like everyone else. But no dice. I suppose I could have signed up with a fake account but that didn't feel right, so I just moved on. I did write him back, however.

"I want you to know that you are free to steal all of my qigong secrets," I wrote. "You don't even need to tell anyone else they are mine. You can sign up with a fake account. But please—take my secrets!"

I don't know if he ever took me up on my offer, although it's possible. I do know that some qigong teachers have "stolen" my secrets, rebranded them, and taught them without giving me credit. To this I say: good for you!

It baffles me that some people don't want to learn as much as they can. I understand that beginners shouldn't rush around trying to learn everything; they need to focus on the fundamentals. But intermediate and advanced practitioners who have been doing qigong for years? Why don't they go learn *all the things*?!?

I chased teachers across Asia, Europe, the US, and Central America. I spent thousands of dollars on qigong books and DVDs. And today, I have a growing library of online courses as well. One day, if I can simply upload qigong skills to my head like in *The Matrix*, I'll probably do that too!

All of these learning opportunities—the online courses, the in-person workshops, the books, the DVDs—were completely unavailable to past qigong masters. If you had given them the option, I'm sure they would have taken full advantage. Give Hua Tuo an internet connection and a credit card, and I guarantee that he would rack up a sizable bill on books and online courses!

There Are No Secrets

Modern practitioners of qigong often forget that the art comes from a long tradition of strict secrecy. Because they don't understand this tradition, they underestimate the momentum that secrecy still carries in the twenty-first century. They dismiss it, to their own detriment.

For example, it's common for qigong and tai chi teachers to say, "There are no secrets." They are referring to a popular tai chi book by Wolfe Lowenthal, but what they really mean is that the secrets are found in the fundamentals. In other words, if you diligently practice the fundamentals of qigong or tai chi, you will unlock the secrets as a matter of course, or so they say.

Historically speaking, this simply wasn't true. Qigong practitioners, who were often martial artists as well, guarded their secrets carefully. They intentionally withheld critical pieces of information from their students, sometimes for decades. And some still do!

For example, one of my teachers intentionally put a red herring into his DVDs. He gave misleading instructions in order to protect his secrets. He then taught the correct techniques to his top disciples.

To understand the Chinese phenomenon of secrecy, let's go back in time. Imagine that you're living in China roughly four hundred years ago. Imagine that you're Chinese, you're male (I'll explain this in a moment), that you can read (most could not), and that you come from a wealthy family.

In one of your family's scrolls, you read something about qigong. You're fascinated, and you want to learn more. After spreading the word and using daddy's connections, you find a teacher who everyone agrees is a master.

You can't simply walk up to the master and ask for lessons, so you use daddy's connections to get a local magistrate to write you a letter of recommendation. Next, you buy some gifts. You (or rather daddy) spend the equivalent of present day two thousand US dollars on an amazing box of ginseng. (Yes, you really can spend that much on ginseng.)

Next, you go to the master's house with your letter of introduction and your box of ginseng. You knock, and when the door opens, you're already kowtowing, your gift and letter extended as you touch your head to the ground.

"Master, please teach me," you say.

The master looks at you, takes the gift and letter, and then shuts the door, saying nothing. Day one complete!

You return the next day, kowtowing again and begging to be taught. This time, you bring a rare piece of jade as a gift. Again, the master takes the gift and then closes the door.

This pattern repeats for seven days in a row. On the seventh day, the master still says nothing but leaves the door open. And thus your training begins. Woohoo!

During the first week of training, you learn the Horse-Riding Stance and nothing else. The master shows you how to take a stance roughly double the width of your shoulders, how to sit deeply in the stance with your back straight, how to hold your fists at your waist, and how to breathe.

Sitting in the stance, your legs begin to tremble after just a few minutes. When you rise up in the stance to give your legs a rest, the master simply tells you to sit back down again. That's it.

You go to the master's house every day to practice. And I mean practice! There is virtually no instruction. What little instruction you receive involves the master whacking or poking you with a thin bamboo cane saying, "Not correct." Your legs are so sore that you can barely walk, but you persist.

After two weeks, the master teaches you another exercise called Lifting the Sky. He shows you the form but doesn't mention the breathing. You copy his breathing as best as you can.

So now your practice sessions consist of grueling bouts of the Horse Stance followed by easy sessions of Lifting the Sky. You look forward to Lifting the Sky because it's so much easier than the Horse Stance. You take short breaks to drink some tea, and then you rush back to practicing, eager to prove your commitment to the master. You are persistent because you don't want to bring shame to your family by quitting.

You learn nothing about the theory of qigong, very little about breathing, and the main piece of instruction that you receive is "not correct" without ever learning what actually *is* correct. Not once does the master say, "good job!" or even "correct." Whenever he looks at you but says nothing at all, you feel proud of your progress!

On your 108th day of training, the master says, "Fang song" in Chinese, which means "release and soften." He shows you how to relax more in both the Horse Stance and Lifting the Sky. You're amazed at how big a difference this makes! He also teaches you a new exercise called Three Levels to Earth, which involves squatting up and down. It's a nice break from the monotony of the Horse Stance.

Every few months, the master gives you a new piece of instruction. Just one tiny piece. "Relax the jaw like this," he says one day, and then leaves you to practice. "Breathe like this," he says two months later.

This teaching method continues for three years. You see other students come and go. Most don't make it past the first three months, but one student, Chee, has persevered. Now there are two of you practicing in the master's courtyard!

You feel proud of yourself when the master shows you a new exercise called One Finger Zen. It's much more complicated than anything else you've learned, but you follow it as best as you can.

When you get home that evening, you replay the master's performance in your mind over and over.

"Never in front of others, not even Chee," the master says the following day as you begin your One Finger Zen practice. It is crystal clear to you that you are to keep the One Finger Zen technique hidden from all the other students, or else you will not learn more. When other students are around, you practice the Horse Stance. When they leave, which is always before you do, then you switch to One Finger Zen.

Gradually, the master teaches you more about One Finger Zen, always in private.

"Direct the qi to the finger," he says one month. He demonstrates, and you can see the tip of his finger vibrating in an unusual way. But he doesn't say anything about trying to vibrate the finger, so you don't try to do that. You simply try to direct the qi to the finger, whatever that means.

"Swallow your saliva down to dantian," he says one day. Luckily, you know where dantian is from your studies. It takes you weeks of trial and error before you get a glimpse of what this instruction actually means.

More months pass. "Open the five gates," the master says. You look at him, confused, but say nothing. With his hand, he taps on his lower belly and says, "One." Then he taps his opposite shoulder and says, "Two." Then his elbow. "Three." Then his wrist. "Four." Finally, he gently taps the ends of his fingers. "Five," he says.

Dantian, shoulder, elbow, wrist, fingertips, you think to yourself. *Five gates.* You vaguely remember reading something about these Five Gates in a scroll, but you can't remember where. You say them over and over in your mind as you practice and when you get home, you write everything down.

In fact, you've written down literally every instruction that your master has said to you over the years. All of it fits on a single scroll the length of your forearm.

One day, not long after the tenth anniversary of beginning with your master, he invites you to tea. This isn't the first time, but it's a rare event. By now, you know ten different exercises (literally one exercise per year), you know some qigong theory, and you can feel the qi starting to move.

Over tea, the master tells you some of the subtleties of One Finger Zen. He talks about theory, about practical tips, and he talks about his own experience. Then he does something he's never done before.

"Questions?" he says.

In ten years, he has never opened himself for questions. But you're prepared. You've kept a running list of questions in your mind for years! He seems pleased and answers each question carefully and thoughtfully. Of course, you write all his answers down later.

During the next practice session, the master helps you to implement all the new information from the tea conversation. While you are practicing, the master gently touches a series of energy points on your back. You've read some medical classics, and you have a rough idea which points he touched. You make a mental note to write these down later.

Then, suddenly, One Finger Zen comes alive. You feel the qi stronger than ever. You don't know if it was the information, the touch from the master, or both, but you're thrilled at your progress.

"Tell no one," the master says. "Not until I die. Swear it to me."

So you take a solemn vow, no small thing in your culture, to keep the details of One Finger Zen a complete secret. Later, when you are taught more secrets, the master reminds you of your vow. You can't tell your family or your wife, and you definitely can't tell your classmates.

In this story, I mentioned that you were a Chinese man, as opposed to a woman. This is because women were often not taught qigong or martial arts. While there are many famous female martial artists and qigong masters, they are the exception, not the rule.

In many families, the daughter was not taught the family style of kung fu for fear that the secrets would then leave the family once she married.

My point with the story is that even if you were born under ideal conditions—even if you were a Chinese man, even if you were literate, even if you came from a wealthy family—you *still* had to work hard to earn the secrets from the master. And once you learned them, you kept them!

So when white men who don't speak a word of Chinese tell me that there are no secrets, I can't take them too seriously.

I'm white, but I speak some Chinese, I've been to Asia many times, and I understand Chinese etiquette. I've met masters who would not teach me because I'm white, even though I spoke Chinese. I've also met masters who would not teach women. And if you happen to be a black woman who wants to learn? Fuggetaboutit!

More commonly, I've met many masters who I suspect have considerable hidden knowledge. Perhaps they will pass it on to a few disciples. Or perhaps their secrets will die with them.

When Lightning Strikes

Let's continue the story above. Imagine that the master has passed away, and you're finally free to speak about your art. Two years after you take your first student—wham! You get struck by lightning, and you're dead.

Hey, I didn't say this was a happy story!

All that survives of your art is what you taught your student in two years, and the notes that you wrote. The rest of it—all those hard-won secrets and experience of One Finger Zen—are lost forever. Your student, even if he could read, would never be able to piece together the secrets from your scrolls.

Luckily, the secrets of One Finger Zen are *not* lost in real life. I inherited them, and so did many of my classmates. I hope you'll learn these secrets one day, because One Finger Zen is pretty amazing.

But imagine how many powerful secrets have been lost through the centuries. An amazing art like One Finger Zen lost to posterity because of secrecy? I love qigong so much that it hurts my heart to think of it. The truth is that we'll never know. Those secrets are gone forever, like priceless works of art lost to a fire.

The best we can hope to do is somehow re-create what was lost. And that is exactly what is happening. It's happening as more and more people share the qigong secrets that they've learned, and I'm one of them. Not only do I openly share qigong secrets with my students—but I share them with my *online* students! I learned many secrets the hard way; not as hard as the story above, but much, much harder than my students now have it. The information is presented on a silver platter.

I believe that this is the future of qigong, but it has advantages and disadvantages. Students who learn secrets so easily often don't appreciate them. And that's one reason why students don't know that there *are* secrets. I'm unusual in that I teach secrets openly and early. I don't make you wait three years, like traditional masters do.

It's important to remember just how secretive these arts were throughout most of history. Not only was there no internet back then (gasp!), but books on the subject were almost impossible to find. And even if you did manage to find a good book—for which you likely paid as much as a gently used car—and even if you also knew how to read, you *still* might not be able to decipher the book.

That's because classical qigong texts were cryptic. Often, they were just training notes like in the story above. Sometimes, they used poetic language to describe a process, but without any instruction. For example, a classical text on the Small Universe might tell you to direct the energy from Dantian, to Huiyin, to Lingtai, to Baihui, and then down to Tan Zhong.

But even if you knew where those energy points were (remember, no googling!), and even if you already knew *how* to move qi in your body (remember, no YouTube!), then you probably wouldn't have done enough preliminary qigong to have sufficient qi to successfully do the technique. In other words, unless you already had the skill being described, the text would be relatively useless.

Don't get me wrong. I'm incredibly grateful that past masters wrote their experiences down, but perhaps not for the reasons you might think. I did not need classical texts to learn the skills of qigong. I learned the old-fashioned way—through the master/disciple oral tradition.

However, I'm grateful for classical texts because when I read them (in translation now since I've forgotten most of my classical Chinese), I feel connected to those past masters. I know exactly what they're talking about because my experience of practicing qigong, thousands of years later, is similar.

And that's friggin' cool! It's a great time to be alive because we have access to so much high-quality information about qigong. As long as we remember that qigong is to be experienced, not just studied, this information boon is a wonderful thing!

Don't Forget the Healers

We've talked about the martial artists and how they were important stewards of the art of qigong. But let's not forget about the healers. Three famous healers, who were also qigong masters, are worth mentioning:

Hua Tuo 華佗 (c. 140–208 AD)

Hua Tuo (pronounced "Hwah Too-aww") was an eminent Chinese physician who lived from roughly 140–208 AD. He was skilled in acupuncture, moxibustion, herbal medicine, and also qigong. Fun fact: historical records show that Hua Tuo was the first person to successfully use anesthesia during surgery. Yes, surgery! In the second century AD! Wowzers.

In the qigong world, he's most famous for creating a set called the Five Animal Play (Wuqinxi, 五禽戲). Most people believe that Hua Tuo invented the Five Animal Play by observing the movements of five animals: tiger, deer, bear, monkey, and crane. Legend has it that he then formalized his observations into dynamic qigong patterns similar to Lifting the Sky. This is a reasonable interpretation, but I have a different theory.

I believe that Hua Tuo's Five Animals were not meant to be five formalized exercises, but rather five descriptions of spontaneous energy flow. This phenomenon is something of special importance to me and my students. For those who know the secret of Flowing Breeze Swaying Willow, it makes perfect sense. When we get the qi flowing spontaneously, it can manifest in different ways depending on where your energy blockages are. We'll talk more about Flowing Breeze Swaying Willow and spontaneous qigong later.

I believe that Hua Tuo codified spontaneous qigong into five archetypes. For him, the energy of each of the five main meridians resembled the movement of a different animal:

1. Heart Meridian = Bird
2. Liver Meridian = Deer
3. Spleen Meridian = Monkey
4. Lung Meridian = Tiger
5. Kidney Meridian = Bear

In other words, if the energy flows vigorously through the Heart Meridian, then your spontaneous movements may resemble that of a bird. Having taught spontaneous energy flow to thousands of students, I can say with confidence that this is precisely what happens. You'll learn more about this amazing skill soon and also be able to experience it for yourself.

Zhang Zhongjing (張仲景; 150–219 AD)

Zhang Zhongjing (pronounced "Jahng Jawng Jing") was another famous Chinese physician. He is sometimes called the Chinese Hippocrates because he codified all the Chinese Medicine knowledge until his time. His masterpiece, the Shanghan Zabing Lun (傷寒雜病論), otherwise known as the *Treatise on Febrile Pathogens and Miscellaneous Diseases*, influenced the development of Classical Chinese Medicine for hundreds of years. It is still used today.

He was also one of the first to talk about qigong as a form of medicine. Specifically, he talked about qigong being able to prevent disease, a novel idea at the time. This theory is now foundational in most schools of qigong.

Sun Simiao (孫思邈, 581–682 AD)

Sun Simiao (pronounced "Soon Suh Meow") was another famous Chinese physician who practiced and taught qigong. At one point, he was called the King of Medicine (Yaowang, 藥王) for his contributions to Classical Chinese medicine. Not a shabby title!

In addition to writing two massive texts, he also taught "the Thirteen Measures to Stay Healthy." This was a series of simple qigong techniques, like combing the hair, washing the face, and rolling the eyes. I still teach many of these exercises today. They can be found in Phase Five of the Five-Phase Routine, which you'll learn about soon.

Today, we've inherited the wisdom and experience of both groups of past masters: the healers and the martial artists. Over the centuries, the two traditions mixed and cross-fertilized. The medical knowledge from the healers spread to the martial arts camp. Meanwhile, the discipline and courage of the martial artists flowed back to the healers. Students today get to stand on the shoulders of these giants, making it much easier for us to get amazing results with qigong.

Success Story: Liz

Liz is a forty-two-year-old American who had migraines from the age of five. Roughly eight years ago, they got so bad that she couldn't string two thoughts together. Her pain was off the charts, she had severe aphasia (inability to speak normally), and many nights she could be found in a fetal position on the floor thinking about suicide.

She saw several neurologists and tried pharmaceuticals, but these didn't even come close to solving the problem. Next, she tried TruDente, an interesting combination of orthodontics and sports medicine. This helped reduce the migraines by 85 percent, which seemed like a dream come true.

Unfortunately, the treatment began to plateau and eventually stopped working altogether. The migraines began to creep back into her life. Liz was desperate.

Two years ago, she started studying qigong, but the results were not good. She wasn't expecting miracles, but she was hoping for something.

Then, about a year ago, she switched to Flowing Zen Qigong. She started practicing the Five-Phase Routine religiously and saw rapid progress in three areas—her sex life started to improve, she had greater mental clarity, and she had more energy. Given that fatigue and mental fog were huge problems, she was grateful for this progress.

Then, about six months ago, she had a breakthrough in her practice that utterly changed everything. "I can stop a migraine in its tracks in ten to thirty minutes," she recently told me. "I have my life back and one of the main things I'm grateful for in this world is your teachings!"

CHAPTER 4
Qigong Theory and Philosophy

Before we dive into the theory and philosophy of qigong, let me say something that may surprise you: To get results with qigong, you don't need to know any theory. Zero. Zip. Zilch. Nada. In other words, you don't need to know how qigong works to make it work for you.

In fact, many masters throughout history knew hardly any theory at all. Some of them were illiterate, and if they were lucky enough to know how to read, they may not have had access to qigong or medical texts. Remember, books (or scrolls) were rare and precious commodities throughout most of human history, including ancient China.

Nevertheless, certain theories—like the theory of yin and yang, the meridian theory, and the theory of Five Elements—were central to ancient Chinese culture. Past masters were likely exposed to the basics of these theories whether they could read or not. Since Western culture doesn't typically teach these theories, it's helpful to have a basic understanding of them.

As you learn about the theory behind qigong, please don't feel like you must memorize any of it. You will not be quizzed on this material!

We should be aware of three main concepts:

1. Yin-Yang Theory
2. Meridian Theory
3. Five-Element Theory

The Thang about Yin and Yang

Yin-Yang Theory has influenced countless Chinese arts since it first appeared over 2700 years ago. Arts that incorporate the theory of yin and yang include:

- qigong
- acupuncture
- Chinese herbalism
- feng shui
- Chinese massage (tui na)
- Tai Chi Chuan

You've heard about yin and yang, of course. At the very least, you recognize this image:

This is the tai chi tu (taijitu), a symbolic representation of the philosophy of yin and yang. A symbol is helpful here because yin and yang are, ultimately, impossible to describe. I like Lao Tzu's reminder about naming and describing things:

"The tao that can be told
is not the eternal Tao
The name that can be named

is not the eternal Name.
The unnamable is the eternally real.
Naming is the origin
of all particular things."
   —Tao Te Ching (Stephen Mitchell translation)

The universe is, ultimately, a mystical interplay between yin and yang. But let's see if we can crack open that mystery a little.

The Big Yin Yang Bang

We spoke earlier about the *I Ching* (Yi Jing) and its reference to "tai chi"—not the martial art but the philosophy. This is the earliest known reference to the theory of yin and yang, and it dates back to roughly 700 BCE. For clarity, from now on I'll refer to the philosophy using the modern spelling of taiji to differentiate it from the martial art we know as tai chi.

The *I Ching* didn't use the familiar yin-yang circle to represent this theory. Instead, it used something called "hexagrams," which are broken or unbroken lines in pairs.

It was not until later that the taiji symbol came into use. But for our purposes today, it is much more useful than the hexagrams.

The taiji symbol starts with an empty circle. This point often gets missed, but it is important. Yin and yang are not the beginning. Wuji is the beginning.

Wuji (無極) is the great void that existed before the Big Bang, the void that still exists somewhere behind the veil of our cosmos. It's what will exist after the heat death of this universe.

Out of wuji comes a duality that we call taiji. From that duality, from that positive and negative, the entire universe is born.

Here is a quotation from Stephen Mitchell's 1988 translation of the Tao Te Ching:

> "The Tao gives birth to One.
> One gives birth to Two.
> Two gives birth to Three.
> Three gives birth to all things."

What does this mean? In modern terminology, we might say that the Tao gave birth to the Big Bang, the Big Bang gave birth to positive and negative, and positive and negative gave birth to all the elements. That's the idea here, even if my science isn't perfect.

The ancient Greeks used the concept of chaos (χάος) and cosmos (κόσμος). According to Brian Muraresku, author of a fascinating book called *The Immortality Key*:

> "*Chaos* is the 'infinite darkness' of 'unformed matter' that existed in the 'first state of the universe.' While *cosmos* is 'the natural order' of the final product that we now glimpse in the night sky."[1]

From this, we can arrive at the following working definition: Yin and yang are opposite, complementary, interdependent, and inseparable forces that, together, form a complete and harmonious whole.

The classical example of this is night and day. Let's look closer at this:

- Night and day cannot be separated. They are interdependent.

- Night and day are opposite, as evidenced by expressions such as: "It was like night and day."
- Night and day are complementary. The entire concept of a "day" comes from the changing of nighttime into daytime, and vice versa.
- Night and day are not absolute. Day and night don't turn on and off like a light bulb. Rather, they flow into one another. Night gradually turns into day, and day gradually turns into night.
- Night and day are relative. For example, day and night flow differently at the equator than they do in the arctic. And night and day mean different things on Venus than they do here on Earth.

So when we're talking about yin and yang, there is always a viewpoint, or a point of comparison. In the example of night and day, we're talking about planet Earth. Similarly, the Chinese classics are typically speaking from the perspective of ancient China.

The Four Types of Disharmony

For those qigong practitioners who are interested in self-healing, Yin-Yang theory is most useful as a symbol of balance within the human body. This balance can be energetic, physical, mental-emotional, or a combination.

Chinese Medicine talks about four types of disharmony of yin and yang:

1. Excess yin
2. Excess yang
3. Deficient yin
4. Deficient yang

What's the point of comparison here, you ask? Good question. If yin and yang are not absolute, then what does excess yin or deficient yang even mean?

In Chinese Medicine and qigong, we're talking about the human experience—not trees, not four-legged mammals (although they share some similarities), and not six-eyed aliens. So deficient yang presents itself in a specific way in humans. For example, deficient yang in the Kidney Meridian will typically show patterns of soreness in the low back, pain in the knees, an aversion to cold weather, erectile dysfunction, fatigue, infertility, and loose stools.

If we supplement the deficient yang in the Kidney Meridian with qigong, acupuncture, and herbal medicine, then those symptoms will begin to resolve. In other words, when we harmonize yang in the meridian system, we become healthier (and happier).

This is another way of saying that you want your yin and yang to be harmonized all through your body. You want balance. In many ways, this is all you need to know about yin and yang.

In physiological terms, a balance of yin and yang means that your body's immune and repair functions are in harmony with the countless bacteria, viruses, toxins, and trauma that bombard your body daily. If you are sick or in pain, it means that there is an imbalance between yin and yang.

Common Misrepresentations of Yin and Yang

Yin and yang is widely misunderstood and misrepresented in the West. For example, the Oxford dictionary defines the two words as follows:

- Yin: the feminine or negative principle (characterized by dark, wetness, cold, passivity, disintegration, etc.) of the two opposing cosmic forces into which creative energy divides and whose fusion in physical matter brings the phenomenal world into being.

- Yang: the masculine or positive principle (characterized by light, warmth, dryness, activity, etc.) of the two opposing cosmic forces into which creative energy divides and whose fusion in physical matter brings the phenomenal world into being.

All of this is somewhat true, but can you identify the flaw? I'll give you a hint: Einstein would spot it immediately!

There is no absolute definition of yin and yang because the definition depends on the point of reference. For example, a woman might be considered yin when compared to a man, but what happens when you compare her to her own daughter? In that case, the relativity would flip, and the woman would become yang.

When it comes to qigong and Chinese Medicine, the point of reference is typically assumed. As such, many terms have come into common usage. For example:

- Lung Yin Deficiency
- Kidney Yang Deficiency
- Liver Yang Rising

The point of reference here is always human physiology. Despite the great variation in appearance among humans, we all share the same anatomy and physiology. Some things remain the same regardless of your gender, sex, age, body composition, ethnicity, height, or weight.

Tan and Pale Meridians

Whether you realize it or not, your body has twelve Primary Meridians and eight Secondary Meridians. These meridians have a set reference point for yin and yang. For example, the three meridians that run from your armpit down to your fingers are yin, whereas the three meridians that run from your fingertips up the outside of your arm to the top of your shoulder are yang.

There's an easy way to remember this: The yin meridians run along parts where the sun doesn't shine. No seriously. The paler your skin, the more yin the meridian (weird tan lines aside). Look at your forearm and you'll see that one side is tanner than the other. That's because one side naturally faces out and thus gets more sun. That side is more yang.

Meanwhile, your armpit doesn't get nearly as much sun as your outer forearm. Even if you were to walk around naked all the time, this area would be less tan because it gets less sun.

And just for the troublemakers out there, let's be clear that the amount of sun is not what causes yin or yang meridians. If you walked around on your hands with your legs spread apart and got lots of sun where it doesn't usually shine—those meridians would still be yin. Perhaps if you did that for a million years, thereby altering the evolution and physiology of the human body, your meridians might shift. Let me know how that works out for you.

The Meridian System

Meridian Theory is robust, sophisticated, and time tested. It has been a common thread among the Chinese healing arts for thousands of years:

- **acupuncture** (the use of hair-thin, sterile needles to stimulate the flow of qi along the meridians)
- **acupressure** (similar to acupuncture, but it uses finger pressure instead of needles)
- **moxibustion** (the burning of the herb mugwort on acupoints to promote healing)
- **Chinese herbal medicine** (the use of herbal decoctions and tonics to stimulate the flow of qi along the meridians)
- **kung fu** (Chinese martial arts, including tai chi)

- **shiliao** (Chinese food therapy)
- **Taoist bedroom arts** (Chinese sexual practices that promote health and longevity)
- **tuina** (Chinese massage therapy)
- **die da** (Chinese traumatology for bruises and breaks)
- **qigong** (the art of life-force cultivation)

The Chinese term for meridian is *jingluo* (經絡, pronounced "jing-low"). This translates to "channel," as in a channel that water runs through. In this case, it's qi, or life-force energy, that flows through the channels.

There's an additional connotation here. The second character, 絡, means "net-like." So the jingluo are a net-like series of channels through which qi flows. Think of a highway system, with big inter-states as well as smaller roads, all forming a complex network. With the meridians, it's qi that flows along the network rather than cars.

Even though the word "channel" is a better translation, I continue to use the word "meridian" because it is already in common usage. Even Google translates the Chinese word "jingluo" as "meridian." Sorry, but I'm too busy with my teaching and personal practice to pick a fight with Google right now.

Most of the Chinese Medicine classics compare the flow of qi to water, drawing on the natural dynamics found in rivers, streams, springs, and seas. It's important to remember that the concept of qi is ancient. Back then, they didn't know about protons, neutrons, or electrons. They had no electric lights, no electric cables, and (gasp!) no Wi-Fi.

In the twenty-first century, it's natural to think of qi as a form of energy, like a current running through a wire. And this is acceptable if we remember that the ancient masters didn't share this paradigm. They had no concept of wires or electricity, so they looked to natural, observable phenomena for inspiration.

Where Are the Meridians?

The Chinese classics tell us that the Kidney Meridian runs from the bottom of your foot, up your inner leg, through your groin, and then up your chest. But if you were to cut into your leg (ahem, please don't do this at home), you wouldn't see your Kidney Meridian. Even if you were to scan your leg with a Magnetic Resonance Imaging (MRI) machine, you still wouldn't find it.

In Western culture, this is confusing, because we like things to be visible and tangible. The fact that the meridians are not readily visible is enough reason for many people to dismiss them as pseudoscience.

But are the meridians really invisible?

In his book *Anatomy Trains: Myofascial Meridians for Manual and Movement Therapists*, Thomas Myers uses modern Western anatomy to argue that fascia lines are well correlated with the ancient Chinese meridian lines. In short, the reason the meridians were not obvious to Western anatomists is because they weren't looking at the fascia. Or rather, they were looking at fascia all wrong.

If you've ever cut up a raw chicken, then you've seen a clear layer of stringy stuff on the breast. That membranous tissue is called fascia. It might not seem like much, but it just may contain the most convincing modern explanation of Meridian Theory!

Every good surgeon uses fascial planes as a map of where to cut and dissect. Researchers know that cancer spreads through fascial lines. Mobility and strength experts recognize the importance of fascia and nurture it daily. Chronic pain experts point to fascial tension as the root cause.

Despite all of this, anatomists have overlooked the fascia for decades. As Daniel Keown, author of *The Spark in the Machine*, puts it, they "ignored the one thing that was everywhere, covering everything, connecting everything, almost transparent and invisible, yet immensely strong . . . like a man looking for his glasses when they were on his face."[2]

The idea of an invisible network of meridians with a mysterious energy called qi flowing through them is foreign to most of us. And even if we accept this ancient theory, it's helpful to have a modern parallel. I believe fascia theory gives us that parallel.

Pronounced either as "fash-ee-uh" or "fey-shuh," fascia has only recently gained the interest of orthodox Western Medicine. In fact, most of the research is only ten to twenty years old. The conversations we're now having about fascia—in both Eastern and Western circles—couldn't have happened thirty years ago. It's that new.

Fascia is hard to define. In fact, the definition keeps changing as more research is done. As of this writing, the definition from the International Fascia Research Congress is as follows:

- **A fascia** is a sheath, a sheet, or any other dissectible aggregation of connective tissue that forms beneath the skin to attach, enclose, and separate muscles, nerves, and internal organs.

- **The fascial system** consists of the three-dimensional continuum of soft, collagen-containing, loose, and dense fibrous connective tissues that permeate the body. It incorporates elements such as adipose tissue, adventitiae and neurovascular sheaths, aponeuroses, deep and superficial fasciae, epineurium, joint capsules, ligaments, membranes, meninges, myofascial expansions, periostea, retinacula, septa, tendons, visceral fasciae, and all the intramuscular and intermuscular connective tissues including endo-/peri-/epimysium. The fascial system surrounds, interweaves between, and interpenetrates all organs, muscles, bones, and nerve fibers, endowing the body with a functional structure, and providing an environment that enables all body systems to operate in an integrated manner.[3]

So when we talk about fascia, we're not only talking about a wide range of connective tissue; we're also talking about an entire system that includes several different types of tissue as well as many different functions. In this sense, the fascial system is comparable to any of the eleven organ systems of Western anatomy. If you're rusty on these systems, here they are:

1. Integumentary system
2. Skeletal system
3. Muscular system
4. Lymphatic system
5. Respiratory system
6. Digestive system
7. Nervous system
8. Endocrine system
9. Cardiovascular system
10. Urinary system
11. Reproductive system

These systems are a lens through which Western Medicine views the human body. The ancient Chinese masters looked through a different lens. According to ancient Chinese Medicine theory, you have twelve Primary Meridians (十二经脉), as follows:

1. Taiyin **Lung** Channel of the Hand (手太阴肺经)
2. Shaoyin **Heart** Channel of the Hand (手少阴心经)
3. Jueyin **Pericardium** Channel of the Hand (手厥阴心包经)
4. Shaoyang **Sanjiao** Channel of the Hand (手少阳三焦经)
5. Taiyang **Small Intestine** Channel of the Hand (手太阳小肠经)
6. Yangming **Large Intestine** Channel of the Hand (手阳明大肠经)
7. Taiyin **Spleen** Channel of the Foot (足太阴脾经)
8. Shaoyin **Kidney** Channel of the Foot (足少阴肾经)
9. Jueyin **Liver** Channel of the Foot (足厥阴肝经)

10. Shaoyang **Gallbladder** Channel of the Foot (足少阳胆经)
11. Taiyang **Bladder** Channel of the Foot (足太阳膀胱经)
12. Yangming **Stomach** Channel of the Foot (足阳明胃经)

You'll notice that each meridian is associated with an internal organ. This is confusing because it leads us to think of each meridian as an organ rather than a system, which is incorrect. Even though we typically call a meridian by its main organ, it is still a system with functions beyond the scope of that particular organ.

This happens in the Western paradigm too. For example, the respiratory system involves more than just the functions of lungs. It also includes the functions of the nose, sinuses, pharynx, and the diaphragm. Similarly, the Lung Meridian involves more than just the lungs. It is a system with many functions.

The fascial system is similar. It is not just a piece of connective tissue, but rather a complex system with a variety of functions. Here are some facts about fascia that will be helpful:

- Fascia is the most abundant tissue in the body.[4]
- Fascia is intimately tied to the nervous system.
- Fascia has ten times more sensory receptors than muscle tissue.
- Fascia interpenetrates and surrounds all organs, muscles, bones, and nerve fibers.
- Fascia forms a 3D, contiguous matrix of structural support in the body.
- Fascia is a force transmitter, dispersing external forces and thereby helping to prevent injury in a particular muscle, joint, or bone.
- Mood influences fascia, and vice versa.[5]
- Fascia is an electrical conductor and resistor, and also generates its own piezoelectric energy.[6]

Recently, researchers *discovered* what they think is not only a new organ, but the largest organ in the body! This new organ is called the *interstitium*, and it contains tiny fluid-filled structures filled with interstitial fluid (IF).[7]

The interstitium is a system of tiny spaces below the surface of the skin. These spaces are given a framework or scaffolding by connective tissues that are composed of collagen and elastin. Because of this, the interstitium can be viewed as a form of fascia.

Interstitial fluid drains into the lymphatic system. The lymphatic system is a body-wide network of tissues and mini-organs that rid the body of toxins and waste materials. It does this by transporting lymph, a watery fluid containing infection-fighting white blood cells, throughout the body. This fluid is similar to blood plasma.

Once IF enters the lymphatic system, it is called lymph fluid. The lymphatic system is closely related to the immune system. However, the immune system is not considered an organ system.

As you can see, it gets confusing. Is lymph just a form of interstitial fluid, or vice versa? What are we to make of the overlap between the interstitium, the fascia, and the lymphatic system?

The ancient Chinese masters solved this problem with the concept of qi. Qi is what flows between and through all these overlapping systems.

These masters understood something about fascia that we are only now beginning to comprehend. In fact, they devoted two full meridian systems, the Triple Burner and the Pericardium, to the fascia. It was that important to them.

We can think of all the meridians as lines of fascia, interstitium, and lymph. Together, they form a complex network that reaches every part of the body and encompasses a wide range of functions. This is a highly plausible explanation for the many healing benefits that we receive from practicing qigong.

As Daniel Keown eloquently puts it: "An electrical force held in a fabric into which our body is woven: this is science that is beginning to sound like Chinese medicine and Qi."[8]

The Mighty Psoas

What if I told you that there is a muscle in the body that is a perfect, modern representation of the mind-body connection, a muscle that not only connects the upper and lower parts of the body but also connects your physical and mental-emotional systems as well? What if I told you that this muscle provides a direct, two-way link to the central nervous system, and that it is, in some traditions, called the "muscle of the soul."

This muscle exists. It's called the psoas (pronounced "so-as"), and it's arguably the most important muscle in qigong. Some people, including Jo Ann Staugaard-Jones, author of *The Vital Psoas Muscle*,[9] even argue that the psoas is the most important skeletal muscle in the human body.

If it's so important, then why have most people never heard of it? Or if they've heard of it, why don't they know how vital this muscle is to so many functions? The psoas is but another example of Western Medicine not having it all figured out . . . yet.

Today, most physicians don't understand the role of the psoas despite the growing research. Even alternative medicine practitioners don't fully comprehend its importance. This is quickly changing in the twenty-first century, however, and that's a good thing for you and me! But you don't need to wait for the world to catch up before applying this information.

Your psoas is a deep muscle that runs from your lower spine, through your core, and then connects to the top of your thigh bone. Without the psoas, you couldn't walk, climb stairs, or bend over. Any movement that involves hinging the top and bottom of the body uses the psoas, as does flexing the hip joint.

What modern research is discovering is that the psoas is also intimately linked with the nervous system. Some people call it the "fight or flight" muscle. This will help you to understand why the muscle is so important in qigong.

When things go awry with the psoas, the result can be awful. I know this from experience because, for several years, I suffered from severe low back and hip pain. Qigong helped tremendously, but it didn't give me the full relief that I needed. And that's because, at the time, I didn't understand the psoas.

Once I started working on the psoas, then everything changed. This release can be done with qigong as well as some auxiliary myofascial exercises, but the key is to *release* the psoas, a task that is harder than it sounds. The Five Animal Play, a qigong technique that is central to my teachings, involves releasing the psoas along with deep-rooted emotional blockages. You'll learn more about the Five Animal Play later. For now, just know that releasing the psoas can lead to psycho-emotional releases, which in turn can lead to deeper and more long-lasting healing.

The Five Elements

The next concept we need to examine is the Theory of Five Elements (Wu Xing, 五行). This philosophy is central to many Chinese arts, including qigong, acupuncture, herbal medicine, therapeutic massage, and feng shui. A basic understanding of this theory will help you to get more out of your qigong (and perhaps out of life in general).

First, you need to understand that the Five Elements are not really elements. This is not a periodic table containing elements like hydrogen and oxygen. The ancient Chinese masters didn't believe that the cosmos was made of only five physical elements.

The Chinese term *wu xing* is surprisingly hard to translate. Here is a half dozen translations, which I hope will give you a broader perspective:

1. The Five Elements
2. The Five Phases
3. The Five Agents

4. The Five Movements
5. The Five Processes
6. The Five Stages

The ancient Chinese masters discovered that a wide variety of phenomena in the universe could be explained by a five-phase paradigm. These five phases were described using symbols: Fire, Earth, Metal, Water, and Wood. You'll typically see the Five Element chart presented in this order:

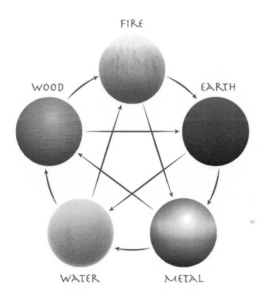

However, in older versions of the Five Elements, you find Earth at the center of the cycle. In that version, Earth was not viewed as a season like the other Elements, but rather as the end of each of the four seasons when the energies return to the Earth.

Each of the Five Elements is associated with one of the Meridian systems. Furthermore, each Meridian System is associated with an emotion:

ELEMENT	ORGAN	EMOTION
Fire	Heart	Joy
Earth	Spleen	Worry
Metal	Lungs	Grief
Water	Kidneys	Fear
Wood	Liver	Anger

You don't need to memorize these associations unless you're studying acupuncture. What you do need to understand is that stuck emotions affect the meridians, which affect the organs, which affect your health. When we clear the emotional blockages that clog up the organ systems, people begin to heal again.

Five Element Theory is thus useful for qigong practitioners to better understand the flow of energy and emotions through the body. The health of your organs depends on the health of your emotions. We'll talk more about energy blockages and emotions later, but in summary, know that the only bad emotion is a stuck emotion.

Dantian Theory

The Chinese word dantian (dāntián, 丹田) literally means "elixir field," but a better translation might be "energy center." These energy centers are in several places:

- Upper Dantian (上丹田, shàng dāntián), located in the center of the forehead slightly above the eyebrows.
- Middle Dantian (中丹田, zhōng dāntián), located in the centerline of the chest at the level of the heart.
- Lower Dantian (下丹田, xià dāntián), located in the lower belly 2–3 inches diagonally below and behind the navel.

Of these, the lower dantian is the most important. This is the home base for your body's energy. It is important not only for healing arts like qigong, but also for martial arts like tai chi chuan and Shaolin Kung Fu.

Unfortunately, searching for dantian with your fingers isn't terribly helpful. If you haven't already cultivated qi at dantian correctly for a few years, there isn't much to feel. Beginners often have trouble feeling dantian because they are looking too hard for what the classics describe as a "golden pearl."

Interestingly, dantian usually starts out bigger and gradually gets smaller with practice. It may start out the size of a softball or even a volleyball. That's because the energy hasn't consolidated yet.

I don't pretend to understand the physics behind this phenomenon, but dantian seems to shrink as you advance. Over the years, my dantian progressed from feeling like nothing, to the size of an amorphous softball, to a tennis ball, to a golf ball, and finally to a large marble. However, that's just the core of the field. The energy from the core still radiates out in all directions, like the light from the sun.

There are other energy fields that you'll feel as you progress. The Gate of Vitality (mingmen, 命門), located on the midline of your spine just below the spinous process of the second lumbar vertebra (L2), is one of the most important. To locate it, find the shallow part of the natural curve of your lower back. This spot should be almost exactly opposite your navel.

I should mention that there is some discrepancy regarding the location of mingmen among qigong schools. The location I described above is the one I learned in acupuncture college, and the one that feels right to me when I practice qigong. However, whenever we're talking about energy fields like dantian or mingmen, we're talking about an area, not a tiny little point. It therefore makes sense that different masters might have a slightly different experience.

To start feeling energy at mingmen, rub the area with a finger. Then close your eyes and try to feel some warmth or activity there. If you can't feel any activity, don't worry. Just try to feel the lingering sensation where you rubbed your finger. That gentle awareness is what we're after.

Typically, we close a qigong session by bringing awareness to the lower dantian, but we can close with mingmen instead. If you are pregnant, if you have any issues in the lower belly, or if you have issues with libido and sexual dysfunction, then it's better to finish your qigong session with mingmen rather than the lower dantian.

My advice to students with less than three years of regular qigong practice is not to worry too much about dantian or mingmen. New students often try to chase sensations at dantian, and this is a mistake. It's like opening a long-term investment account and expecting to get rich in a few months. With dantian, as with your retirement account, the gains will be seen over time.

What Is Jing (精)?

In the Chinese tradition, the human condition is seen as a balance of three things, called the Three Treasures (san bao, 三寶). This can be viewed as an ancient Chinese version of our modern concept of a mind-body-spirit connection.

The Three Treasures are as follows:

1. Jing (精)—essence
2. Qi (氣)—energy
3. Shen (神)—spirit/mind

The Chinese word *jing* (精) is difficult to translate, but it's worth looking at closely. The most common translation is "essence," and that's probably as close as we will get with one word. But this word doesn't tell us much about what jing actually is.

Jing is sometimes equated with semen, but this is not accurate. It's true that the jing you have came from your father's sperm, but it is also the result of your mother's DNA, as well as the conditions during her pregnancy. Jing is much more than just semen, or even just DNA.

Here's a quotation from Daniel Keown that sums it up better than I can:

> "Jing is the fount of our life, the alchemy of Yin and Yang that we inherit from our parents, our constitution. It is the seed of life from which our body springs, flowers and then seeds. This energy is stored within and by our Kidneys, it creates our body, guides its development, manifests its change into adulthood, and its decline leads us into our old age and senescence."[10]

We all want more jing whether we realize it or not. Think of someone you know who can work long hours, who has a seemingly endless supply of energy, who stays thin with minimal effort, who can eat whatever they want without getting bloated, who can function without sleep even into their forties and beyond—these people were born with a lot of jing. I hate them as much as you do.

In the West, we might say that these people were born with good genes, or that they have a strong constitution. The Chinese would say that they exhibit great jing. However you describe them, the idea is the same: some people were born rich in terms of vitality.

Jing is what guides our growth as an embryo and a child, it is what moves us through puberty and into adulthood, and it is also what declines as we age. The ancient Chinese believed that jing was "stored" within the Kidney Meridian. This is one of the reasons why the Kidney Meridian is of special importance in qigong. If you want more vitality—and who doesn't—then nurture this important meridian. You'll be happy to know that nothing nurtures the Kidney Meridian better than qigong!

Interestingly, the Kidney Meridian is the only one that doesn't have any diagnoses with excess. You can have too much qi in any meridian except the Kidney Meridian. In essence (pun intended!), your Kidney Qi is a clock that is counting down from the moment you were born to the moment you die.

People always think they want more qi, and they do, sort of. But really, they want more jing, or they want qi to support the jing that they already have. I certainly do because I was born with less of it.

I've been through comprehensive diagnoses with many skilled acupuncturists, so I have objective information about my own levels of jing. But a lack of jing is easy to spot. For example, I'm 5'7" whereas my brother is almost 6' tall. On top of that, my teeth have always been bad, I've had low back issues since I was a teenager, and I started balding in my early thirties. All of this suggests a low dose of jing at birth. For whatever reason, I was born with less vitality than most people, including my older brother. You might even call me the runt of the litter. (Sorry, Mom!)

And you know what? That's okay. Lots of people are born with less qi. Millions, possibly even billions. Among these people you will find many artists, spiritualists, and thinkers who changed the world. Stephen Hawking is a good example.

Thanks to qigong, it's hard to tell that I was born with less qi. In fact, many of you who know me are probably surprised to hear me mention it. You probably thought that I was overflowing with qi. And I suppose I am, but the qi that I have now is not the qi that I was born with.

This brings us to the twin concepts of Pre-Heaven Qi and Post-Heaven Qi.

Pre-Heaven Qi (Yuan Qi 元氣)

This is sometimes called prenatal qi, but the concept is simple: this is the energy that you were born with, and it is closely related to jing. This is your initial dose of vitality that you get from your parents and the conditions during your gestation.

Post-Heaven Qi (Houtian Zhi Qi 後天之氣)

This is the qi that you cultivate through eating, drinking, breathing, and through your lifestyle choices. The more you cultivate, the less you will tap into your Pre-Heaven Qi and jing.

It's useful to be aware of how much qi you were born with. If you're not sure, then an acupuncturist can help you to figure this out. Learning that you were born with less qi comes as a welcome relief to many people. When you've spent a few decades struggling to keep up with other people, it's a relief to learn that it's an unfair race.

The good news is that people who are born with a lot of qi typically aren't attracted to arts like qigong. Why would they be? They're like rich kids who don't need to worry about budgeting.

On the other hand, some of the greatest tai chi and qigong masters throughout history were originally attracted to the art because they were sickly. Illness is what gave them the motivation to practice and achieve mastery. Cheng Man-ch'ing, a famous tai chi master who suffered from tuberculosis as a child, is a good example.

In the qigong world, you'll often hear that Pre-Heaven Qi is fixed, that it's what you were given at birth and there's nothing you can do about it. Whether or not this is true is difficult to prove, and luckily, it doesn't really matter.

The truth is that we can effect change in our overall energy through things like qigong, acupuncture, diet, and other lifestyle adjustments. Whether this replenishes our Pre-Heaven Qi or supplements it with Post-Heaven Qi is irrelevant. The result is the same: a life filled with more vitality.

You'll often hear pre-heaven qi talked about as if it's synonymous with genetics. Here's the problem with this view: the way we've talked about genetics is wrong. In general, most people view genetics as something fixed, like you're just born with certain genes and there's nothing you can do about it.

The field of epigenetics, which simply means "above genetics," is a fairly recent development. Epigenetics is to genetics what quantum physics was to Newtonian physics. In other words, the new field totally revamped the older one and is a paradigm shift.

Traditional genetics explains the way genes are passed through the generations. Epigenetics, on the other hand, explains how genes are USED. In short, we have much more influence over our genetics than we thought. A gene can express itself in different ways, and it's not as simple as an on/off switch. It's more like a musical composition where you've only got so many notes, but they can be expressed in countless ways.

Both the theory of epigenetics and the theory of Pre-Heaven Qi agree that you can exert tremendous influence over your genes, your vitality, your qi, and your life by altering your lifestyle. Even your beliefs seem to alter genetic expression! Qigong is arguably the single best way to influence your genes and your jing. In fact, if you do only one thing to improve your vitality, qigong is the way to go. This is why I always tell students to add a daily qigong habit before trying to make other lifestyle changes! Start with the best!

One final thought about jing: I would be remiss if I didn't mention the connection between qigong, jing, and sexual vitality. There is a millennia-long tradition of cultivating sexual energy with qigong called The Art of the Bedchamber (fang zhong shu, 房中術), often just referred to as Taoist sexual practices. Unfortunately, some people mistakenly think that qigong is *only* about cultivating sexual energy.

Sexual vitality is, in the end, just energy. In Chinese theory, sexual energy is typically connected to jing. If you have more jing, then you'll have more sexual vitality and a stronger libido. Although there are specific techniques for this, any holistic style of qigong will strengthen your sexual vitality!

What Is Qi (氣)?

What is qi? You'll find all sorts of definitions of qi out there. You'll even find people who are upset that qi has all sorts of definitions. Me, I like things simple.

Qi is life-force energy. Whether it is the energy that moves food through your digestive system, or the energy that mobilizes your immune system, or the energy that powers your cells—all of that is qi.

Again, it's worth remembering that ancient masters didn't have microscopes. Although Chinese Medicine did an amazing job with human anatomy and physiology—far better than Western Medicine until the invention of the microscope—they couldn't see the invisible miniature world of cells. The concept of qi arose to explain the various processes and phenomena of human anatomy, and, indeed, of all living things.

An analogy may help. Newtonian physics, which is what I learned in high school, turns out to be totally wrong. When viewed from the perspective of quantum physics, Newtonian physics just isn't true. It does not accurately describe the workings of the cosmos.

But there's something critical here that we can't forget: Newtonian physics is incredibly useful! In fact, you can't really build a bridge without it. In this sense, Newtonian physics is still "true."

On the macro level, the ancient Chinese masters were correct, just like Newton was correct about physics. Qi accurately explains the various processes in the human body that were invisible until the microscope was invented in 1590. Remember that Chinese Medicine had already been used for nearly two thousand years by that point!

The modern practitioner need not view qi as a mysterious energy flowing through the body that is yet undetected by science. Instead, we can simply view qi as a metaphor for the many functions that *have* been detected by science, from the flow of interstitial fluid to the electromagnetic impulses of the heart to the neurotransmitters in the brain. All of this is qi, and if you want to heal, then you want all of it to flow better. Qigong will help you to do exactly that.

What Is Shen (神)?

Shen, the last of the Three Treasures, is typically translated as "spirit." This word has so many meanings that we need to dig deeper to make sense of it. In Chinese, the character can mean "demigod," "deity," or "spirit." For our purposes, it's best to think of the modern "mind, body, spirit" trope. In this comparison, shen is analogous to spirit.

But we get into trouble because "shen" is also mind, which ruins the mind-body-spirit comparison. Perhaps a better translation of shen is "personality." Your current personality has a direct relationship with your qi (energy) and jing (essence). For example, when faced with adversity in your life, how do you react? Do you step up to the challenge and summon strength that you didn't know you had? If so, then you are using your shen to marshal your energy and even your genetics. Your personality can change over time, which is another aspect of shen.

Consciousness is another word that may help us understand shen. The first thing you need to understand about consciousness is that Western medicine still cannot explain it. There are many theories that attempt to locate consciousness in the brain, but all of them fall short. In many ways, shen is precisely what is missing from Western medicine. The rise of psychology in the early twentieth century was an attempt to fill this void, and it worked to a certain degree. But there's still something missing.

Shen is said to be stored in the Heart Meridian, similar to the way that jing is stored in the Kidney Meridian. Many of the functions that Western Medicine associates with the brain would be associated with the Heart in Chinese Medicine. The strength of a person's shen is said to be reflected in their eyes, and this makes sense. If you imagine someone who is extremely wise and spiritually advanced, you would also imagine being able to see some of that in her eyes. What you would see is what they called shen.

In qigong, shen is critical for getting results. If I had to point to one reason why modern students don't get the results that they deserve, it's because they aren't focusing their shen during their session. With Flowing Zen Qigong, Phase 1 of the Five-Phase Routine is dedicated entirely to focusing our shen.

And don't worry. Even when your shen is scattered and weak, like mine was while I was depressed, you can still summon your shen for a fifteen-minute qigong session. With practice, your shen will improve and your qigong practice along with it.

SUCCESS STORY: CHRISTINE

Christine started feeling unwell in 2011 with symptoms of fatigue, anxiety, and depression. Lab work showed nothing significant, so she adjusted her diet and decided to start running. But the symptoms continued, and her doctor couldn't offer an explanation.

In 2012, Christine finished a marathon. But in 2013, as she was training for another marathon, she became so dizzy that she couldn't stand up. Her fatigue got so bad that she couldn't walk a block without having to sit down. On top of that, she couldn't think straight, had difficulty speaking, suffered several panic attacks, and was extremely sensitive to both light and sound.

She saw a cardiologist, an infectious disease specialist, a neurologist, and a psychiatrist. These doctors offered diagnoses, but no solutions. The symptoms continued and Christine felt like a shell of her former self.

Finally, after checking off thirty-five different symptoms from an online checklist, she diagnosed herself with chronic neurological

Lyme's Disease. A few weeks later, she found a Lyme specialist nearby who confirmed her diagnosis.

His treatment involved a massive course of antibiotics. She was taking 5 different antibiotics and 123 different supplements for a total of 36 pills, four times per day.

This protocol lasted all of 2014, at which point symptoms slowly started to fade. But because of the antibiotics, her gut microbiome was a mess. She developed several food sensitivities and had required a severely restricted diet.

Despite the treatments, she experienced two relapses over the next few years. She tried going back on antibiotics, but her stomach couldn't tolerate them. She also tried homeopathy, attended local qigong classes, and stuck to a "Lyme" diet.

In 2019, Christine found the Flowing Zen programs and began to practice. She told me that she followed the program "consistently but not perfectly" for an entire year. By the end of that program, her fatigue was gone, her CNS symptoms were gone, her anxiety was gone, and her foot pain was gone. She also resumed cardio training, which she had not been able to do for years.

She's no longer taking any prescription medication for Lyme. More importantly, she has let go of the constant fear of relapse and feels stronger than she has in years.

"I truly believe I've found a practice that will support my overall health for as long as I practice," she told me. "I've somehow survived this pandemic with relative ease and peace thanks to twenty-five minutes a day of this amazing practice."

"It's important that you know that, even though we've never met, you've changed my life and I am forever grateful."

Notes

1. Brian Muraresku, *The Immortality Key* (New York: St. Martin's Press).

2. Daniel Keown, *The Spark in the Machine* (Jessica Kingsley Publishers, Kindle Edition), 14.

3. "About Fascia," Fascia Research Congress, https://fasciacongress.org/congress/about -fascia/.

4. Thomas W. Myers, *Anatomy Trains: Myofascial Meridians for Manual and Movement Therapists* (Amsterdam: Elsevier Limited, 2020).

5. R. Louis Schultz and Rosemary Feitis, *The Endless Web: Fascial Anatomy and Physical Reality* (Berkeley, CA: North Atlantic Books, 1996).

6. Daniel Keown, *The Spark in the Machine* (Jessica Kingsley Publishers, Kindle Edition), 12.

7. Benias, P.C., Wells, R.G., Sackey-Aboagye, B. et al., "Structure and Distribution of an Unrecognized Interstitium in Human Tissues," *Scientific Reports* 8, no. 4947 (2018), https://doi.org/10.1038/s41598-018-23062-6.

8. Daniel Keown, *The Spark in the Machine* (Jessica Kingsley Publishers, Kindle Edition), 12.

9. Jo Ann Staugaard-Jones, *The Vital Psoas Muscle: Connecting Physical, Emotional, and Spiritual Well-Being* (Berkeley, CA: North Atlantic Books, 2012).

10. Daniel Keown, *The Spark in the Machine* (Jessica Kingsley Publishers, Kindle Edition), 108.

CHAPTER 5
How to Explain Qigong to a Skeptic

The original Greek root of the word *skeptical* means "to doubt." And when it comes to learning an esoteric art like qigong, doubt is natural for Westerners. There's nothing wrong with being skeptical.

In fact, I like skeptics because they ask good questions. Often, a skeptic will simply voice a question that a non-skeptic had in the back of their mind. This provides an opportunity to answer a question not just for the skeptic, but for the entire class.

In this chapter, I'll address the most common questions that skeptics have asked me in my classes. With this information, you'll be positioned to do what countless skeptics have done — open your mind and give qigong a try. Or if you're not skeptical, then the same information will nevertheless help you to understand qigong on a deeper level.

Is Qigong Too Antiquated?

Traditionalists sometimes criticize me for using modern terminology when talking about qigong. For example, I talk about the vagus nerve, the parasympathetic nervous system, the fascia, and other modern concepts that all relate to the practice of qigong.

Similarly, modernists sometimes criticize me for continuing to use ancient terminology. For example, they don't like the term qi, or the concept of the Five Elements. They want to use a purely Western paradigm.

To me, there is no contradiction in talking about our life force flowing through our meridians in one sentence, and then talking about this same energy decreasing your levels of the stress hormone cortisol. Flowing back and forth between different paradigms isn't difficult, and it need not be threatening to our world view. We need not argue about whether qi is just lymph fluid, or if it's connected to the fascia system, or if it refers to hormones.

Qi is all of these things, and also none of them. It's all these things because the flow of qi absolutely influences the healthy flow of lymph fluid, the flow of bioenergy through your fascia, and the production of your hormones. And yet, qi is none of these things. For thousands of years, qigong masters knew nothing about hormones and yet they did amazing things with qigong.

I believe that in the twenty-first century, we have no choice but need to look through multiple lenses. We can't go back to the old ways and view the world through a purely ancient perspective. Nor does the modern perspective offer us a complete picture. This is one reason why people are drawn to ancient wisdom. If Western Medicine had all the answers, then most people wouldn't bother with ancient arts like qigong.

Western Medicine still knows very little about consciousness, internal energy, chronic pain, and self-healing. That's why, despite the amazing things that Western Medicine can do, we still look to the East for answers. We look for practical solutions and we find them in arts like qigong.

This goes in the opposite direction too. Western Medicine excels at a great many things. For example, if you have a badly broken leg or a ruptured appendix, then the emergency room is your best choice. Western Medicine offers us practical solutions to many things, especially acute problems.

When it comes to many chronic problems, however, Chinese Medicine has the edge. For example, if you're suffering from chronic pain and the only solution that your MD offers you is an opioid, Chinese Medicine can offer you better options. Acupuncture and qigong can both offer you pain relief without the dangers of opioids.

In the end, we should be grateful for the opportunity to choose the lens that we want to look through. We can choose to look through the Western Medicine lens for things like surgery and emergency medicine. And we can choose to look through the Chinese Medicine lens for things like chronic pain, depression, autoimmune disorders, and chronic fatigue.

Is Qigong Scientific?

When I first started teaching qigong back in 2005, it was harder to answer skeptics because there wasn't a lot of research. Today, things are much different. Anyone who says that there's no evidence about the benefits of qigong is simply ignorant. In fact, qigong is more evidence-based than some of the pills and procedures people receive from their MDs, who unfortunately cling to disproven treatment protocols despite the evidence.[1]

If you do a quick search on PubMed, you'll find the following for each search:

- qigong = 856 results
- qi gong = 2,085 results
- tai chi = 2,993 results
- mindfulness = 19,298 results

For those who don't know PubMed is a service of the US National Library of Medicine® that "provides free access to MEDLINE®, the NLM® database of indexed citations and abstracts to medical, nursing, dental, veterinary, health care, and preclinical sciences journal articles." In other words, it's the main database for research studies.

Of course, not all of the research studies listed above were conclusive or even positive. That's true of any treatment, whether it's a drug, a surgery, or a therapy. However, many of the qigong and qigong-related studies showed promising results, which is precisely why more research is being done every year.

A student of mine, who is also a pharmaceutical researcher, said this regarding the research on qigong: "If you saw that much positive research on a drug or a device, you would see billions of dollars being poured into research and patents."

That's the nature of the world that we live in. There are no patents for qigong, tai chi, meditation, or yoga. Without patents, companies can't make huge profits. And yet, despite this, the research is still overwhelmingly positive.

Based on the research, we can confidently say that qigong helps with the following issues:

- Qigong helps lower blood pressure.[2][3][4][5]
- Qigong & tai chi help to improve physical balance.[6][7][8]
- Qigong relieves depression and anxiety.[9][10][11]
- Qigong helps relieve chronic pain.[12][13][14]
- Qigong & tai chi build muscular strength.[15][16][17]
- Qigong & tai chi increase bone density.[18][19][20]
- Qigong & tai chi strengthen the immune system.[21][22][23][24]
- Qigong relieves arthritis pain.[25][26][27][28]
- Qigong & tai chi improve cognitive function.[29][30][31]

Over the next decade, I'm sure that the list of benefits will increase, as will the strength of the evidence. But we don't need to wait for more research to get started with our own healing. The verdict is already in. Qigong works!

Nevertheless, I believe that there are some practical ways to improve qigong research over the next few decades. Here are my ideas:

1. Many tai chi studies actually include qigong.

Whenever a new study comes out, I read the fine print. I dive as deeply into the study as possible with my knowledge and experience, both Western and Eastern. And here's what I often find with tai chi studies: It's not really tai chi.

The terminology is a problem here. If a "tai chi" study involves fifteen minutes of qigong exercises plus fifteen minutes of tai chi forms—is that really tai chi? No, it's a combination of qigong and tai chi.

Sometimes, it's not easy to tell what the participants were actually practicing. I would need to watch a video or speak to the teacher to find the truth. It's reasonable to conclude that many of the 2,993 tai chi studies above included some qigong.

2. The importance of the teacher is underappreciated.

One of the first things I do when looking at research is to search for the actual teacher. It's not always easy to find! Often, the studies just say things like: "Subjects were taught tai chi for eight weeks." The teacher is not mentioned, nor are they listed as an author in the study.

With arts like qigong, the role of the teacher is critical. There is a long tradition of honoring the "heart-to-heart transmission" from teacher to student. This isn't mystical; it's simply pointing out the importance of high-quality teaching from a caring instructor. If you are going to study the effectiveness of qigong for a particular health issue, then the teacher is part of the equation. The better the teacher, the better the result.

3. Qigong doesn't treat symptoms.

Most research studies will test the effectiveness of qigong on a particular disorder or pathology, like depression or diabetes. That makes sense when you're in the Western paradigm, but not so much from the Eastern paradigm. In fact, there's no such thing as depression or diabetes in Chinese Medicine. The paradigm is totally different.

Chinese Medicine is more proactive. It doesn't just try to reverse disease. Rather, it focuses on rooting out underlying issues and bolstering fundamental physical and mental-emotional processes in order to actively promote health.

Because of this, qigong treats the individual person, not the disorder. In fact, many types of qigong are not designed to treat symptoms at all. Rather, they are designed to be used as a long-term solution to the root causes of pathology. So while you're testing whether or not qigong will help one hundred people with diabetes, it may actually be getting fantastic results in other areas that you're not testing. As such, the broader benefits of qigong are often underappreciated.

4. Qigong studies aren't long enough.

So far, I have not seen a years-long study of qigong, let alone a decades-long study. Most of the trials range from a few weeks to a few months long. Compare this to nutritional studies, which sometimes go on for years or decades.

Qigong is meant to be a lifestyle. In fact, one of my goals as a teacher is to get students hooked on qigong so that they practice for the rest of their lives. (This means you, dear reader.)

If you really want to see the power of qigong, do a study on people who've been practicing for ten years, and measure *all* of their benefits, not just one or two. The results will knock your socks off!

5. Placebo isn't the enemy.

The gold standard for Western research is the double-blind randomized controlled trial (RCT). This is a study in which neither the participants nor the experimenters know who is receiving the treatment. This is done to prevent bias—especially bias due to the placebo effect, which is controlled for.

See the problem here? How do you study something like qigong if neither the teacher nor the student knows if they are learning qigong? And do you exclude the placebo effect, which is just another word for mind-body healing?

There are no easy answers to these questions. But for starters, we need to stop viewing placebo as the enemy. After all, placebo is concrete, scientific proof of the healing power of the mind.

Is It Just the Placebo Effect?

If I hear one more person say that the benefits of qigong are "just placebo," I'm going to kick them right in the placebo. The word *just* is what gets my goat. After all, the only reason to put the word *just* in front of the word *placebo* is to discount it. When someone says, "just the placebo" to me, this is what I hear:

> "It's *just* a natural healing phenomenon that has been documented to spontaneously reverse a wide range of severe, chronic disorders without using any drugs or surgery. Just that little thing."

Because of my training in qigong and Chinese Medicine, I understand what the placebo really is. For the life of me, I can't understand why people aren't jumping up and down at the discovery of this amazing phenomenon. We should be embracing it rather than rejecting it.

The term "placebo" first came into use in the twentieth century. Dr. Henry Beecher was so fascinated by what he witnessed after giving fake morphine to soldiers in WWII that he wanted to investigate further. Good for you, Dr. Beecher! Thank you for exploring the placebo effect rather than rejecting it!

In essence, the healing power of the placebo effect results from the deep-seated belief that a medical treatment will bring benefits. In other words, the placebo effect proves that your beliefs and thoughts have a measurable effect on your health and well-being. And yet, this powerful phenomenon is being largely ignored in the West.

It is critical to understand that the placebo effect is not just a psychological phenomenon. It's not just in your head. Research on the placebo has shown measurable improvements that cannot be explained by mere psychology.

Here's a quote from a book called *Mind Over Medicine: Scientific Proof That You Can Heal Yourself* by Dr. Lissa Rankin, MD:

> "Is there scientific data to support the seemingly miraculous stories of self-healing that float around? You betcha. There's proof that you can radically alter your body's physiology just by changing your mind. There's also proof that you can make yourself sick when your mind thinks unhealthy thoughts. And it's not just mental. It's physiological."

We've established that the placebo effect is solid, scientific proof of the mind-body connection. We've also established that Western Medicine prefers to ignore this phenomenon. Classical Chinese Medicine, on the other hand, has been exploring the phenomenon for thousands of years.

Of course, Chinese Medicine has never used the term "placebo." Aside from the fact that "placebo" is a Latin word, Chinese Medicine has never needed a word for placebo because it never denied the mind-body connection in the first place.

Here's another way to think about it. Before Sigmund Freud, the mind and its role in healing was virtually nonexistent in Western Medicine. Western Medicine was extremely mechanistic.

The reason why Freud started a revolution is because Western Medicine desperately needed the field of psychology to bring it some balance.

Today, the fields of Mind-Body Medicine and Integrative Medicine are bridging the gap between the physical and psychological sides of Western Medicine. Psychology has come a long way from the talk therapy of Freud's era. Modern therapies like Acceptance and Commitment Therapy (ACT), Mindfulness-Based Cognitive Therapy (MBCT), Internal Family Systems (IFS), and Somatic Experiencing (SE) are proving to be more promising than Freudian-inspired psychoanalysis, thereby bridging the gap more effectively.

But let's not forget that in Chinese Medicine there is no need for a bridge because there was never a gap to begin with. If you went back in time and asked Hua Tuo, the famous Chinese physician, whether he believed in the power of the mind to heal the body (i.e., the placebo effect), he would have been confused. He would probably wonder why this time traveler from the future was asking questions with such obvious answers. In Chinese Medicine, the idea that the mind could be separated from healing is just crazy nonsense. Of course, the mind and body are connected. Duh!

Here's an example that will help you to appreciate the power of the mind over the body. This example is extreme and also painful, but it will illustrate my point.

Imagine that you received an email from a trusted friend saying that your beloved _____ [child, parent, spouse, pet] has just died. Within seconds, your blood pressure spikes, your cortisol levels rise, your heart rate increases, your breathing changes, and epigenetic changes begin to form in your genes. All of these physical reactions came from an email, or rather, from the thoughts and beliefs induced by the email.

Now imagine that the email was actually some sort of cruel hoax. No one died. In other words, all your physiological reactions were not only based on thoughts and beliefs—but they were based on *false* thoughts and beliefs. This analogy, as terrible as it may be, is highly accurate for us. Most of us have false beliefs that are wreaking real physiological havoc on our body.

In my opinion, the #1 false belief in the Western world, a belief that is epidemic and devastating in its consequences, is the belief that the placebo effect is something we should be skeptical of. What if you changed that belief? What if, rather than setting the placebo effect aside, you went deeper into it and cultivated its raw power instead?

Is Pain Just in Your Head?

Let's look at chronic pain. Typically, we think of pain as purely physical. We assume that there's a structural issue causing the pain. Unfortunately, Western Medicine still perpetuates this myth despite overwhelming evidence to the contrary. Of course, chronic pain is *sometimes* caused by a structural problem, but more often, it's not.

For example, herniated discs are often the diagnosis given to explain chronic low back pain, something I've battled since I was seventeen. According to this theory, the fluid in our vertebral discs leaks out, or herniates, thereby causing pain. But modern research using MRIs shows that this theory is not true at all.

For example, here are four options when it comes to herniated discs and chronic back pain:

1. Herniated discs with chronic pain
2. Herniated discs without chronic pain
3. No herniated discs with chronic pain
4. No herniated discs without chronic pain

Studies have shown that there is no correlation between herniation and pain.[32] In these studies, you can find people in all four of the categories above, thereby disproving the correlation theory.

People can have herniations with or without pain, and they can have pain with or without herniations. In other words, herniations are not the source of the pain to majority of the time.

So why do doctors still believe that herniations are the cause of pain? Not all of them do. Many doctors, like Dr. David Hanscom, who is a spine surgeon, are pushing back against this kind of diagnosis. I recommend his book, *Back in Control*. If you read it, you'll see that his mind-body approach to back pain sounds a lot like qigong!

When it comes to dealing with chronic pain, Western Medicine is failing hundreds of millions of people. It is failing because it is looking for answers in the wrong place. It is looking for pain in the physical structure of the body while ignoring the mind

I know what it's like to suffer from terrible chronic pain. I know what it's like to be in pain in every position—standing, sitting, and lying down. I know what it's like to feel like you're losing your sanity because the pain is so bad and so constant. I know what it's like to wash down pills with alcohol in a desperate attempt to find relief—any relief—from the pain.

You could say that suffering taught me to be more compassionate toward others who are suffering. It's common to dismiss people's pain as "all in their head." Please don't do that. Be compassionate instead.

Pain is a complex and confusing subject. Many of our ideas are firmly ingrained even though they are incorrect. Years ago, a sixty-something man with a disheveled, gray ponytail attended an open house at my qigong studio. We'll call him Craig. He cornered me at the event and grilled me with questions about qigong for back pain. I did my best to answer all his questions and told him about my own experience beating chronic pain.

"Maybe you just imagined that your pain was gone," he said with a slight smirk. It was one of those comments that, if I had questioned it, would be explained away as a joke. "Just kidding," he would say if I had taken offense. But I knew where Craig was coming from and what he was really asking.

I noticed a military tattoo on his forearm, and I decided to tell him a story. "Have you heard of Henry Beecher?" I asked. Craig shook his head. "Dr. Beecher was a military doctor during World War II," I explained. "When he ran out of morphine, he was desperate to help the wounded soldiers, who were in terrible pain. So he gave them harmless saline injections but told them that it was morphine."

Craig was listening attentively now. His smirk was gone.

"It worked amazingly well," I said. "These soldiers, who received zero morphine, still got relief. So let me ask you this: do you think that they just imagined that their pain was gone?"

This line of thinking must have worked, because Craig ended up joining my beginner's class. I guess you could say that he had a change of heart. It turned out that Craig battles PTSD, as do so many veterans today. Qigong helped him to better manage the chronic pain as well as his PTSD.

Craig was probably parroting what he had heard somewhere else. Others had dismissed his pain as being just in his head, and so he tried to dismiss my pain the same way. But in his heart, I think he knew it was wrong.

If you think that Western Medicine has pain all figured out, then you are mistaken. Over fifty million Americans suffer from chronic pain. If Western Medicine had pain all figured out, then 15 percent of the country wouldn't be suffering from it. Let's take a closer look so that we can have a deeper understanding of how and why Western medicine is failing so many Americans when it comes to pain relief.

Here are four examples to show you just how complex it can get:

- **Example 1: Phantom Pain.** After a limb is amputated, patients often report having terrible pain in the missing limb.[33] In other words, even though there are no peripheral nerves left to transmit pain signals, people still experience severe pain. This is a real phenomenon. Don't dismiss it as imaginary or "in the head." I recommend that you have a two-minute conversation with someone who has phantom pain. It will open your mind as well as your heart.

- **Example 2: Simulated Surgery.** In studies, fake surgery is sometimes used as a placebo (rather than a pill). For example, a 2013 study showed that a simulated surgery was just as good as real surgery at reducing the pain from torn knee cartilage.[34] In other words, fake knee surgery eliminated pain even though it didn't fix the torn cartilage.

- **Example 3: Herniated Discs.** Many patients with herniated discs don't have any pain whatsoever. Often, the X-rays and MRIs look like the patient should be unable to walk—and yet the patient is in no discomfort.

- **Example 4: No-Cause Back Pain.** Patients with terrible chronic pain often go through a barrage of tests, which conclusively show that the cause of their back pain is—unknown. But the pain is often so severe that it is debilitating for the patient.

In the West, we like to think that pain must be due to some sort of structural problem, that something must be broken, like a broken watch. The four examples above prove that this kind of thinking is flawed. In examples one and four, there was pain where there shouldn't be pain. In examples two and three, there was no pain where there should have been pain.

As much as we would like pain to be a physical and structural problem, many times it just isn't. This begs the question: is our entire way of thinking about pain fundamentally flawed?

What Is Pain Anyway?

Let's have fun with two thought experiments:

1. Imagine that you go to the doctor because of terrible back pain, but their high-tech tests reveal that nothing is physically wrong. Does this mean that you're not in pain?
2. Now imagine that you have no pain, but a scan shows that you have two herniated discs, or spinal stenosis, or spinal arthritis. Does this mean that you're actually in pain?

The truth is that there is only one person on the planet who can measure your pain: you. The most common method for measuring pain in both Eastern and Western medicine is to ask the patient to rate their pain on a scale of one to ten. For example, when I was in acupuncture college, we had to memorize the following phrase: "On a scale of one to ten, with ten being the worst pain imaginable and zero being no pain at all, what is your pain level right now?"

This method is a terrifically accurate way to measure pain. But it's also extremely frustrating to the Western, reductionist view of pain. That's because this method is subjective rather than objective.

There is no objective way to measure pain. There is no such thing as a PRI (Pain Resonance Imaging) machine. Pain is 100 percent subjective, and Western researchers hate this fact. That's probably why researchers at Stanford started working on "a diagnostic tool that could eliminate a major hurdle in pain medicine—the dependency on self-reporting to measure the presence or absence of pain."[35]

A major hurdle? The problem with the Western approach to pain medicine is not in the diagnosis; it's in the treatment. Western doctors *know* that there's pain; they just don't know how to get rid of it!

Well, that's not entirely true. Getting rid of pain is easy. All you need to do is write a script for opioids or muscle relaxants! Today, there is a lot of mistrust in the pain industry because too many patients have gotten addicted to opioids. Once they are addicted, they may lie about their pain levels to continue being prescribed their meds. This is to be expected, but this isn't their fault. It was the Western medical system that prescribed addictive opioids in the first place.

As I said earlier, it's better to start with compassion. Just like in our justice system, people should be innocent until proven guilty. We should trust people when they say that they are in pain, and we should give them solutions that don't involve highly addictive substances. We need to have compassion toward people who are in pain, and also toward people who become addicted to prescription drugs through no fault of their own.

There is something missing from the Western approach to pain, something important. The Western solutions are ineffective precisely because pain isn't just a physical or structural problem. In order to fully understand pain, you must look at the mind-body connection. In other words, you must treat humans as thinking, feeling beings rather than as robots.

All over the world, people are turning to acupuncture, meditation, qigong, yoga, and other Eastern therapies. And they are getting results—better results than they did with Western therapies. For example, many folks find me only after having tried everything else first. They've already been to the Mayo Clinic, they've seen pain specialists, they've had surgery, they've been medicated—and yet they're still in terrible pain.

Qigong often works even when all else has failed. In other words, my small business, with little ole me and 1.5 employees, is sometimes more effective than the Mayo Clinic, a $12 billion nonprofit that employs over 63,000 people. If Western Medicine were doing a good job, this wouldn't be possible, and I would be out of business.

Things are changing, albeit slowly. Western Medicine is reluctantly embracing Mind Body Medicine and Integrative Medicine. The Mayo Clinic has even started offering tai chi! Progress!

As Western Medicine brings other therapies and arts into its embrace, let's not forget *why* this is happening. The Mind Body Medicine, Integrative Medicine, and Functional Medicine movements all began *within* the Western Medical community. These movements started precisely because Western Medicine was doing such a lousy job, especially with chronic pain. In other words, the rise of these movements is a signal that the Western medical model has already failed.

The sooner Western Medicine admits defeat when it comes to chronic pain, the sooner people can start feeling empowered to find their healing outside of the allopathic model. But don't wait for Western Medicine to fully embrace therapies like qigong because this might take another ten to twenty years to happen. Take the initiative and start now. You're ahead of the curve.

What Can We Heal?

Let's do another thought experiment. This experiment has the potential to forever change the way you view healing. For the experiment, we'll be talking about cancer. But first, a caveat. In the US, it is illegal for anyone other than oncologists to treat cancer. Let me be absolutely clear that this is just a theoretical discussion, not medical advice. I am not a medical doctor.

For the experiment, I'll ask you a simple question. Please think about the question for a moment before you answer. Here it is:

In theory, can cancer be reversed without chemotherapy, radiation, surgery, or any medication whatsoever?

Let me be clear that I'm not asking whether you *believe* cancer can be reversed. I'm talking about facts. According to the available evidence, can cancer be reversed or not? Okay, got your answer?

Hopefully, you answered "yes." If you answered "maybe" or "no," then I've got news for you, and it's wonderful news! The medical literature is full of cases where cancer reversed itself without any external intervention. In other words, there is scientific evidence that the human body can heal itself of many kinds of cancers—without drugs, chemo, radiation, or surgery.

We're talking about a well-known phenomenon called "spontaneous remission" or "spontaneous regression." For example, a 2008 study found that spontaneous regression/remission occurred in 22 percent of all breast cancer patients.[36] Spontaneous remission is not nearly as rare as we once believed. In fact, it seems to happen all the time. Back in 1993, researchers decided that spontaneous remission was something that should be studied rather than ignored. Together, they compiled the largest database of medically reported cases of spontaneous remission in the world, with more than 3,500 references from over 800 journals.

The result is a publication called *Spontaneous Remission: An Annotated Bibliography.*[37] This bibliography shows that spontaneous remission is all of the following:

1. Widely documented in the world medical literature since the end of the nineteenth century.
2. A phenomenon that occurs across a broad spectrum of diseases and is not limited to cancer, though cancer does make up the bulk of the reports.
3. Potentially an extremely rich area of research that can allow us to see important, little-known biological and psychological processes in a way that may provide important clues to understanding the self-regulating processes in the body.[38]

Coming back to my original question, we now have a good answer: The human body is capable, at least in theory, of reversing some forms of cancer. If you were suffering from cancer, you would absolutely want to be one of the lucky souls to undergo spontaneous regression because it would involve no surgery, it would incur no nasty side effects, and it would save you a few hundred thousand dollars. So how can you pour yourself a nice cup of spontaneous remission? Well, you can't, at least not according to Western Medicine.

Unfortunately, doctors and researchers are too busy fighting the "war" on cancer to pay attention to something like spontaneous remission. Who cares that it is arguably the most important medical discovery in the last one hundred years? We've got a war to fight!

The many cases of spontaneous remission are proof that it's at least *possible* to reverse cancer, even if researchers don't yet understand the mechanism for this kind of healing.

For our purposes, the simple fact that cancer can theoretically be reversed gives us half of the equation we're searching for. It shows us what we can, in theory, heal.

Now let's talk about the other half. Let's look at something that the human body simply cannot heal. And let's use an example that Western Medicine is also incapable of fixing.

A young woman once approached me after a workshop and asked, quite innocently, if qigong could regrow a limb. You see, this woman, a college student with a bright future, was an amputee. A rare medical condition had required that she have a leg amputated at a young age.

My heart went out to her. It was one of those moments where you just want to lie and say that everything is going to be okay, but I told her the painful truth. "I'm sorry," I said, "but to the best of my knowledge, that's not possible, not with qigong or any other method."

As far as I know, there are no recorded cases of entire human limbs being regrown. You can comb the medical literature and never find a single case of this ever happening. Not even one. So it's safe to say that this kind of thing is outside the window of possibility.

On the other hand, qigong did help this woman to relieve the phantom pains associated with the amputation. I've seen this happen many times. But I've never seen or even heard about anyone regrowing a limb. It's just not something that the human body is capable of doing.

These two examples, cancer and an amputated limb, give us a simple equation for the range of possibilities with self-healing arts like qigong. I call this the Self-Healing Map.

For example, the evidence suggests that cancer is on the Self-Healing Map. This doesn't mean that every case of cancer can be reversed, but it absolutely does mean that *some* cases of cancer can be reversed. In other words, it's possible to reverse cancer.

On the other hand, regrowing a limb is not on the Self-Healing Map. It's simply not within the range of healing for the human body. Maybe it will be possible one day using stem cells or other technological methods, but it's not possible with self-healing.

What other health problems are on the map? Well, the first thing you should do is look through the Spontaneous Remission Bibliography Project. If your problem is on the list, then you can reasonably theorize that it's possible—at least in theory—to heal yourself. Does that mean you'll definitely heal? No. There are many other factors involved, but isn't it wonderful to know that it's possible to heal?

What about things that are not on the list? Remember that spontaneous remission, by its nature, is not easy to record. Do you think that there are more than thirty-five hundred cases of spontaneous remission in modern history? You bet there are, and you can also bet that most of them were never documented. For example, I have a student who reversed Crohn's disease. Her doctors have confirmed that there are no longer any signs of Crohn's present, and she's also completely off her medication. But I can't find that disease on the list.

If you suffer from Crohn's and you want more evidence, then you should comb the internet for other cases of people who healed themselves of the disorder, even if it wasn't with qigong. I'm betting that there are cases of people doing it with many different forms of self-healing. Do a few hours of focused research and find out if the human body has ever healed your particular issue.

And of course, if your condition is something that often heals itself, like low-back pain, arthritis, depression, or migraines—then it's definitely worth trying qigong. These issues often respond quickly to a steady qigong practice.

Regardless, let's not miss the crucial lesson—the body is capable of all sorts of amazing healing! Let's come back to our original question: What can we heal with qigong, at least in theory? Lots!

What If You Don't Heal?

So far, we've talked about theory. But as we know, theory and practice don't always see eye to eye. Just because qigong can theoretically heal something doesn't mean that it will. When it comes to healing with qigong, there are many factors, like the quality of your practice, your deeply held beliefs, the food that you eat, your age, and even the people you surround yourself with.

In the qigong world, we call these "blockages." There's nothing mysterious here; we all have them. Let's imagine that you've been practicing qigong for two years. You've gotten good results, but you still have a few lingering health problems. The strangest thing is that some of your classmates have been able to overcome these exact issues using qigong. And yet you can't seem to do the same for yourself. Why?

I've seen this many times. For example, I once had two students literally standing next to each other in a class. One of them had overcome arthritis in only six months using qigong. The other student, however, was still suffering from it even after two years of practice. This is a perfect example of the gap that exists between theory and reality. In theory, your problem can be healed, but, it may not be so easy.

I've seen people reverse arthritis many, many times. People all over the world are reversing it with diet, acupuncture, chiropractic,

tai chi, and other methods. So there's no question that—in theory—
many cases of arthritis can be reversed. Then why does arthritis
reverse itself in some people, but not others? To find the answer,
look for the blockages.

The human body is an incredibly complex healing machine,
and there are many things that can potentially block your energy. I
developed something called the Blockage Wheel (see below) to help
students figure out where they might be blocked. The wheel helps
identify twelve blockages that students often run into.

Here's a perfect Blockage Wheel. In other words, this person
has no major blockages in any of the twelve major areas.

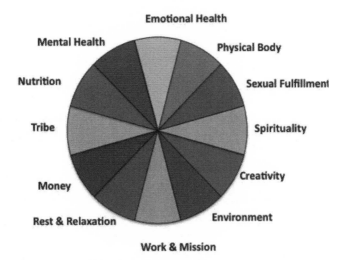

But smooth blockage wheels like this are rare. For most of us,
some areas are better than others. Maybe you eat well and exercise
religiously, but you don't rest enough. Or maybe you smoke and
drink, but you have healthy relationships and a strong sense of purpose in life.

The end result for both of these examples is that your ride
is bumpier than it should be. Here's a typical blockage wheel for
humans in the twenty-first century:

Let's take a closer look at each blockage.

1. Emotional Health

Are your emotions stuck? In qigong theory, all physical ailments have an emotional component; in fact, each of the Twelve Primary Meridians has an emotion directly associated with it. For example, if you are fearful, then there may be a blockage in your Kidney Meridian, and this blockage may be contributing to your back pain.

Trauma is a big issue too. We could place it in several categories since it affects our physical body as much as our emotions, but I'll put it here because I think that trauma is, at its core, an emotional event. The far-reaching effects of trauma on both children and adults is still not widely acknowledged. I could write an entire book about qigong and trauma, and perhaps I will one day. In the meantime, read *The Body Keeps the Score* by Bessel Van Der Kolk, as well as *Waking the Tiger* by Peter Levine. These two books will give you an eye-opening introduction into the repercussions of trauma, as well as ways that we can heal. Qigong fits in beautifully and in fact is mentioned by both authors.

2. Physical Structure

How is your posture? Do you have an unnatural curve in your lower back (called lordosis)? Do you have a slight hunch in your upper back (called kyphosis)? In Chinese there's a saying: "You need not worry about getting old so long as your spine is straight and healthy." Sometimes, this is referred to as a person's "structure." Physical strength and flexibility (or a lack thereof) are also factors that can affect your structure and your health. If your structure is off, then your fascia will be kinked up and your qi will not flow the way it was designed to.

In the twenty-first century, few people have a perfect structure. Based on my experience, as well as conversations with several acupuncturists and chiropractors, I estimate that over 90 percent of modern humans have structural issues that are blocking them from healing. Qigong is an effective way to work on your structure and alignment.

3. Sexual Fulfillment

The qigong masters viewed sexual energy as a critical aspect of human vitality. We are sexual beings, and this energy is part of being alive. If your sexual energy is blocked, then it can cause all kinds of problems, both emotional and physical. This is true even for celibate monks and nuns. Qigong can help to clear sexual blockages. This is how the Shaolin monks and nuns remained healthy for years despite their vows of celibacy. On a side note, I would argue that the lack of these blockage-clearing qigong techniques is precisely what has led to so much perversion and abuse in the Catholic Church. Sexual blockages can cause tremendous harm to our children and our world.

4. Spirituality

Are you connected to something bigger than yourself? Do you view life, our planet, and the cosmos with a sense of awe? How often do you have peak experiences? Sometimes, a blockage can be lodged deep in the spirit. If you don't feel a connection to God, Nature, Source, Your Original Face, or the Tao, then the natural exchange of energy between you and the cosmos will be blocked. This applies to atheists too. A connection to something bigger than oneself can be as simple as spending time in nature or appreciating fine art in a museum. Qigong is an easy way to practice mindfulness. The practice of mindfulness can help us to stay more present, which in turn helps us to stay more connected. It is this connection that will help to heal spiritual blockages.

5. Creativity

Resist the temptation to dismiss creativity as something you don't need. It is an important part of healing. Twenty thousand years ago, humans were painting on cave walls, weaving baskets, sewing functional and beautiful boots, sculpting pottery, designing ornate necklaces, and carving useful tools. Creativity is not just for artists; it's in our DNA.

Unfortunately, artistic expression is not what it once was, especially in the US, where funding for the arts is constantly being cut. Children who are raised without the arts don't pursue creativity as adults. This creates blockages.

Adults who take up a creative hobby often see a dramatic improvement in their health as a result. Qigong is a wonderful way to build up the energy and the courage required for creative pursuits. After practicing qigong for a few years, don't be surprised if you decide to write that novel or take up piano lessons!

6. Environment

Energy flows in and through your environment. Your house, your workplace, the climate where you live—these things have a profound effect on your health. In fact, there is an entire field of study called *Feng Shui* (pronounced "fung shway") that deals with the flow of qi in and through spaces.

In my experience, bad Feng Shui can be a major source of energy blockages. When students improve the Feng Shui in their environment, they often see big improvements in their own healing. Similarly, the Feng Shui at our mountain retreat in Costa Rica is so good that students benefit even after just 1 week in that environment.

7. Your Mission

Are you clear about your life purpose? If so, are you fulfilling it? Many famous psychologists, including Ernest Becker and Viktor Frankl, believed that a sense of purpose was the single most important thing in a person's life. I tend to agree with them. If your work is pure drudgery, if there is no time during the week where you feel that you are making strides in your mission, then this could be causing an energy blockage. Many times, I've watched students quit their job and start a new career. As a result, they quickly began to heal in ways that they never imagined possible!

8. Rest

Sleep is one of the ways your body replenishes and restores itself. Let's be honest, you probably don't get enough of it. Humans should be getting eight to ten hours of *quality* sleep every night. If you've been getting six hours of restless sleep for years, then that could be part of the problem.

In my experience as a teacher, students who don't wake up feeling rested won't get the full benefits of qigong. Practicing qigong can certainly help, but you may also need to make other changes. For example, you may need to go to bed earlier, or limit screen time in the bedroom, or even buy a new mattress.

9. Money

If you're constantly stressed out by your finances, then this is a big drain on your energy. I see this blockage all the time in students. They just can't relax into working on their health until they fix some of their financial problems. On a more personal note, I totally get it. Financial stress was my default mode until my forties. When I finally started to clear some of these blockages, I felt like a massive burden was taken from my shoulders. My qigong improved dramatically after I cleared these blockages!

10. Community

Research has shown that belonging to a community can have a profound effect on your overall health and longevity. In fact, one study suggests that loneliness has the same impact on mortality as smoking fifteen cigarettes per day![39] By all means quit smoking, but quit loneliness too! We all need a community, whether that's at church, a football game, a book club, or a local tai chi class. For people who live alone, pets are a great way to combat loneliness. Even just sitting in a cafe surrounded by other people can help to start clearing these blockages.

11. Nutrition

You are what you eat. Duh. You knew this already. But what should we eat? There is no easy answer. You will find scientific data to support everything from veganism to the carnivore diet to everything in between.

"The Masai subsist on cattle blood and meat and milk and little else," wrote Michael Pollan, author of *In Defense of Food*. "Native

Americans subsist on beans and maize. And the Inuit in Greenland subsist on whale blubber and a little bit of lichen. The irony is, the one diet we have invented for ourselves—the Western diet—is the one that makes us sick." [40]

In other words, avoid the Standard American Diet, no matter what else you do. But making dietary changes is not easy. That's why I always recommend that students start with qigong. The additional energy and willpower that you build from adding a daily qigong routine will help you to make dietary changes and figure out what works best for you.

12. Mental Health

Your thoughts and your beliefs affect your health, your energy, and your biology. If you haven't yet read it, I highly recommend *The Biology of Belief* by Bruce Lipton. This book, written by a Western scientist, explains the fascinating world of epigenetics— a world where your thoughts and beliefs can change the expression of your genes!

Mental health can also refer to your clarity of mind. If your mind is dull, if you can't concentrate, then you won't be able to learn the things you need to fix your health. That's a blockage too.

And, of course, if you are depressed or anxious, then this will affect your health too. I know from experience how this can become a negative feedback loop. The more depressed you are, the worse your health gets. And so you get more anxious and more depressed. And then your health gets worse and so on.

Qigong is a great way to break the cycle. In Chinese Medicine, what we call the "mind" is in the heart. So we could say that qigong starts by treating the heart-mind. When your heart-mind begins to heal, then the rest will quickly follow.

SUCCESS STORY: HOLLY

Holly suffered multiple compression fractures to her spine and was in constant pain. Understandably, she became fearful of movement even though she knew that exercise was important for her overall health. She had already tried several rounds of physical therapy and didn't know where else to turn.

Then she discovered qigong. After trying a few local studios, she finally found our online classes. For Holly, the combination of clear instruction along with an accessible teacher is what helped her get over her fear. Here's what she wrote me in an email: "I appreciate your systematic way of teaching. I've tried learning qigong from two other instructors in the past but without great results. With your method, I feel I am making real progress and things are starting to make so much more sense to me! You helped me to break the cycle of chronic pain and also restored my confidence that it was safe to exercise without exacerbating my condition."

As her fear of movement gradually subsided, Holly's nervous system was able to downregulate, thereby allowing her qi to flow more freely. And as her qi flowed freely, her pain gradually dissolved. Today, Holly is able to engage in other forms of exercise in addition to qigong. Her follow-up scans also showed an improvement in bone density. This is an example of the holistic benefits of qigong. Holly just wanted to get out of pain, but she got so much more with qigong!

Notes

1. David Epstein and ProPublica, "When Evidence Says No, but Doctors Say Yes," The Atlantic, February 22, 2017, https://www.theatlantic.com/health/archive/2017/02/when-evidence-says-no-but-doctors-say-yes/517368/.
2. Suphannika Ladawan et al., "Effect of Qigong Exercise on Cognitive Function, Blood Pressure and Cardiorespiratory Fitness in Healthy Middle-Aged Subjects," Complementary Therapies in Medicine 33 (Aug. 2017): 39-45, https://doi.org/10.1016/j.ctim.2017.05.005.
3. Liye Zou et al., "A Systematic Review and Meta-Analysis Baduanjin Qigong for Health Benefits: Randomized Controlled Trials," Evidence-Based Complementary

and Alternative Medicine 2017, no. 4548706 (March 2017): 1–17, https://doi.org/10.1155/2017/4548706.

4. Hongchang Yang, Xueping Wu, and Min Wang, "The Effect of Three Different Meditation Exercises on Hypertension: A Network Meta-Analysis," *Evidence-Based Complementary and Alternative Medicine* 2017, no. 9784271 (April 2017): 1–13, https://doi.org/10.1155/2017/9784271.

5. B. Cheung et al., "Randomised Controlled Trial of Qigong in the Treatment of Mild Essential Hypertension," *Journal of Human Hypertension* 19, no. 9 (May 2005): 697–704, https://doi.org/10.1038/sj.jhh.1001884.

6. Timothy C. Hain et al., "Effects of T'ai Chi on Balance," *Archives of Otolaryngology—Head & Neck Surgery* 125, no. 11 (November 1999): 1191–5. https://doi.org/10.1001/archotol.125.11.1191.

7. Liye Zou et al., "A Systematic Review and Meta-Analysis Baduanjin Qigong for Health Benefits: Randomized Controlled Trials," *Evidence-Based Complementary and Alternative Medicine* 2017, no. 4548706 (March 2017): 1–17, https://doi.org/10.1155/2017/4548706.

8. Rafael Lomas-Vega et al, "Tai Chi for Risk of Falls. A Meta-analysis," *Journal of the American Geriatrics Society* 65, no. 9 (September 2017): 2037–43, https://doi.org/10.1111/jgs.15008.

9. Roger Jahnke et al., "A Comprehensive Review of Health Benefits of Qigong and Tai Chi," *American Journal of Health Promotion* 24, no. 6 (July-August 2010): e1-e25, https://doi.org/10.4278/ajhp.081013-LIT-248.

10. Hector W. H. Tsang et al., "Effect of a Qigong Exercise Programme on Elderly with Depression," *International Journal of Geriatric Psychiatry* 21, no. 9 (September 2006): 890–7, https://doi.org/10.1002/gps.1582.

11. B. Cheung et al., "Randomised Controlled Trial of Qigong in the Treatment of Mild Essential Hypertension," *Journal of Human Hypertension* 19, no. 9 (May 2005): 697–704, https://doi.org/10.1038/sj.jhh.1001884.

12. Roger Jahnke et al., "A Comprehensive Review of Health Benefits of Qigong and Tai Chi," *American Journal of Health Promotion* 24, no. 6 (July-August 2010): e1-e25, https://doi.org/10.4278/ajhp.081013-LIT-248.

13. Marlene Fransen et al., "Physical Activity for Osteoarthritis Management: A Randomized Controlled Clinical Trial Evaluating Hydrotherapy or Tai Chi Classes," *Arthritis and Rheumatism* 57, no. 3 (March 2007): 407–14, https://doi.org/10.1002/art.22621.

14. Alison Hammond and Kaye Freeman, "Community Patient Education and Exercise for People with Fibromyalgia: a Parallel Group Randomized Controlled Trial," *Clinical Rehabilitation* 20, no. 10 (October 2006): 835–46, https://doi.org/10.1177/0269215506072173.

15. Liye Zou et al., "A Systematic Review and Meta-Analysis Baduanjin Qigong for Health Benefits: Randomized Controlled Trials," *Evidence-Based Complementary and Alternative Medicine* 2017, no. 4548706 (March 2017): 1–17, https://doi.org/10.1155/2017/4548706.

16. Joseph F. Audette et al., "Tai Chi versus Brisk Walking in Elderly Women," *Age and Ageing* 35, no. 4 (April 2006): 388–93, https://doi.org/10.1093/ageing/afl006.

17. Roger Jahnke et al., "A Comprehensive Review of Health Benefits of Qigong and Tai Chi," *American Journal of Health Promotion* 24, no. 6 (July-August 2010): e1-e25, https://doi.org/10.4278/ajhp.081013-LIT-248.

18. Roger Jahnke et al., "A Comprehensive Review of Health Benefits of Qigong and Tai Chi," *American Journal of Health Promotion* 24, no. 6 (July-August 2010): e1-e25, https://doi.org/10.4278/ajhp.081013-LIT-248.

19. Kaiming Chan et al., "A Randomized, Prospective Study of the Effects of Tai Chi Chun Exercise on Bone Mineral Density in Postmenopausal Women," *Archives of Physical*

Medicine and Rehabilitation 85, no. 5 (May 2004): 717–22, https://doi.org/10.1016/j.apmr.2003.08.091.

20. Hsing-Hsia Chen, Mei-Ling Yeh, and Fang-Ying Lee, "The Effects of Baduanjin Qigong in the Prevention of Bone Loss for Middle-Aged Women," *The American Journal of Chinese Medicine* 34, no. 5 (2006): 741-7, https://doi.org/10.1142/S0192415X06004259.

21. Roger Jahnke et al., "A Comprehensive Review of Health Benefits of Qigong and Tai Chi," *American Journal of Health Promotion* 24, no. 6 (July-August 2010): e1-e25, https://doi.org/10.4278/ajhp.081013-LIT-248.

22. Hidetaka Hamasaki, "Exercise and Gut Microbiota: Clinical Implications for the Feasibility of Tai Chi," *Journal of Integrative Medicine* 15, no. 4 (July 2017): 270–281. https://doi.org/10.1016/S2095-4964(17)60342-X.

23. Juan M. Manzaneque et al., "Assessment of Immunological Parameters Following a Qigong Training Program," *Medical Science Monitor: International Medical Journal of Experimental and Clinical Research* 10, no. 6 (June 2004): 264–70, https://pubmed.ncbi.nlm.nih.gov/15173671/.

24. Penelope Klein, "Qigong in Cancer Care: Theory, Evidence-Base, and Practice," *Medicines* (Basel, Switzerland) 4, no. 2. (January 2017), https://doi.org/10.3390/medicines4010002.

25. Chenchen Wang et al., "Comparative Effectiveness of Tai Chi Versus Physical Therapy for Knee Osteoarthritis: A Randomized Trial," *Annals of Internal Medicine* 165, no. 2 (May 2016): 77–86. https://doi.org/10.7326/M15-2143.

26. Marlene Fransen et al., "Physical Activity for Osteoarthritis Management: A Randomized Controlled Clinical Trial Evaluating Hydrotherapy or Tai Chi Classes," *Arthritis and Rheumatism* 57, no. 3 (March 2007): 407–14, https://doi.org/10.1002/art.22621.

27. Jeong-Hun Shin et al., "The Beneficial Effects of Tai Chi Exercise on Endothelial Function and Arterial Stiffness in Elderly Women with Rheumatoid Arthritis," *Arthritis Research & Therapy* 17, no. 380. (December 2015), https://www.ncbi.nlm.nih.gov/pmc/articles/PMC4718020/.

28. Ray Marks, "Qigong Exercise and Arthritis," *Medicines* (Basel, Switzerland) 4, no. 71 (September 2017), https://doi.org/10.3390/medicines4040071.

29. Suphannika Ladawan et al., "Effect of Qigong Exercise on Cognitive Function, Blood Pressure and Cardiorespiratory Fitness in Healthy Middle-Aged Subjects," *Complementary Therapies in Medicine* 33 (June 2017): 39–45, https://doi.org/10.1016/j.ctim.2017.05.005.

30. Theresa H. M. Kim et al., "The Mental-Attention Tai Chi Effect with Older Adults," *BMC Psychology* 4, no. 29 (May. 2016), https://doi.org/10.1186/s40359-016-0137-0.

31. Peter M. Wayne et al. "Effect of Tai Chi on Cognitive Performance in Older Adults: Systematic Review and Meta-Analysis," *Journal of the American Geriatrics Society* 62, no. 1 (2014): 25–39, https://doi.org/10.1111/jgs.12611.

32. Tuncer Tascioglu and Omer Sahin, "The Relationship Between Pain and Herniation Radiology in Giant Lumbar Disc Herniation Causing Severe Sciatica: 15 Cases," *British Journal of Neurosurgery* 1-4 (December 2020), https://doi.org/10.1080/02688697.2020.1866168.

33. "Phantom Pain," Wikipedia, update February 24, 2021, https://en.wikipedia.org/wiki/Phantom_pain.

34. Joseph Walker, "Fake Knee Surgery as Good as Real Procedure, Study Finds," *The Wall Street Journal*, December 25, 2013, https://www.wsj.com/articles/SB10001424052702304244904579278442014913458.

35. Tracie White, "Does That Hurt? Objective Way to Measure Pain Being Developed at Stanford," *Stanford Medicine*, September 13, 2011, https://med.stanford.edu/news/all-news/2011/09/does-that-hurt-objective-way-to-measure-pain-being-developed-at-stanford.html.

36. Per-Henrik Zahl, Jan Maehlen, and H. Gilbert Welch, "The Natural History of Invasive Breast Cancers Detected by Screening Mammography," *Archives of Internal Medicine* 168, no. 21 (2008): 2311-6, https://doi.org/10.1001/archinte.168.21.2311.

37. Marilyn Schlitz, "Spontaneous Remission: An Annotated Bibliography," Institute of Noetic Sciences, January 1, 1993, https://noetic.org/publication/spontaneous-remission -annotated-bibliography/.

38. Caryle Hirshberg, "Introduction—Spontaneous Remission: The Spectrum of Self-Repair," *Spontaneous Remission: An Annotated Bibliography* (Sausilito, CA: Institute of Noetic Sciences, 1993), 4, http://noetic.org/wp-content/uploads/2020/10/SRB-intro.pdf.

39. Nick Tate, "Loneliness Rivals Obesity, Smoking as Health Risk," WebMD, May 4, 2018, https://www.webmd.com/balance/news/20180504/loneliness-rivals-obesity-smoking -as-health-risk.

40. Michael Pollan, *In Defense of Food* (New York: Penguin Books, 2008), Kindle.

CHAPTER 6
It's All about the Qi

Roughly ten years into my teaching career, I started to feel like there was something missing from my method. I wanted something to help students understand the various skills that past qigong masters possessed. So I dove into both classical and modern qigong texts, experimented with different teaching tips, and also meditated on the subject.

During this time, I stumbled on a famous Zen quotation, one that had inspired me in the past and continues to inspire me today. I've already referenced this quotation, but it bears repeating:

"Do not seek to follow in the footsteps of the wise; seek what they sought."

—Zen Master Matsuo Basho

In seeking what the past masters sought, I built upon their knowledge, and then added a modern understanding and experience of qigong. The result is something that I now call the Twelve Skills of Qigong.

Of course, past qigong masters get all the credit for discovering and developing these twelve skills. My work has been to organize, arrange, and teach them in a modern context. I didn't invent any of this. Special credit goes to Dr. Roger Jahnke, a qigong master, acupuncturist, and mentor. My conversations with him, as well as the contents of his book *The Healing Promise of Qi*, formed the original basis for these Twelve Skills. Without his help, it would have taken me much longer to codify the Twelve Skills.

These skills are not mysterious. With proper training and diligent practice, anyone can learn and enjoy all Twelve Skills. As you read about them, remember that they are not linear. These aren't levels like in a video game. A lifelong practice of qigong will involve many laps through the Twelve Skills, going deeper and deeper with each successive lap. Realistically, most people will jump around a bit too, especially since it's hard to learn all Twelve Skills.

Also, remember that the Twelve Skills are universal, meaning that they will apply to all schools of qigong. Different schools may use different techniques and different terminology, but the skills are the same. Humans can only do so many things with qi and I've arranged all of them into the Twelve Skills.

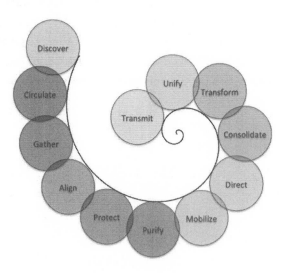

The Twelve Skills of Qigong

Skill #1: Discovering the Qi

To go deeply into qigong, you need to become more sensitive to the qi in general. In other words, you must discover the qi that already exists in and around your body. Discovering the qi is a gradual process of quieting the mind, relaxing the body, and heightening the internal awareness. In Flowing Zen Qigong, we use an ancient technique called Entering Zen (ru jing, 入靜) to change the state of our nervous system, shift our brainwaves to the Theta state, and heighten our awareness. It is from this state that we are better able to sense the qi in and around our bodies.

The opposite of this state of mind is what the ancients called the Monkey Mind. You're already familiar with this state because you've lived in it for years. The Monkey Mind is the constant stream of thoughts in your head, the radio station that you can't seem to turn off. A central theme of my teaching is the importance of shifting from the Monkey Mind to the Zen Mind at the very beginning of each practice session. In other words, use Skill #1 at the beginning of each session except for the Two-Minute Drill.

Skill #2: Circulating the Qi

The smooth flow of qi is critical for health and happiness. Once you learn the skill of circulating the qi, you'll want to continue practicing it for the rest of your life. Circulating the qi is what brings fast results, especially in terms of pain management, improved digestion, emotional healing, and immune response. It's also what makes you feel energized. In Flowing Zen Qigong, the main circulation technique is a beautiful and rare exercise called Flowing Breeze Swaying Willow (Phase 3 of the Five-Phase Practice Routine). You'll learn more about this amazing technique soon, and also in the book bonuses. As with Skill #1, we use Skill #2 in every practice session except for the Two-Minute Drill.

Skill #3: Aligning the Qi

If your physical structure is not aligned, if your muscles, tendons, fascia, and ligaments aren't working optimally, if your spine is unhealthy—then your qi will not flow properly. The solution is to gradually build strength, flexibility, and balance while simultaneously softening the tissues in your body. This will gradually realign your structure and also your qi. Luckily, qigong helps people to accomplish this regardless of their fitness level or age. With Flowing Zen Qigong, we use a variety of techniques to align the qi. Different people will need different techniques for their current body structure. If you've ever done a qigong technique and noticed that, even on a purely physical level, it felt great—then it's probably because you were aligning your qi.

Skill #4: Gathering the Qi

The more qi you have, the more of the main ingredient you have to work with! Having more qi also unlocks greater possibilities with the other twelve skills, especially the skills of consolidating, transforming, and transmitting the qi. More qi also means higher energy levels and greater vitality.

There are several ways to gather more qi, but the main method in Flowing Zen Qigong is called zhan zhuang (pronounced "john joo-ahng"). This is a mouthful, so I often call them the warrior stances instead. This type of qigong involves statically holding a posture for minutes at a time, but without becoming rigid. It's a tricky skill to master, but once you get the hang of it, then gathering more qi becomes straightforward, like placing solar panels in the sun.

Skill #5: Protecting the Qi

No matter how good you are at the other skills, no matter how much you practice, you'll plateau in your development if you don't protect your qi. The food you eat (or don't eat), your lifestyle habits, your environment, your finances—all of these can drain your qi. You want to protect yourself from these external influences.

This skill is less about qigong exercises proper and more about lifestyle changes. For example, you may need to improve the quality of your sleep, make common-sense dietary changes, or strategically remove negative habits like smoking. Change is hard, and that's why I recommend adding a daily qigong habit first. Once you do this, qigong can act as a gateway to other healthy habits. In other words, don't start with this skill, but rather add it gradually as you progress with your qigong habit.

Skill #6: Purifying the Qi

To reach higher levels of qigong mastery, you must purify your thoughts and emotions. Whereas Skill #5 is focused on external influences, Skill #6 is focused on internal influences. In other words, Protecting the Qi deals with stuff outside of us whereas Purifying the Qi deals with stuff inside of us.

With Flowing Zen Qigong, we have a variety of techniques to accomplish this, including One Percent Forgiveness, Loving Kindness Meditation, the Gratitude Spark, the Five Animal Play, Maranasati Meditation, and Dispelling 1000 Thoughts. These techniques will help you to balance your emotions and regulate the Monkey Mind, thereby enabling you to go into a deeper state of Zen. They'll also help you to be a better human being.

Skill #7: Mobilizing the Qi

In the past, internal martial arts masters could instantly summon their qi and direct it into a punch, a kick, or a throw. This is known as fajin (發勁), or exploding power. It sounds like stuff of kung fu movies, but there's nothing mysterious about it. This skill is all about using your strength, fascia, and body mechanics as efficiently as possible.

Even if you have no interest in martial arts, this skill will help you to get in touch with the spirit of the peaceful warrior, which will make you more courageous, more decisive, and help you to draw better personal boundaries. This is also one of the best ways I've found to regulate hormones. In Flowing Zen Qigong, we typically Mobilize the Qi using techniques from a set called the Eighteen Arhat Arts, or from an art called One Finger Zen.

Skill #8: Directing the Qi

You can't call yourself a master of qigong unless you can easily direct your qi to any part of your body, including any organ. Although this may sound fantastic to beginners and skeptics, most students can begin to do this after a year of dedicated practice.

With Flowing Zen Qigong, we use a variety of techniques to direct the qi to different areas. For example, we use Nourishing Kidneys to direct qi to the Kidney Meridian (duh), Pushing Mountains to direct qi to the hands, and Separating Water to direct qi to the Lung Meridian. But the real skill is not in the technique that you choose. In fact, if you are skillful, then you can direct the qi without any physical movement at all.

Skill #9: Consolidating the Qi

Gathering the qi isn't enough; we also need to consolidate it in the lower dantian. This skill goes hand-in-hand with Gathering the Qi, but it is more focused on consolidating the qi rather than just gathering it. If you've been practicing qigong or tai chi for years but still can't feel the golden sphere of energy at dantian, then you need to spend more time consolidating.

In Flowing Zen Qigong, we do this in Phase 4 of the Five-Phase Routine. We also use other techniques, including Three Centers Merge and Dantian Breathing. Over time, you'll start to feel that golden sphere in your lower dantian, which in turn will give you a larger overall capacity of qi.

Skill #10: Transforming the Qi

The Small Universe (Xiao Zhou Tian, 小周天), sometimes called the or Microcosmic Orbit, is a famous qigong technique that directs a strong current of qi in a loop along the Ren and Du meridians. This loop runs from your lower lip down the centerline of your chest, down to your perineum, up the centerline of your back, over the top of your head, down your face, then back to the starting point. By circulating the energy in this way, we transform qi (energy) into jing (essence) and shen (spirit).

The Small Universe can be done standing or seated, and it involves very little physical movement. To an observer, it would look like you were doing standing or sitting meditation. That observer would probably get bored watching you.

Your experience, however, will be anything but boring. In many ways, all other forms of qigong are child's play compared to the Small Universe. This is an advanced technique that comes with some risks, which I've blogged about. But if you have good instruction and have spent time with the previous nine skills, then the risks are small. It's certainly safer than crossing the street or getting in your car.

By the time you learn the Small Universe you'll already be in love with qigong. But once you finally learn it, you'll feel like you're just getting started with this art! It's a game changer!

Skill #11: Unifying the Qi

Qigong is nonreligious, but the art can take us into a blissful state of union with something much larger than ourselves. It doesn't matter if you call that the Tao, the infinite, Source, Shiva, God, or simply Nature. It also doesn't matter if you are an atheist.

When you practice a qigong technique called Dantian Breathing at an advanced level, you begin to breathe not just with your belly, not just with your dantian, not just with your body—but with the entire cosmos. Think of this as a deep, quiescent state of cosmic awe.

For those who have struggled with sitting meditation, qigong can be a wonderful substitution. For example, Dantian Breathing can be done sitting, or in several standing postures. There are also other techniques, like the Small Universe and also the Big Universe, that can lead us to this blissful state of unification.

Skill #12: Transmitting the Qi

With the twelfth skill, we complete the cycle by giving energy back to others. Qi can be transmitted from the hands, and also from the heart. This is not as mystical as it sounds. For example, when I teach a class, I'm transmitting qi from my heart.

I also do hands-on healing where I transmit energy to a student, similar to Reiki. Typically, this involves opening some of the major energy points, thereby helping the student to go deeper with their own practice. But the same skill can be used by any healer.

With Flowing Zen Qigong, the main techniques for transmitting qi to another person (or pet) are Cosmos Palm and One Finger Zen.

Skill vs. Technique

As you learn about the Twelve Skills, please make sure that you understand the difference between skill and technique. Here's the simplest way to understand the difference: Techniques are more visible; skills are more invisible.

When we're talking about the Twelve Skills, we're talking about invisible skills. For example, if I direct the qi to my index finger, you probably won't notice unless you can somehow sense qi. (Some people can do this naturally.)

On the other hand, if I practice a qigong technique called Shooting Arrows, the physical form is pretty obvious. My body is moving in a particular way that is easy to see. Shooting Arrows happens to be a great *technique* for applying the *skill* of directing the qi to the index finger, but the skill and the technique are separate. Once you become skillful, you can even direct qi to the index finger without using Shooting Arrows.

Let's look at three simple examples to drive this point home:

- **Example #1:** Mary is performing the qigong technique called Shooting Arrows, but she is unable to direct the qi to her index finger even though the physical form of the exercise is perfect.

- **Example #2:** Tom is performing the qigong technique called Shooting Arrows, and he is also able to direct the qi to his index finger.

- **Example #3:** Jane is standing upright and motionless with her eyes closed. She is not performing the technique Shooting Arrows, but she is nonetheless able to direct the qi to her index finger.

Can you see how the technique and the skill are different? Can you see how one can happen without the other?

Another thing to remember is that skill is a journey, not a destination. Rather than thinking about the Twelve Skills of qigong as a straight line, think of them as a spiral. Imagine that, by the time you've learned the twelfth skill, you've also arrived back at the beginning, albeit at a deeper level.

Our galaxy is a spiral. The "Golden Number" of mathematics maps out to a spiral. Our genes form in the shape of a helix, which is a spiral structure. In many ways, the natural order of the universe is a spiral, not a line. Qigong also follows the natural order of the universe.

I've been through all twelve skills, and I can perform each skill. Does that mean I'm done? Am I an Enlightened Mega Grandmaster? Um, no.

I like to compare myself to a fifth-degree Black Belt. In Karate, there are ten degrees of black belt, with the tenth degree reserved for the patriarch of the particular style, usually an elderly Japanese man. This is just an analogy to remind you that mastery has many levels.

It's a lesson that I never forgot from my karate days—that black belt is only the beginning. If we continue using the karate belt analogy, then you need to understand this: You'll be mastering the Twelve Skills not only from white belt to black belt, but also through all ten ranks of black belt.

I've been practicing the twelve skills for over two decades and plan to continue practicing them for several more decades. For example, I still practice discovering the qi (Skill #1) every single day. It's not a beginner skill that I learned years ago and then left behind. If anything, I am discovering the qi in new and beautiful ways.

I also don't always proceed in order through the skills. One day, I might focus on gathering the qi. Another day, I might focus on consolidating. Or I might spend a month deepening my skill of transforming. This is what the journey of mastery really looks like.

I've arranged the Twelve Skills in a pretty chart. But your journey won't look like that. Mine certainly didn't. For example, many of you reading this have probably learned some of the Twelve Skills, but not all of them. That's okay. You've got the rest of your life to learn and develop the other skills.

What Qi Really Feels Like

Feeling qi helps us to gauge our progress. It tells us that we are practicing correctly, that we are successfully entering into a meditative state, relaxing the body, and cultivating the energy. It also signals that, with continued practice, we will see more and more health benefits.

But more importantly, feeling qi is essential when it comes to cultivating the Twelve Skills. How can you direct qi if you can't even feel it? How can you consolidate qi at dantian if you can't feel dantian?

Over the years, I've received tons of emails from sincere students who still can't feel much in the way of qi. Many of them have been practicing qigong for years. A few were even instructors with more than ten years of experience!

When I started teaching qigong in 2005, I printed up brochures to hand out to prospective students. I knew nothing about marketing, but a friend told me that I needed a slogan. After thinking about it, I chose the following for my brochures: "No Qi, No Fee!"

I meant this slogan to be amusing, but I also wanted to put my money where my mouth was. I literally promised prospective students that I would give them their money back if they didn't feel qi by the end of my twelve-week intro course. No one ever asked for a refund—not a single student.

It should not take years to feel qi, let alone decades. The truth is that anyone can feel qi if they follow the right method. I'm not saying that my method is the only way to feel qi—but I am saying that if you can't feel qi after two years of practice, then you need a new method.

Qi can feel like many things. I'm hesitant to put it into words because if you try to chase after specific sensations, you might miss it. The truth is that sensations of qi vary from person to person, especially for beginners. Here are some common sensations that students describe:

- Tingling in the hands
- A flow of warmth in the chest
- A refreshing coolness through the limbs
- Insects crawling on the skin (but in a good way somehow)
- A buzzing in the limbs
- Hair standing up on the skin
- A feeling of inspiration flowing into the body
- A sense of magnetism in the hands
- Electricity vibrating through the limbs
- A subtle momentum moving through the body like a gentle breeze

All of these descriptions are good, but remember that they are just pointers. Your own experience might be a little different. Or your experience may be similar but you might choose different words. After all, words always fall short of the actual experience.

On top of these sensations, there are also other ways to feel qi. For example, imagine that you sprain your ankle. It swells up, and it's painful.

Then imagine that you practice some qigong techniques in a chair since you can't stand comfortably. You do this several times over a twenty-four-hour period. After that, you notice that the pain has dissipated, and the swelling has gone down.

I've got news for you: that's qi too! Feeling a reduction in pain and swelling is absolutely a qi sensation. The same is true of an elevated mood after practicing qigong, or an increase in energy levels. Tangible benefits like these are clear signs that your qi is moving. So while you may not be able to feel the qi directly, you can sense it indirectly.

As you practice qigong and cultivate the Twelve Skills, you'll get better and better at feeling qi directly. But how do we feel qi anyway? Which of the five senses is involved?

If you think that you've only got five senses, then I'm sorry to say that modern researchers don't agree with you. The theory of the five senses actually dates back to Aristotle (b. 384 BCE), so it's a wee bit outdated. Unfortunately, the researchers have not yet reached a consensus. The only thing that researchers agree on is that there are definitely more than five senses.

It turns out humans might have as many as twenty senses or as few as eight. Some of this depends on classification, and some of it depends on further research.

Don't believe me? Try the following experiment:

1. Sit or stand comfortably.
2. Close your eyes.
3. While keeping your eyes closed, touch your nose with the pinky of your left hand.

Easy, right? But which of the traditional five senses did you use to touch your nose?

Sight? Your eyes were closed! Hearing? You can't hear your pinky! Smell? Maybe your dog could find your stinky pinky like that but not you. Taste? You didn't even touch your tongue. Touch! That must be it! But wait, you didn't actually touch anything until the very end. So how did you find your nose?

The answer is that you used your sense of proprioception. Congratulations. You now have at least six senses!

I was able to sense my qi long before I could explain how I was doing it. I knew I could sense it, but didn't know how. Maybe it's because I was raised as a classical violinist and have a finely tuned auditory faculty, but for years I swore that I could actually "hear" my qi. Other people told me they could see it, but that wasn't my experience. Others said they felt a tingling sensation in the hands and body, and I felt that too. But I also heard something, a vibration, or a sound. And yet, it wasn't in my ears.

I had a similar experience in acupuncture college while learning what is known as Chinese Pulse Diagnosis. I learned to sense dozens of different pulse qualities with the tips of my fingers. If you get good at it, then you can be amazingly accurate at diagnosing patients.

Once you get the hang of Chinese Pulse Diagnosis, you realize that you're not just using your fingers. There are other senses involved too, no question. For me, it always felt like I was "listening" to the pulses. But how can you listen with your fingers?

If we stick with the outdated paradigm of the five senses, then we're stuck with only five words: see, hear, smell, taste, and touch. The words people typically use to describe qi are almost always connected to the five traditional senses. Some students describe feeling a tingling or a buzzing in the hands. Some describe seeing energy moving through the body. Others, like me, talk about hearing the energy.

I believe that people describe sensations of qi using words that relate to their dominant sense organs—usually sight, hearing, or touch. In the end, however, these are just words. And words suck because they encourage the Monkey Mind. In the Zen tradition, this is akin to the expression of the "finger pointing at the moon". Words are the finger, and they point to the moon, but they are not the moon. Therefore, don't concentrate on the finger or you will miss all the heavenly glory. (Yes, I just quoted Bruce Lee from *Enter the Dragon*.)

My advice to students who want to sense the qi is simple: Learn to quiet your mind to the point where words are no longer necessary. In the Zen Mind, we don't need words like "sight" and "hearing." From that deep meditative state, we can just sense the energy directly—without any need for a description.

As I mentioned earlier, if you've been trying for years to sense the qi and you're still unsure, then you may need a new method. Many students have been blown away by their ability to sense the qi with Flowing Zen Qigong. My method certainly isn't the only one that will help you to feel qi, but it's a good option.

Other teachers may have different methods for helping students to feel the qi. If the method works, then great. But if it takes a few decades just to feel the qi, then I suggest that you try my method for a year instead. You can go back to the other methods later, but with a greater sensitivity to qi.

Qi is the main ingredient in qigong, so sensing it is an important part of mastering the art. When you work on strength, it's easy to see that you're getting stronger because you can lift heavier weights and your muscles start to grow. But with qigong, it's not so apparent.

Mastery in qigong is invisible. Don't listen to anyone who tells you that mastery involves picture-perfect form. That's nonsense. Any ballerina could display picture-perfect qigong form with three months of practice because of her superb body control, but this doesn't mean she's a master of qigong.

Similarly, someone who can sit in a perfect full-lotus meditation posture is not necessarily a meditation master. And vice versa, an elderly master might not be able to sit in a perfect full lotus posture. Internal arts like qigong and sitting meditation have invisible skills, so we need to look elsewhere to measure progress.

Flowing Breeze Swaying Willow

I've mentioned a qigong technique called Flowing Breeze Swaying Willow (搖風擺柳, yao feng bai liu) several times in this book. Of the hundreds of qigong techniques that I've learned, this is arguably the most useful when it comes to getting healthier. Unfortunately, this technique and the relevant skills have been kept secret for centuries, so it is not well known in the qigong community. That's a shame because it's one of the most amazing life skills that you can learn, and it's one of the main reasons that my students get such awesome results.

Flowing Breeze Swaying Willow, often abbreviated as FBSW, is the single best technique I've ever found for circulating the qi (see Skill #2 on page 157). In Chinese Medicine, the main goal is to restore the smooth flow of qi through the meridians. This is true whether we're talking about acupuncture, herbal medicine, Chinese massage, or qigong. When the qi flows smoothly, then you will be healthier and happier.

And vice versa, if your qi is not flowing smoothly in one or more meridians, then you will experience pain and illness. Wherever there is pain in the body, and whenever there is an illness, there is a blockage in the flow of qi.

We call this a "disharmony of yin and yang." When you boil it down, all illness and pain are ultimately due to a disharmony of yin and yang. This disharmony can manifest in countless ways, like depression, cancer, hypertension, back pain, or a zillion other disorders. But one way or another, there is disharmony.

If you go see an acupuncturist, the first thing they will do is diagnose you using the traditional methods—pulse diagnosis, tongue diagnosis, and asking diagnosis. The goal is to figure out where the qi is blocked so that the physician can work on clearing this blockage with needles and/or herbs.

With qigong, we don't need a diagnosis. In fact, if you try to self-diagnose, you're likely to get yourself into trouble. Here's why. Imagine that you've got a torn ligament in your knee. It would seem logical to direct the qi to your knee. And it is logical; but it's not Chinese Medicine.

According to Chinese medical theory, the Liver Meridian nourishes the ligaments. Therefore, it's likely that your knee problem isn't just in your knee; it's also in your Liver Meridian. This explains why acupuncturists don't just insert needles in the problem area. For example, to fix your knee problem, a skillful acupuncturist may nourish your Liver Meridian by putting needles in your foot.

I have taught at a few different acupuncture colleges over the years. I love acupuncture students, but they are a pain in the ass to teach! While learning acupuncture, students are excited about the diagnostic side of Chinese Medicine, and rightly so. It's cool stuff. But when these students start to learn qigong, they want to diagnose themselves. Or worse—they have already been given a Chinese diagnosis. And so they try to *do* things with their energy.

And this is a mistake. Your body has a deep, innate wisdom; we unlock this wisdom with Flowing Breeze Swaying Willow. If you try to direct your energy somewhere, like your Liver Meridian or your painful knee, then you will undercut the natural healing wisdom of your own body.

The beauty of FBSW is that it *allows* the energy to flow wherever it needs to go. Our main task while practicing FBSW is to let go of mental, emotional, and physical tension, thereby allowing the energy to circulate freely.

If the body is so good at healing, then why are so many people suffering? It's a fair question. I asked the same one decades ago. Back then, my teacher only offered traditional explanations, which weren't satisfying. Today, I have a better answer for my students.

I'm a Star Trek geek, but you don't need to be a big fan to understand this analogy. Imagine that the starship *Enterprise* is being attacked by the Klingons. What's the first thing that Captain Kirk says?

"Shields up!"

Then Scotty, the ship's engineer, diverts energy from non-critical systems to boost the shields, hence his most famous line, "I'm givin' her all she's got, Captain!" To survive the attack, Scotty diverts power from the science lab to the shields. And this makes sense, right? The shields matter more than the science lab during an attack.

Your body does the exact same thing. In fact, it's designed to do this. When confronted with a threat—a saber-toothed tiger, for example—your body quickly shifts gears into the Sympathetic Nervous System (SNS). This is the "fight or flight" response that we've all heard of.

Just like Scotty, your body will divert energy away from non-critical systems, like digestion, cellular repair, and organ function.

It diverts all that energy to the muscles and the cardiovascular system so that you can either run from the tiger or fight it. (Note: unless you have some friends with long spears, I highly recommend running.)

On the *Enterprise*, once the attack is over, the captain will turn the shields off, and power will be restored to the science lab. The human body is designed to do the same thing. After escaping the tiger, you are *supposed* to shift gears back to the Parasympathetic Nervous System (PNS), which puts us back into "rest and restore" mode. Unfortunately, this doesn't happen for most modern humans.

The Yin and Yang of Your Nervous System

The two branches of the nervous system, the Parasympathetic Nervous System (PNS) and Sympathetic Nervous System (SNS), form what the qigong masters would have called a yin-yang harmony. Imagine the PNS as the dark side of the yin-yang symbol and the SNS as the light side. Together, they form the Autonomic Nervous System, which we could compare to the entire yin-yang symbol.

(Side note: An easy way to remember the two terms is as follows. Parasympathetic = peaceful; Sympathetic = stressful.)

The SNS (stressful) is like the body's accelerator, and the PNS (peaceful) is like its brake. The two branches move together in a rhythm, just like your breath. In fact, every inhalation you take stimulates your Sympathetic Nervous System and every exhalation stimulates the Parasympathetic.

Whenever you inhale deeply, you mildly activate the SNS, your heart beats a little faster, and your nervous system ramps up a little. Whenever you exhale deeply, you mildly activate the PNS. Your heart slows down a little and your nervous system relaxes. If you've ever been to a yoga class, this is why your teacher probably encouraged you to lengthen the exhalation—to stimulate the PNS.

The SNS diverts blood and energy to the muscles for immediate action (fighting or flighting), just like Scotty diverting energy to the shields. It does this by stimulating the adrenal glands, which in turn speeds up the heart rate and increases blood pressure. The PNS promotes self-healing and self-preservation functions, like digestion, wound healing, and cellular repair. It does this by releasing a neurotransmitter called acetylcholine, which basically acts as a brake to the SNS. The PNS lowers the heart rate, relaxes the muscles, and lowers the blood pressure.

Today, you can measure the relative health of your nervous system with something called a Heart Rate Variability (HRV) monitor. Many devices are now available to measure HRV, something that was hard to do even just a few years ago. Keep in mind that different devices will return totally different HRV scores. You might register a baseline of 21 on an Apple Watch, 123 on a chest monitor, 52 on an Oura Ring, or 85 on a WHOOP Strap. If you're going to use HRV as a metric, the key is to use the same device for at least two weeks and establish a clear baseline.

HRV monitors give us a useful snapshot of the overall health of our nervous system. With HRV, a higher score is better, which is confusing because it's the exact opposite of resting heart rate. But it makes sense if you think about it. A healthy Heart Rate Variability score means that there is *more* variability between your PNS and SNS. In other words, your nervous system can easily flow between fight-or-flight mode and rest-and-restore mode.

Unfortunately, modern humans are pretty terrible at shifting back to the PNS. This is a quirk of modern living, and it explains why we have trouble healing. For humans living twenty thousand years ago, it was clear when there was a life-or-death threat. Those threats looked like tigers and rhinos. Simple! But for us in the twenty-first century, it's not so clear. Have you ever felt your stomach drop when receiving a bill in the mail? It's just a piece of paper, and yet your body shifted into SNS. To your nervous system, that piece of paper was the same as a tiger.

Is a bill a life-or-death threat? Foreclosing on your mortgage is serious business, but it probably won't kill you. And yet it *feels* like you'll die. The bill in the mail, the reprimand from our boss, the argument with our spouse—these are all tigers as far as your nervous system is concerned. In other words, modern humans, despite our tiger-free lifestyles, feel as if we are being chased by far more tigers than our ancestors.

The reason you aren't healing is because your nervous system lacks yin-yang harmony. It does not flow back and forth between SNS and PNS the way it should. Because you're stuck in a constant state of fight or flight, much of your body's energy is diverted away from your healing systems. Imagine if Scotty never diverted energy *back* from the shields because the Klingons kept attacking 24/7.

In other words, you aren't healing because your natural healing system is constantly turned off. Your healing juices just aren't flowing. The good news is that, with practice, you can train your nervous system to shift out of fight-or-flight mode and back into rest-and-restore mode. When you do that, the body's healing juices start to flow again.

This is why it's critical to let the energy flow freely with FBSW. When we get the energy circulating again, the body will naturally start to heal itself, repair cells, heal wounds, and lower inflammation. In fact, with the help of qigong, it will heal better than ever before.

Healing with Flowing Breeze Swaying Willow

When it comes to regulating the nervous system and self-healing, nothing beats Flowing Breeze Swaying Willow (FBSW). Although this technique is mentioned in several qigong classics, its form was never described, leading some people to dismiss it. But there's a good reason why the form was never mentioned: Flowing Breeze Swaying Willow is formless.

Actually, there is a physical form to FBSW, but it changes from person to person. This technique falls into the category called Spontaneous Qigong. In short, the flowing form arises spontaneously as the energy flows.

If you were to watch someone practicing FBSW, it might look like a drunk person wobbling on their spot. In fact, I was once stopped by two cops while practicing FBSW in Isham Park in New York City. "Everything okay there, buddy?" one of them asked. He probably thought I was drunk. I stopped my flow, quickly brought my energy to dantian, and explained to them that I was practicing a stress reduction exercise (hey, it's true!). They just smiled and moved on.

You won't necessarily be practicing in public like I did, and in the beginning your FBSW might not even be visible to another person. For most people, it starts out very subtle. If someone were to watch you closely, they might notice a slight swaying motion. Otherwise, they would probably just be bored.

Why does the body sway during FBSW? Past masters would say that the qi is flowing freely through the meridians. Today, we might explain it further by talking about nervous system regulation. As we shift from SNS back into PNS, the nervous system relaxes. As we've already discussed, fascia is intimately tied to the nervous system. I believe that FBSW releases the fascia throughout the body thereby allowing the entire nervous system to switch into healing mode.

The fascia in and around the psoas muscle is of particular importance. Remember that the psoas is sometimes called the "muscle of the soul," and it connects the upper body to the lower body. Relaxing the psoas creates movement between the upper and lower body, which in turn translates to gentle swaying.

As a result of this fascial release and nervous system regulation, all your body's fluids will flow better. In other words, FBSW gets your blood, lymph, synovial fluid, cerebrospinal fluid, interstitial fluid, pericardial fluid, and even your saliva flowing better. When all these healing juices are flowing, it means that your qi is flowing. And when your qi is flowing, it means that you are healing! Even if you only spend five minutes per day practicing Flowing Breeze Swaying Willow, it can transform your life.

Instead of talking about what Flowing Breeze Swaying Willow looks like, let me try to describe what it feels like. The first time you experience this, you're likely to be amazed. After doing specific qigong techniques in a specific order, you feel totally and completely relaxed. Everything is loose—your jaw, your face, your shoulders, and your knees, but you also feel emotionally relaxed. There's a deep sense of tranquility and ease. You feel carefree, perhaps for the first time in years.

Then, as you move into Flowing Breeze Swaying Willow, you start to feel a gentle momentum building in your body. What you'll feel is your body swaying gently as you stand on your spot, almost as if you are losing your balance. But you're not losing your balance. Your qi is starting to flow!

Remember that the human body is filled with many fluids—lymph fluid, synovial fluid, cerebrospinal fluid, saliva, plasma, and of course, blood. You also have intracellular fluid flowing inside every cell of your body—all thirty trillion of them! When you practice Flowing Breeze Swaying Willow, the qi starts to flow smoother, and as a result, all your fluids also start to flow smoother too. The result is that you feel the body starting to sway very gently—almost like a willow tree in the breeze!

More importantly, when the energy and the fluids start to flow, the body starts to heal itself! Every time you practice Flowing Breeze Swaying Willow, you restore and enhance your natural healing capacity. The most obvious sign of this is that you'll feel fantastic after completing a session with FBSW.

The Five-Phase Routine

Unfortunately, Flowing Breeze Swaying Willow is such a subtle, internal skill, that it's not easy to learn, let alone practice. The truth is that you need to implement a half-dozen qigong secrets just to initiate the internal qi flow. Obviously, you need to know these secrets, but that's only half the battle. Knowing the secrets is one thing; remembering them is another!

That's why I developed something called the Five-Phase Routine (5PR). The entire routine only takes ten to fifteen minutes, and it is an easy way to implement the most important qigong secrets into your daily practice. The Five-Phase Routine is at the heart of everything we do in Flowing Zen Qigong. I formulated this routine early in my teaching to bring together the most important secrets of qigong into every single practice session. I still practice and teach this routine today because it is so effective.

For many students, the Five-Phase Routine is revolutionary, even if they have decades of prior experience. Here's an example:

> "I've been practicing qigong and tai chi for over twenty years, but your Five-Phase practice routine was a game changer for me. All I can say is *wow*! Within weeks, my back pain dissolved, and my mood improved considerably. I now incorporate your routine into my daily sessions, even when doing my tai chi forms."
>
> —Scott Baker, retired teacher

Although I learned something similar to the Five-Phase Routine when I was a disciple, it was not organized. When you understand each of the Five Phases, you'll be more likely to practice them correctly. And if you practice correctly, you'll get at least twice the benefits compared to people who don't use the Five-Phase Routine. That's a sweet deal!

This routine contains five distinct phases, which are as follows:

- Phase 1: Opening Sequence
- Phase 2: Energy Cultivation
- Phase 3: Energy Flow
- Phase 4: Energy Consolidation
- Phase 5: Closing Sequence

Let's look at each phase in more detail to understand why this routine is the pinnacle of modern qigong practice.

Phase 1: Opening Sequence

If you were to watch one thousand modern practitioners begin their qigong sessions, probably 998 of them would begin moving within ten seconds. Perhaps they would close their eyes for a few moments and settle into a rooted stance, but few of them would spend more than ten seconds on this phase. And that's just not enough time to relax the nervous system and enter a meditative state. Hell, some people just dive straight into moving techniques, skipping it altogether.

This is a huge mistake, and it will doom you to mediocre results. As already mentioned, it's critical to first enter a meditative state, a process that we call Entering Zen. That's what Phase 1 is all about.

First, we walk around briskly. This can mean walking around the house or the room if you're practicing inside during winter. Or it can mean taking the dog for a nice walk. Walking like this gets the blood flowing, calms the mind, and primes the body for deeper relaxation.

Next, we stand upright and begin a head-to-toe relaxation sequence. In short, we systematically relax the body from head to toe—with an emphasis on some key areas, like the jaw, the chest, and the knees. Then, for good measure, we use a vocalization along with a simple visualization: relaxing the body twice as much while simultaneously making a sighing sound. It's amazing how much physical tension you can release this way.

Then we use an ancient and powerful technique called Smiling from the Heart. This is easier to experience than to describe. If you haven't already done so, try the guided meditation in your book bonuses. For now, just know that it involves finding your inner smile and letting it blossom.

Smiling from the Heart takes the Head-to-Toe relaxation to a deeper level. It relaxes you on a mental-emotional level. I might even argue that it relaxes you on a spiritual level. Many students, when they first experience this technique, shed tears of joy. Later, they share that it felt like coming home.

All of this, from the moment we begin walking to the moment we Smile from the Heart, can take anywhere from one minute (if you are very skillful) to five minutes (if you are a fresh beginner). Phase 1 allows us to relax the nervous system, enter into a meditative state of mind, shift the brainwaves away from the everyday state, and open the energy systems of the body, especially the Heart Meridian, which is often called the emperor of all the meridians.

Phase 2: Energy Cultivation

Phase 2 is what most people imagine when they think of qigong. There are literally thousands of different qigong techniques out there—and all of them go here in Phase 2. Whether it's Lifting the Sky, Double Dragons, One Finger Zen, or even a complete tai chi form, it belongs in Phase 2.

This phase may vary from day to day, depending on which exercises you choose to practice. In Flowing Zen Qigong, students are encouraged to choose a handful of their favorite exercises. By choosing favorites you'll not only be more likely to practice, but you'll also enjoy the session more—something that is critical for getting results.

How many exercises should you do? For beginners, the sweet spot is three to six techniques. For intermediate students, it's three to twelve. For advanced practitioners, it's three to eighteen. If you are new to the Five-Phase Routine but not to qigong, then it's better to do fewer techniques so that you can focus on the internal skills.

Different techniques cultivate the energy in slightly different ways, but all qigong techniques are holistic, especially when used within the Five-Phase Routine. Even if an exercise emphasizes, say, the Lung Meridian, you cannot help but also cultivate qi in the other Eleven Primary Meridians. That's because the meridians are not separate; they all work together holistically.

Our purpose in Phase 2 is to enjoy ourselves, to loosen and strengthen the body, and to get our qi flowing more vigorously, and to cultivate the qi in various ways. Phase 2 also prepares us for the next phase, which is crucial for getting results.

Phase 3: Energy Flow

This is the phase that is most often missing in qigong, and that's unfortunate. In Phase 2, we got the qi flowing, but that's not enough. Once the qi is flowing, we need to let it flow!

When we let the qi flow, the result is a gentle swaying of the body called Flowing Breeze Swaying Willow. You might also yawn, sigh, or step off your spot. The imagery of the willow tree is beautiful, but it's just an analogy. We should in no way imitate an actual tree. Instead, we should allow our qi to flow. We do this by letting go of physical hidden tension in the body, by letting go of thoughts, and by letting go of worries. Let go, and then go with the flow (that's been organically primed and started)!

It's during this phase that the real healing work is done. Because your nervous system is relaxed and your qi is flowing, your body can do massive amounts of healing work in just five to ten minutes. Doing FBSW daily is like getting a powerful acupuncture treatment—but without the needles or the commute!

Phase 4: Energy Consolidation

After we let the energy flow for five to ten minutes, it's time to bring it back home. Imagine that your dogs have been running around outside for a while, but it's time to call them back inside. Of course, the dogs need to be trained to respond to your whistle, but that's also what Phase 4 is about.

By bringing the awareness gently to the lower dantian, you call the energy home. You can also place the palms on the dantian to increase your awareness of the area. Even if you don't feel much energy at dantian (it can take a while), you can still feel centered, solid, and stable.

When you do this, the gentle swaying of FBSW will gradually calm down. You may still sway a tiny bit, but it will be much more subtle than in Phase 3. That's because the qi is settling down. Think of a snow globe. You shake it up, and the snow falls everywhere. If you keep shaking it, the snow will keep falling. But if you put it down and let it sit for a few minutes, then the snow will settle back down.

Don't be rigid, and don't try to stand perfectly still. Instead, seek what we call Flowing Stillness, where we are still, but not rigid. Whether your hands are on dantian or hanging loosely by your sides, you are enjoying the Flowing Stillness.

Another analogy that may be helpful is that we are saving our work on the computer before closing the laptop. I realize that laptops now save things automatically, but it wasn't always like this. Trust me! I lost a few term papers that way in college! After saving your work in Phase 4, you can pick up where you left off in your next session.

Phase 5: The Closing Sequence

Phase 5 utilizes a series of self-massage techniques and gentle acupressure. As I mentioned earlier, many of these techniques come from the famous sixth-century physician Sun Simiao. At first, the techniques might seem overwhelming, but don't worry. With practice, the steps are easy to remember. You can watch an instructional video in your book bonuses, but here are the twenty steps of the closing sequence for your perusal:

The Closing Sequence:

1. Rubbing the Palms
2. Warming the Eyes
3. Patting the Eyes
4. Washing the Face
5. Combing the Hair
6. Acu-Point Massage: Inner Corner of Eye
   (Bladder 1, jing ming, 睛明)
7. Acu-Point Massage: Inner Edge of Eyebrows
   (Bladder 2, zhan zhu, 攢竹)
8. Acu-Point Massage: Stroking the Eyebrows
9. Acu-Point Massage: Middle of Eyebrow
   (Extra Meridian 3, Yuyao, 魚腰)
10. Acu-Point Massage: Outer Edge of Eyebrow
    (Sanjiao 23, si zhu kong, 絲竹空)
11. Acu-Point Massage: Outer Edge of Eye
    (Gallbladder 1, tong zi liao, 瞳子膠)
12. Acu-Point Massage: Below the Eye
    (Stomach 1, cheng qi, 承泣)
13. Stroking Under the Eyes
    (Stomach 1, cheng qi, 承泣)
14. Acu-Point Massage: Inner Corner of the Eye
    (Bladder 1, jing ming, 睛明)
15. Stroking the Nose
16. Acu-Point Massage: The Base of the Nose
    (Large Intestine 20, ying xiang, 迎香)
17. Acu-Point Massage: The Temples
    (Extra Meridian 5, tai yang, 太陽)

18. Acu-Point Massage: Behind the Ears
    (Sanjiao 17, yifeng, 翳風)
19. Rubbing the Ears
20. The Twenty-Four Heavenly Drums

There are five main benefits to the closing sequence:

1. It helps us to transition from a deep meditative state back to our everyday reality.
2. It brings much-needed qi to the acu-points around the eyes, helping to keep our eyes (and our eyesight) healthy.
3. It stimulates the acu-points along the scalp, particularly the baihui (GV20) point at the top of the head. This point is known to relieve stress and anxiety, reduce fatigue, and clear brain fog. It is also said to boost brainpower.
4. It stimulates the acu-points in the ear, which are actually a microcosm of the entire body. So by stimulating these points, we stimulate the entire meridian system.
5. It brings energy to the entire face, making us look younger. (I sometimes jokingly call this a Qigong Facelift.)

You can also do the Closing Sequence any time during the day. Afterward, you'll feel refreshed and your head will be clearer. I like to do it as a quick break when I've been staring at a computer for too long.

Why the Five-Phase Routine Is So Effective

Remember all those ancient Chinese secrets we talked about in chapter 3? I extracted the most important secrets from thousands of years of qigong development and stuffed them all into the Five-Phase Routine! You're welcome!

From the structure of the routine to the little details like relaxing the jaw, to Flowing Breeze Swaying Willow—the routine itself is a living encyclopedia of the most important qigong secrets. If you practice the Five-Phase Routine, you cannot help but implement these secrets because they are built right in.

Knowing a secret isn't enough though; you must practice it. This is true of both Eastern and Western philosophy. In Eastern philosophy, the emphasis was on experience and practice rather than book-learning. In fact, Bodhidharma, the man in the cave mentioned earlier, once encouraged his disciples to burn their books! He wasn't trying to impose censorship like the Nazis did during the Holocaust, but rather he was trying to remind students that books only pointed the way. But books themselves are not the way.

The ancient Greeks had a similar philosophy. They used the term "gnosis" (γνῶσις) to refer to experiential knowledge, as opposed to theoretical knowledge, which they called "epistemology." Socrates and the other great philosophers encouraged their students to practice philosophy in an active way that improves one's life, not just book learning or memorization.

Unfortunately, we don't have a good differentiation like this in English. Other languages do. For example, in German, the word *kennen* refers to experiential knowledge, whereas the verb *wissen* refers to facts and theoretical knowledge. French and Spanish have similar differentiations.

My point is that intellectually knowing an ancient qigong secret is not sufficient; you must implement it. Knowing a secret, such as the importance of relaxing the jaw, is not enough. Even knowing why, the secret is important (because it relaxes the vagus nerve and in turn the entire nervous system) is not enough. Relaxing the jaw must be an experience for you, and eventually it should become a daily habit.

By practicing the Five-Phase Routine, you'll be implementing literally thousands of years of ancient Chinese wisdom. It's all right there, embedded in the routine. For example, there are three different types of qigong exercises:

1. **Quiescent qigong** exercises have little-to-no visible movement, like Entering Zen or zhan zhuang qigong.
2. **Dynamic qigong** exercises are the most obvious and involve visible movements, like Lifting the Sky or Pushing Mountains.
3. **Spontaneous qigong** exercises involve a free flow of internal energy which leads to spontaneous, unrehearsed physical movements, like Flowing Breeze Swaying Willow.

The 5-Phase Routine incorporates all three categories in every session. We begin with quiescent qigong (Phase 1), move to dynamic qigong (Phase 2), then move into spontaneous qigong (Phase 3), back to quiescent qigong (Phase 4), and finally finish with dynamic qigong (Phase 5).

The final result is an amazingly efficient routine for getting remarkable health benefits. I often tell my students that a single session of the Five-Phase Routine is equivalent to one acupuncture session. I've spoken with many acupuncturists about this, all of whom had experience with Flowing Zen Qigong, and they agree with this assessment.

Let's put this into perspective. If you were to pay for daily acupuncture (which is common in China), then it would cost you $23,725 per year if you paid $65 per session. With qigong, you can treat yourself daily by using the Five-Phase Routine. This doesn't mean that you shouldn't get acupuncture, but it puts the value of the Five-Phase Routine into perspective. Ideally, you would do both acupuncture and qigong because of the wonderful synergy created by these two arts. But if you had to choose only one, then I think qigong is the better choice.

The Five-Phase Routine is powerful medicine. If there is a more streamlined and efficient qigong routine for modern practitioners, I have yet to find it. The Five-Phase Routine is, quite simply, the most effective qigong session I know of.

The Five Animal Play

Decades ago, I learned a spontaneous qigong exercise called Zi Fa Dong Gong (自發動功). This translates to "self-manifested spontaneous cultivation," which is a mouthful in both English and Chinese. The technique is similar to Flowing Breeze Swaying Willow, except that the flow of qi is more vigorous.

My first try with Zi Fa Dong Gong was a failure. I had already learned Flowing Breeze Swaying Willow, so I was familiar with spontaneous qigong. As was typical of my qigong routines, I just wobbled gently on my spot.

Many of my classmates had a different experience. About a minute after the teacher led us into Zi Fa Dong Gong, things got pretty loud in the room. Around me were the sounds of people moving vigorously. Then came the vocalizations. When I heard a woman sobbing deeply, I couldn't help but take a peek.

There was the woman crying deeply on her spot. Then there was a young man who looked like he was being electrocuted, except that he had a huge grin on his face. Across the room, a woman was rolling on the ground as if desperate to scratch an itch on her back. Another student had his arms wide open as he laughed gently, like a school kid with a case of the giggles.

For someone with no understanding of spontaneous qigong, the scene would have looked comical at best and insane at worst. Luckily, I knew that these students weren't crazy. They were simply releasing energy blockages—something that I was eager to do for myself!

As we've already learned, each meridian has an organ association as well as an associated sound. Stuck emotions affect the meridians, which affect the organs, which affect your health. To restore health, we need to clear the emotional blockages that clog up the organ systems—this is addressing problems at their root cause.

According to Chinese medicine, and I'm paraphrasing here, the only bad emotion is a stuck emotion. In other words, all our emotions need to be unstuck, including the so-called bad emotions like anger. When deep emotional blockages, some of which have been stuck for decades, begin to release, students will often make some sort of vocalization along with the spontaneous movements.

This makes sense, right? When you feel a strong emotion, you often make a sound. Sometimes, you also add a movement to the sound. For example, if you stub your toe, you will probably curse out loud. Along with that vocalization, you might clench your fists or hop around on one foot.

When you're sad, you cry. When you're happy, you laugh. The same is true of deep emotional releases. On its way out of the body, a blockage tends to make a sound. In this regard, the mouth and throat are the most important organs for clearing deep emotional blockages.

It's essential to understand that people doing Zi Fa Dong Gong are clearing deep-rooted blockages. In some cases, if left untreated, these blockages can be life-threatening. It's no understatement to say that spontaneous qigong can save a life by releasing deep blockages.

I eventually figured out Zi Fa Dong Gong for myself after a few tries and found it an invaluable resource for my own healing. Later, I started teaching the technique to my students—although I was always careful not to expose them to it too soon lest they be frightened away. Your first time doing it in a group setting might be a bit of a shock. It can be unsettling or triggering to hear students yawn, cry, scream, cough, sigh, or even giggle. It's certainly a different experience than a quiet yoga class with gentle music playing in the background.

A decade into my teaching, I decided to substitute the term Five Animal Play in place of Self-Manifested Spontaneous Cultivation. I did this for several reasons, which I'll explain.

The Five Animal Play (五禽戲, Wu Qin Xi), sometimes called the Five Animal Frolics, is an ancient qigong set invented by the famous Chinese doctor Hua Tuo, mentioned in chapter 3. Many people believe that Hua Tuo invented the Five Animal Play by observing the movements of various animals and then mimicking them with five qigong exercises.

Thus, some qigong schools teach the Five Animal Play as five dynamic qigong exercises. These exercises are similar to Lifting the Sky or countless other qigong exercises, but they look a bit like the relevant animals. So the Deer exercise looks a bit like a deer, the Tiger exercise looks a bit like a tiger, etc.

Furthermore, each exercise is correlated to a specific meridian system, a specific sound, and a specific emotion. When we put it all together, it looks something like this:

Exercise	Meridian	Emotion	Sound
Tiger	Lung	Sadness	Sssss
Bear	Kidney	Fear	Chooo
Deer	Liver	Anger	Shhhh
Bird	Heart	Joy	Haaah
Monkey	Spleen	Worry	Hoooh

All of this is fascinating, and it fits in perfectly with Chinese Medicine theory, but the truth is that no one knows for sure exactly what Hua Tuo taught eighteen hundred years ago. The historical evidence about Five Animal Play is limited because of the tremendous secrecy in ancient China.

My perspective is a bit different. Based on my research, my personal experience, and also my experience teaching, I believe that Hua Tuo's Five Animal Play was similar to Zi Fa Dong Gong. In other words, I think it was a form of spontaneous qigong where the internal energy manifests in different physical movements and vocalizations.

The Five Animals of Hua Tuo were not exercises, but rather poetic descriptions of the spontaneous qigong movements. What if, rather than having his students perform a Tiger-like exercise, Hua Tuo was instead inducing a vigorous flow of energy inside them and then encouraging that energy flow to manifest?

Because we all have different blockages, this energy flow will manifest in different ways. I've witnessed this countless times in my classes and private sessions. When the energy flows vigorously in Zi Fa Dong Gong, students move in different ways and make different sounds. Believe it or not, some students end up moving like a tiger or a bear!

I believe that Hua Tuo observed these various movements and sounds in his students and then codified them into five archetypes: Tiger, Bear, Deer, Bird, and Monkey. This makes sense because the ancient Chinese loved to organize phenomena into systems, like the Five Element system discussed earlier.

Remember that Hua Tuo was an acupuncturist and herbalist in addition to being a qigong master. So his qigong students were really patients, and it's likely that he had a thorough diagnosis for them. This would have given him a glimpse into the state of those students' meridians.

I had a similar situation in my studio in Gainesville. My studio was part of a larger wellness center where we offered acupuncture, chiropractic, and massage therapy. Part of the philosophy of our wellness center was to provide complementary care. Thus, my students often gave me permission to discuss their cases with the other healers in the center.

Specifically, this gave me a glimpse into the Chinese diagnosis for many of my students. And because I had attended acupuncture college, I could make sense of this diagnosis. For example, if a student's acupuncture chart said that they were diagnosed with Kidney Yang Deficiency, I understood what that meant.

My point is that, after watching literally thousands of students do Zi Fa Dong Gong, and getting glimpses into hundreds of their acupuncture charts, I started to see patterns. People with Lung Yin Deficiency would tend to move and vocalize in one way, whereas people with Liver Qi Stagnation would move and vocalize in another.

This is why I prefer Five Animal Play over Zi Fa Dong Gong. It fits better with Chinese Medicine theory. Plus, a room full of people doing Five Animal Play is like a room full of different animals making different sounds. It's like a zoo!

This is why I opted for the term Five Animal Play years ago, and I still stand by that decision. But it does cause some confusion because most qigong schools teach Five Animal Play very differently than I do. Nevertheless, I like paying homage to the great Hua Tuo, even if it requires a bit more explanation.

Whether I'm right or wrong about how Hua Tuo taught, we'll never know. Much of these details are lost to the fog of history. I should mention, however, that I am not the only qigong teacher who believes in this theory. A small group of teachers from different lineages have all arrived at a similar conclusion.

Perhaps a more important question is this: which is more useful? I believe that my approach to Five Animal Play is much more useful than the conventional approach. The Five Animal Play, when practiced as a form of spontaneous qigong, is some of the most powerful medicine I've ever encountered. There are already thousands of dynamic qigong exercises out there, so adding a Tiger, Bear, Deer, Bird, and Monkey exercise doesn't contribute much. But Five Animal Play is precisely what is often missing in the world of qigong.

SUCCESS STORY: DAVID

David began practicing qigong for two reasons. First, he had neck and shoulder pain, and second, he wanted a form of moving meditation to complement his sitting meditation. His neck and shoulder pain began to improve within the first few weeks of practicing qigong, but he quickly got far more than he bargained for.

David had spent most of his life thinking that he was just weird and socially awkward. But as he practiced qigong, relaxed his nervous system, and increased his mental clarity, David realized that he suffered from anxiety. In fact, it had ruled his life for years!

This is known as high-functioning anxiety, and it is extremely common. Many people never seek a diagnosis because they just assume that they are weird, like David did. With no diagnosis, these people also don't seek treatment—unless they stumble onto something holistic like qigong.

David told me that practicing qigong helped him to clear "some really intense emotional blockages." It took him about one and a half years of practicing qigong, including FBSW and Five Animal Play, to achieve this, but it was worth the effort. "I can say that now I'm totally anxiety free," he confided.

As he continued to practice, he also became aware of how bad his posture was. Qigong gave him the heightened awareness to gradually correct himself from inside out simply by checking for internal tension (a key skill in qigong). By improving his posture in this way, he not only relieved his neck and shoulder pain but also his chronic tension headaches.

Later, David also stopped getting knee pain whenever he did deep knee bends, possibly because of improving his posture. And finally, his blood pressure dropped from pre-hypertensive to normal.

"I came for tight shoulders and some moving meditation," David said, "but now I'm free of anxiety, my balance has vastly improved, I have better posture than I could have ever imagined, my knee pain is gone, and my blood pressure is totally normal!"

CHAPTER 7
Getting Remarkable Results with Qigong

When it comes to practicing qigong, there is only one thing that really matters: results. You are practicing qigong to make yourself healthier and happier. If you practice qigong correctly for a reasonable period of time, then you should see obvious health benefits. And conversely, if you are not getting results, then something is wrong with your practice.

In this chapter, I'll show you exactly how my students and I get remarkable results with qigong. In the old days, a master would take these secrets to the grave. I'm doing the opposite. I'm shouting these secrets from the rooftops.

When someone says that Flowing Zen Qigong helped them to get amazing results, they're really talking about two things:

1. The Five Phase Routine
2. The secrets revealed in this chapter

In other words, the secret sauce of Flowing Zen Qigong is not found in the various qigong sets or techniques that I teach. I love the sets that are taught, but the truth is that you can get amazing results with many other qigong sets as long as you (a) use them within the Five-Phase Routine and (b) implement the secrets taught in this chapter.

If you're new to qigong, then you'll save yourself time, money, and suffering by reading this chapter carefully. If you've done qigong for years with average or mediocre results, then this chapter will help you double or even 10x your results.

Let's dive in.

Your Qi Diary

If you went to an acupuncturist for twelve weeks, they would keep a chart on your case. Not only would they be able to measure your progress using their own diagnostic methods, but they would be able to remind you of your own subjective measurements. For example, if you rate your own knee pain at a 6/10 on week one and then rate it at a 4/10 on week eight, then you are clearly making progress.

Qigong is all about self-healing. It's empowering to take charge of your own healing. But in doing so, you also must take charge of your own records. If you don't keep records of your progress, no one will.

You need to keep a Qi Diary so that you can track your ups and downs, jot down notes, record your changing experiences, vent your fears and frustrations, highlight favorite exercises, and celebrate small wins.

I like to call it a Qi Diary because it rhymes and sounds cute, but you can call it whatever you like. Use a paper diary or a word document, but not a spreadsheet. Save that for your Qi Chart, which we'll discuss in the next section. If you need to order something like this, do it right now so that it arrives in a few days and it is ready to use.

Here's what will happen if you ignore this advice: You will slow your progress with qigong. If you don't keep some sort of Qi Diary, you will not be able to measure your progress. And if you don't measure your progress, you will lose motivation.

And vice versa, if you can see clear progress, then you will be motivated to continue. The more progress you measure, the more motivated you'll be to practice; the more motivated you are, the more progress you'll make. You'll relax knowing that you're on the right track and that qigong is bringing you many benefits.

Another critical piece of the equation is this: Qigong brings you benefits in many areas, not just the one you're most frustrated with. If you don't keep a Qi Diary, you may not notice these other benefits. Or even if you do recognize them, you won't notice much progress.

Remember the story in chapter 1 about my worst day? A year into my qigong practice, I reached a point where my new worst day was the same as my previous best day from a year prior. That's incredible progress—and yet I didn't even notice it until a class-mate helped me to assess it.

What should you put in your Qi Diary? Here are some examples:

"Back pain seems better today. Still not gone, but I think I'm on the right track and hopefully it'll be gone in a few more months."

"Had a minor depressive episode but bounced back quickly. It only lasted three weeks this time, and it wasn't as severe as the last one, maybe a 6/10 in severity. Such a relief to not fall so deep into the pits of depression."

"Really feeling the energy in my hands now. Not sure what it means, but it's super cool! Feels like warm champagne! Exciting!"

"Major stress from moving and the new job. I'm handling it okay, but my qigong practice has suffered. Need to get back on track. I definitely feel worse without it."

Consider a physical journal or diary that is dedicated to this purpose. Since so much of modern living is already digital, it can be helpful to have something physical. You can buy a nice one online and pair it with a favorite pen. Then set it out somewhere that will remind you to practice qigong.

Your Qi Chart

Now that you've got a Qi Diary, I recommend that you also keep a separate Qi Chart. I admit that this doesn't roll off the tongue as well as Qi Diary, but it's the best I've got.

Your Qi Diary is for words, feelings, and observations, but your Qi Chart is for numbers. Both are important.

With your Qi Chart, you will be tracking subjective progress in a variety of different categories. You'll assign a number from 0 to 4 for each category as follows:

0 = Not at all
1 = A little bit
2 = Moderately
3 = Quite a bit
4 = Extremely

Don't worry. All of this is on the sample Qi Chart found in your book bonuses. But let me explain exactly what you're doing and why.

The Qi Chart is a combination of positive and negative experiences. This means that the higher numbers on the 0–4 scale don't always mean better. For example, a 4 in "feeling depressed" is not the same as a 4 in "feeling grateful." That's okay because all we're trying to do with this chart is measure progress.

Remember that qigong brings a wide range of benefits, including some that probably aren't currently on your radar. The Qi Chart will help you to add more benefits to your radar and notice them.

As you make obvious progress in other areas, you'll gain confidence in being able to reach goals with your main complaint.

Each chart measures twelve weeks of practice. At the end of twelve weeks, look at your numbers. Have you made any progress? If not, then use the troubleshooting section later in this chapter to figure out what's wrong with your practice.

Here's my promise to you: If you practice the Five-Phase Routine every day for twelve weeks (that's one Qi Chart), then you will see remarkable results. This is not to say that you will be healed of all that ails you in just twelve weeks, but rather that you'll get a wide range of obvious benefits. These benefits will give you confidence that you are on the right path and that you should continue with qigong.

Keep in mind that doing the Five-Phase Routine every day, which takes about fifteen to twenty-five minutes, is not easy. Many of you will need to start with the Two-Minute Drill first.

The Two-Minute Drill

Remember when I took a vow to practice Lifting the Sky daily back on New Year's Eve in 1999? At the time, I didn't have a name for it, but today we call this the Two-Minute Drill. In retrospect, I can say with confidence that it is the great secret to creating a consistent qigong practice, or to reclaiming your practice when you lose it.

Back in 1999, I didn't know anything about habits or willpower. Since then, tons of research have been done on the subject. In an effort to help my students (and myself), I've read dozens of books and blogs about willpower and habits. What I can tell you is that my discovery in 1999 happens to be in line with all the modern research on habits and willpower.

Early in my teaching career, I quickly discovered that a huge percentage of students—probably over 70 percent—struggled to practice even though they loved qigong and got early results. I even talked to my master about it. As is typical of Chinese masters, he said that it's not my responsibility to encourage my students to practice. It's up to them.

Of course, I discarded his advice because it was terrible. What is a teacher for if not to inspire students to practice? In 2007, about two years into teaching and a year before opening my brick-and-mortar studio, I decided that I had to do something to help my students develop the qigong habit. That's when I started to do research into the subject.

The result was the development of the Two-Minute Drill. All these years later, the research has continued to prove that the Two-Minute Drill is the secret to building a daily habit. If you struggle to practice, look no further than this.

Your book bonuses will lead you through the Two-Minute Drill, but here is the summary:

1. Find a safe spot and dive into a favorite qigong exercise, like Lifting the Sky or Pushing Mountains.
2. Do roughly two minutes of the exercise, and that's it. In the beginning, you can use a timer to see how many repetitions you typically do in two minutes. For example, you might do twelve repetitions of Lifting the Sky in two minutes. Use that as your rough guide moving forward. In other words, from then on just count about twelve repetitions instead of setting a timer.
3. Finish with a super-abbreviated Closing Sequence: Pat the eyes open, wash your face, comb your hair, and that's it. You can learn the details in your book bonuses.

You'll notice that this is decidedly *not* the Five-Phase Routine. It's basically Phase 2 with a tiny bit of Phase 5. You're skipping all the other parts of the Five-Phase Routine—on purpose.

The Two-Minute Drill is not nearly as powerful as the Five-Phase Routine. Nevertheless, you will feel noticeably better in just two minutes.

The Two-Minute Drill is useful for several reasons:

1. It uses the psychology of what researchers are now calling a "tiny habit," which simply means that it is so small that your typical excuses fall away. We all have two minutes a day and we know it.

2. It feels good. This creates a reward system for your new habit. Knowing that you will feel better in just two minutes motivates you to do it.

3. It becomes a placeholder. If you can do the Two-Minute Drill at the same time every day, then that same time slot will eventually become a longer session.

4. It's easy. Doing a full Five-Phase session requires concentration, privacy, and time commitment. But the Two-Minute Drill can be done any time and virtually anywhere.

You can also use the Two-Minute Drill to increase your overall dosage of qigong. For example, if you've successfully created a habit of doing the Five-Phase Routine in the morning, then use the Two-Minute Drill to carve out a new time slot in the evening. This will not only act as a placeholder but will also give you more mileage for your morning session.

Keep using the Two-Minute Drill until you're able to do the Five-Phase Routine every single day. This might take months or even a few years. For example, you might start with the Two-Minute Drill daily for thirty days, then substitute the Five-Phase Routine on weekends. This is progress!

Gradually, you may work up to doing the Five-Phase Routine five times per week, using the Two-Minute Drill on the other days. And when life gets in the way, then you simply substitute the Two-Minute Drill for a longer session. Or if life really gets in the way and you fall off the horse for weeks, months, or years, then the Two-Minute Drill is how you can get back on track.

The #1 Mistake in Qigong

Whether you're new to qigong or you've been practicing for years, you definitely want to avoid making the #1 mistake, right? The good news is that correcting this mistake is simple. Once you fix it, you'll immediately start seeing better results from qigong. Not three months later, and not even three days later, but immediately.

Without further ado, here's the #1 mistake that people make when practicing qigong for self-healing:

Students pay too much attention to the physical aspect of qigong.

Traditionally, qigong masters spoke of Three Regulations:

1. Regulating the body (tiao shen, 調身)
2. Regulating the breathing (tiao xi, 調息)
3. Regulating the mind (tiao xin, 調心)

"Regulate" isn't a perfect translation, but it's the one most used. A better translation might be to "tune" something, like a violin. This is a task that I know well! Every day for years I would take my violin out of its case and the first thing I would do is tune it.

You must do the same thing with your qigong practice.

In theory, each of these three regulations are equally important. But in the Western world, it's a mistake to treat them equally. When it comes to maximizing your results, Westerners should use this simple equation:

- Put 10 percent of your attention on the physical aspect
- Put 30 percent of your attention on your breathing
- Put 60 percent of your attention on the meditative aspect

I like to call this the 10/30/60 Rule. We're following the ancient advice about the Three Regulations, but we're adjusting it for modern living. Let's look at the 10/30/60 rule in more depth.

The Physical Aspect (10%)

The physical movements and the postures—like Lifting the Sky, Pushing Mountains, or any qigong exercise—should only take about 10 percent of your attention. Learn the techniques as best as you can, but don't obsess. You'll have plenty of time—years or even decades—to gradually improve your form.

The Breathing (30%)

How you inhale, exhale, and pause—and what you feel while doing all this—should account for about 30 percent of your attention. In other words, pay three times more attention to your breathing than to the physical form. In fact, your breathing will likely soften and change the physical aspect of whatever you're doing. For example, as you relax into the breathing of Lifting the Sky, your form is likely to soften as well, and that's a good thing.

The Meditative Aspect (60%)

Meditation is the master key that unlocks the true healing potential of qigong. Unfortunately, this aspect is also the most confusing, probably because we typically try to understand it with our intellectual mind. That's a bit like reading poetry to a robot. When we enter into the Zen state, our brainwaves shift, our nervous system relaxes, and our qi starts to flow. The Zen Mind deserves about 60 percent of your attention because it's integral for self-healing and also because it's the one that we Westerners most often neglect.

But What about Alignment?!?

I'm sure that some of you find the 10/30/60 Rule to be confusing. If you've been learning qigong and/or tai chi for a while, then "alignment" is a buzz word that you've probably come across. Maybe you've heard your teacher say things like:

"Your nose should be aligned with your navel . . ."

"Sink the shoulders, drop the elbows . . ."

"Keep your knee aligned with your toe . . ."

"Sink the chest . . ."

"Don't lean forward . . ."

Or maybe your instructor manipulated your body with his hands. For example, I once took a qigong workshop with an instructor who constantly poked and adjusted a poor sixty-two-year-old woman. This manhandling was all in the name of "proper alignment."

His corrections were futile. One glance at the woman and you could see that she had a pronounced hunch on her upper back. This hunch, called kyphosis, is very common, especially among older adults. Although it can be reversed, it's not a quick fix. And it certainly wasn't going to be resolved in a weekend workshop.

"Alignment is critical," the teacher said to the class as he adjusted her. "Without proper alignment, we can't do qigong."

Is what he said true? Must our alignment be perfect to do qigong?

During the lunch break, I had a little chat with this woman. It turns out she had been doing qigong and tai chi for a few years. More importantly, she'd been getting pretty good results with her arthritis pain. In other words—she'd been getting results *despite* her poor alignment.

Clearly, this woman's alignment wasn't anywhere close to perfect. Nor was it going to improve much over the span of a weekend, or even a month. And yet she was getting results.

I joked about her being the teacher's pet. "I just ignore him," she said. "I don't worry about that stuff at home. I just get into a nice flow." In other words, she was naturally following the 10/30/60 rule, ignoring her alignment and enjoying the flow of the session.

We need look no further than this example for an answer to our question about alignment. People with poor alignment can absolutely get results with qigong. And thank God, otherwise the people who need qigong the most would not be able to use it!

The truth is that most twenty-first century humans have bad alignment. And it's not just the older folks. The younger generation has bad posture too, partially because of cell phones. There's even a condition now called "Text Neck." You can guess what that looks like!

If qigong could only be practiced by people with perfect alignment, then none of us would qualify. I estimate that 90 percent of my students have had alignment issues. If perfect alignment were necessary to get results, then 90 percent of them would have failed!

The qigong teacher above didn't acknowledge how long it takes to restructure the body. Changes like that are measured in years, not days or hours. We can and should work on our alignment, but we shouldn't let bad alignment stop us from enjoying the benefits of qigong now.

Poor posture and poor alignment definitely block the flow of qi. That's life. In fact, everything we do blocks the flow of qi, from the crap we eat to the way we sit. Pointing out things that block the flow of qi is easy! Just close your eyes and point in any direction!

Start where you are. Whatever hand you've been dealt, qigong will make it better.

When it comes to internal martial arts, alignment takes on more importance. This is because we're dealing with self-defense. For example, the Yang Style Tai Chi pattern commonly called "Warding Off" is a defense against a punch to the face. If your alignment is off, then you won't block the punch! Ouch!

These days, tai chi has lost its martial roots, and very few people can use it for self-defense. That's fine as long as they acknowledge that their tai chi is just a form of Medical Qigong. In other words, it's important for teachers to be honest about *why* the alignment should be this one way or another.

An improperly placed toe will not mess up the flow of qi. If you're correcting the toe position for self-defense, that's one thing. Qi flow and self-healing are different.

In chapter 6, we talked about "Aligning the Qi." Notice that I speak of aligning the qi rather than aligning the body. The truth is that we can begin to align the qi even if the physical body is out of alignment.

This is precisely why the woman with kyphosis was able to get results despite poor alignment. The same is true for any alignment issue. Your qi can reroute and flow around blockages and physical issues, including the following:

- lordosis (excessive curvature of the low back)
- scoliosis (abnormal lateral curvature of the spine)
- a hip hike
- flat feet
- a titanium hip replacement
- metal pins in your ankle from a broken bone
- a pacemaker

I speak from experience. Your feet are your root, and I have the world's flattest feet. The angle of your foot determines the alignment of your knee, hip, pelvis, and spine. In that sense, my alignment has never been perfect, and it probably never will be. And yet, I get amazing results from qigong.

I'm able to align my qi despite my flat feet. This is how qigong works in the real world. We're not perfect. We're all just trying to make the best out of the cards we've been dealt. And there's no better art to do that with than qigong.

Mary the Butcher

One of the things you'll often hear me say to students is "butcher the form." This may seem like a strange piece of instruction, but it's super helpful. For many students, it's a huge relief.

Knowing that the form is the least important aspect of qigong is great. Being repeatedly encouraged to butcher the form is even better. For students who wrestle with perfectionism and negative self-talk, this instruction is a game changer.

Here's a real-life example. Years ago, in my studio in Florida, I taught a monthly introduction to qigong. In that workshop, I always taught Lifting the Sky as well as the 10/30/60 Rule. During one of these workshops, I recognized Mary. She had taken the workshop six months prior but was retaking it to review the basics. (This was long before we began teaching online, otherwise she could have just clicked a button to review.)

When I saw Mary performing Lifting the Sky during one of the sessions, I chuckled to myself. Mary's form was beautifully awful; it was *really* bad. In fact, it was one of the worst performances of Lifting the Sky I've ever seen. Physically, that is. Her form was awful, but as we've already learned, form is the least important part of the puzzle.

Most teachers would probably rush to correct her. Some teachers might even chastise her. That's certainly what some of my teachers did to me and my classmates. But I'm not like that.

During the lunch break, I struck up a conversation with Mary. "You took this class six months ago, right?" I asked.

"Yes, Sifu," she said. "And I've been practicing every day!"

"Wonderful!" I said. "How are your results?"

"Amazing! My arthritis pain is almost completely gone, I'm sleeping like a baby, and I've got tons of energy!"

Why on earth would I correct Mary's form when she was getting such good results? She was obviously doing something right. And most importantly, she was practicing regularly.

If I had to grade Mary's qigong performance using the 10/30/60 rule, it would look something like this.

- 4 (of 10) points for the physical aspect
- 28 (of 30) points for the breathing aspect

- 55 (of 60) points for the meditative aspect
- Score: 87 (of 100) points total

An 87 is solid B+, which is great! Mary's form was weak, but her breathing was almost perfect. You could also tell from her facial expressions that she was in a tranquil state of Zen during the sessions. In other words, her overall performance was excellent even though her form was abysmal.

What do you think would've happened if I had corrected her physical form? At best, this would have added five points to her grade. But not so fast! Adding points in one area can take away points from another area.

Here's what might have happened if I had corrected her. First, she would've slipped out of the Zen state as she tried to correct her form. Then she might have experienced negative self-talk: "I can't believe I've been doing it so badly for months. I'm such a dummy!"

As a result, the meditation score would have likely dropped. And once the meditative aspect drops, the breathing aspect will also drop because the nervous system begins to tense up. The new equation, after correcting her form, might look something like this.

- $4 + 5 = 9$ (of 10) points for the physical aspect
- $28 - 9 = 19$ (of 30) points for the breathing aspect
- $55 - 22 = 33$ (of 60) points for the meditative aspect
- Score: 61 (of 100) points total

In this second equation, Mary scored a 61. That's a failing grade, folks. The difference between a score of 87 and a score of 61, in terms of long-term results, is massive. For someone fighting a serious illness, this might literally be the difference between life and death.

Be like Mary. Focus on what's important. Don't be afraid to butcher the form. And if you want to know what's really important in qigong, then follow the Three Golden Rules.

The Three Golden Rules

Learning to pay more attention to the internal aspects is an ongoing process. It's about reconditioning yourself to a new way of thinking. And this takes time.

This is why we have the Three Golden Rules as a guide for practicing. If you come back to the Three Golden Rules over and over, then you'll automatically be following the 10/30/60 equation. The rules help you to focus on what's really important (i.e., what's happening inside).

We live in a physically oriented culture. We perceive the world through our eyes. We notice what looks good. We're more familiar with external arts, where the important stuff happens on the outside.

Qigong, however, is an internal art. This means that the important stuff happens on the inside. In other words, the important stuff is almost invisible!

I designed the Three Golden Rules to help students fully embrace the subtleties of an internal art. Don't be deceived by the simplicity of these rules. I've watched thousands of students dissolve countless problems simply by implementing the Three Golden Rules.

Without further ado, here are the Three Golden Rules:

- Rule #1: Repeatedly let go of your worries.
- Rule #2: Repeatedly let go of your thoughts.
- Rule #3: Try to enjoy the session.

Now let's look at each one in more depth.

Rule #1: Repeatedly let go of worries.

Worrying blocks the flow of qi. This is true during your qigong and tai chi practice, but it's also true throughout your day. Whenever you worry, your energy is stifled. And vice versa, when you let go of those worries, the energy will start to flow again.

Worry will find all kinds of creative ways to sneak into your qigong sessions. That's okay, and it's normal. Don't try to stop worries from creeping in. Instead, get good at letting go of these worries whenever you notice them.

How do you let them go? A gentle exhalation through the mouth may help. Or just say to yourself, "I'm letting this worry go." But whatever you do, don't start worrying about letting go of worries!

Here's a nice quote from a smart guy that sums it up:

"Can any of you, by worrying, add a single hour to your life?"
—Jesus (Matthew 6:25–33)

Worry is an unproductive emotion. It never changes anything. All it does is block the flow of qi in your body.

Also remember that this is a process. Don't expect to let go of 100 percent of your worries on day one and then be done with it. Expect to let go over and over, perhaps dozens of times in a single session. And expect this process to continue for years or even decades.

Rule #2: Repeatedly let go of thoughts

Thoughts will creep in, just like worries. Again, this is natural. It happens to everyone, even masters. Let these thoughts go, over and over.

If you say, "I tried, but I can't!" then here's some news for you. That's a thought too! Let it go. Don't let the letting go of thoughts turn into more thoughts. You can't think your way out of thinking.

Thoughts block you from entering the Zen Mind. If you're following your thoughts rather than letting them go, then you're taking yourself out of the Zen Mind. And if you're not cultivating a meditative state of mind, then you're not getting the best results from your practice.

Rule #3: Try to enjoy the session.

If you're practicing Lifting the Sky, try to enjoy it. It shouldn't be too difficult. Most qigong exercises are incredibly enjoyable. Try to enjoy the movement, or your breathing, or the flow, or the overall feeling you get.

The mind will wander. Gently bring it back to the present moment. Find something to enjoy. As with Rules #1 and #2, you will need to repeat this often.

When you enjoy your qigong session, you automatically deepen the Zen Mind. This, in turn, stimulates the flow of qi. In other words, enjoyment stimulates the flow of qi.

In other words, worrying and thinking both block the flow of qi, whereas enjoyment stimulates it. This is a sweet deal. Not only do you get to enjoy yourself, but you also reap greater benefits *because* of that enjoyment.

Applying the Three Golden Rules

It's amazing how many issues can be resolved with the Three Golden Rules. It's almost like a joke. A student comes in with any problem, and I "solve" it with the Three Golden Rules. Easy peasy!

I put the word "solve" in quotation marks because it's not me doing the solving; it's you. All I did was codify a few ancient qigong secrets into a handy-dandy three-step rule. You did the actual work by practicing the rules.

That's a key point about the Three Golden Rules: they should be practiced, not followed. These aren't concepts or abstractions. These are actual techniques.

Let's analyze some common practice problems, and then solve them with the Three Golden Rules.

Example #1

Problem: You're doing your qigong session, then you start worrying about the form of Lifting the Sky. Should your arms be straighter? What about the stretch at the top? What happens to the shoulders?

Solution: Use Rule #1. Let go of this worry. Remember that the form is the least important aspect of qigong. If this worry comes back, let it go again. And again. Butcher the form. Worrying is worse than any physical mistakes you might be making.

Tip: Intentionally make some mistakes in the physical form. Since the physical form is not that important, these mistakes won't matter. By making mistakes on purpose, you may find that you're able to let go of worry more easily. Try it!

Example #2

Problem: You can't clear your mind of thoughts. It never feels like your mind is completely empty.

Solution: Use Rule #2. Start by noticing the thought. Catch yourself in the act, and then let it go. Also let go of the thought that your mind should be 100 percent empty. It's not true, not even for masters. And even if it were true, thinking about it wouldn't help!

Tip: Try waiting for thoughts, as if lying in ambush. Don't expect the mind to be perfectly clear. Instead, expect thoughts to sneak in, because they will. When you notice them, let them go. Or you pretend to "zap" them, as if playing some sort of video game.

Example #3

Problem: Your daily qigong practice has become a chore, and you are no longer getting the results that you once got.

Solution: Use Rule #3. Do whatever it takes to enjoy yourself. If you can't find something wonderful in a particular qigong exercise, then choose another. There are literally thousands of exercises to choose from!

Tip: Try to notice if your mind is in the present, the past, or the future. Often, we start to regret the past or worry about the future without even realizing that we've left the present moment. Try to notice *when* you are feeling present, like a time traveler trying to figure out what year it is. By doing this, you'll bring yourself back to the now. And it is only in the present moment that we can truly enjoy ourselves.

Never Be Rigid

Softness is a core skill that we must cultivate every time we practice qigong. Whenever we practice, we work on softening the muscles, the nervous system, and the fascia. We also need to soften the most rigid part of the human body—the tissue right between your ears. (I'm referring to your rigid, analytical brain, silly.)

All schools of qigong, no matter how much they disagree on other principles, still agree about softness. Never be rigid in qigong . . . except with this rule. Follow it rigidly!

The concept of softness is foreign to us Westerners. Our approach to physical exercise typically involves the opposite of softness. Even yoga, which is a wonderful discipline, does not emphasize softness in the same way that qigong does. Some yoga practitioners *think* that it involves softness—until they learn qigong.

For example, at the beginning of a yoga session you are likely to stand as follows:

- the feet are close together
- the body is upright
- the core muscles are engaged
- the kneecaps are lifted up
- the sternum is lifting upward
- the shoulders are rolled back

When you stand like this, you feel as solid as a mountain. In fact, I just described Tadasana, or Mountain Pose. Now here's a description of a comparable pose in qigong called the Wuji Stance (Great Void Stance):

- the feet are shoulder width or wider
- the body is upright but soft
- the belly is totally relaxed, including the core muscles
- the knees are unlocked and slightly bent
- the sternum is dropped downward
- the shoulders are soft and sunken forward

As you can see, the qigong approach is different. It's much softer than the yoga approach. To a yoga teacher, a qigong practitioner would probably look like they were slouching.

In fact, yoga practitioners who take my classes often struggle with this. They feel like they are slouching. I need to reassure them that, in qigong, slouching is good!

Always search for softness in qigong. This doesn't mean that you want to be totally limp; it means that you err on the side of softness. In Western culture, we are starting from a place of tension. We have a lot to learn about softness.

A simple experiment will demonstrate this. Hold your hand comfortably in the air in front of your chest. Tense it by opening it stiffly and creating as much tension as you can in the fingers and forearm. Then let the wrist and fingers go totally limp. The hand should hang down from your forearm as if it's a dead fish.

Now find the Goldilocks spot between limp and tense. When in doubt, err toward limpness. The result is a gently curved wrist and fingers that are alive, but not tense.

In qigong, we're trying to do the same thing with the entire body. Remember that this is a skill. It's not a switch you flip once and then you're done. You will be cultivating softness like this for the rest of your life.

Crazy and Non-Crazy Qigong Rules

If you've done any reading about qigong, then you know that there are a lot of weird rules. Some of the rules are pretty crazy. Identifying which rules are crazy is important for modern practitioners.

Qigong saves lives, including mine. But to save lives, it must be practiced. Rules that make it harder to practice can simply be ignored. It's not that the rules have no merit. Rather, it's risk versus reward. When the risk of not practicing outweighs the risk of breaking a rule, then we should break the rule.

Years ago, when I first began searching for books on qigong, I found one with a rule that went something like this: *Don't practice qigong for twenty-four to forty-eight hours before or after having sex.*

I was in my twenties and had a steady girlfriend. There was no way in hell that I was going to follow that crazy sex rule. "Well, I guess qigong isn't for me then," I snorted. A woman standing across the aisle glanced up for a moment, and then looked back at her book.

Thankfully, that crazy rule didn't scare me away from qigong. But that's precisely the danger with rules like this one. For the modern practitioner, prohibitive rules make qigong impractical.

Let's look through the most common qigong rules to see which ones have merit for the modern practitioner.

6 Crazy Rules That You Can Ignore

1. Ignore the no sex rule.

This rule typically prohibits practicing qigong twenty-four to forty-eight hours before or after sex. But it's not even about sex; it's about the ejaculation of semen and the subsequent loss of "essence." If your body does not have the ability to ejaculate semen—well, then you can completely ignore this rule.

If you are capable of ejaculating semen, then you can still ignore this rule unless you are practicing advanced martial or spiritual qigong, in which case, wait thirty-sixty minutes after a qigong session before ejaculating. This lets the qi consolidate at dantian. And it's totally fine to practice qigong immediately after ejaculation.

2. Ignore the barefoot rule.

One of my masters was adamant about not practicing barefoot outdoors. Another one said that practicing barefoot was ideal! Talk about conflicting advice!

Years later, I started to experiment on my own. Instead of wearing shoes outside, as I had done for years, I tried barefoot. I tried qigong in the grass, on sand, on concrete, and indoors—all without shoes or socks.

After a few years of this, I decided that it no longer made sense to tell students not to practice qigong barefoot. There just wasn't a good reason. If practicing barefoot is somehow bad for your energy, then I couldn't find evidence of it.

Today, my advice is to experiment. Try different shoes, and also try barefoot, both indoors and out. The most important thing is to be comfortable.

3. Ignore the noontime rule.

Some masters say you should never practice at noon. Others say noon is one of the four best times to practice (dawn, noon, sunset, and midnight). So who is right?

Chinese Medicine agrees that noon is a bad time for vigorous exercise. This is because the heart meridian is active from 11:00 a.m. to 1:00 p.m. Nevertheless, practicing qigong during this period is fine as long as it's gentle. Save your vigorous qigong or kung fu practices for another time of the day.

4. Ignore the not-while-angry rule.

Some masters say that you shouldn't practice while angry. This makes me angry. Grrr. After practicing qigong, you'll feel less angry. Congrats! You've empirically proven that qigong helps to dissipate anger!

I can safely say that this rule is bullshit. Qigong is excellent for anger management. For depressives, anger management is especially important. That's why I dislike this rule so much.

5. Ignore the in-person rule.

Some people will tell you that qigong can't be learned online. This is verifiably false. It's also dangerous.

We need to remove barriers to learning rather than add them. This is especially important for people battling life-threatening problems, like depression. Online learning removes several barriers, like driving to a class or finding a good instructor nearby.

With some issues, like anxiety, online learning is actually superior. It allows students to learn in the privacy of their home rather than in a group setting, which can aggravate anxiety. Many people have said that, if not for my online programs, they wouldn't have been able to learn.

Since 2014, I've been helping my online students to get amazing results. Lots of other qigong teachers are now following this lead. Don't listen to backward-looking teachers who dismiss online teaching.

6. Ignore the no-peeing rule.

I once heard about a teacher who told his students not to pee for thirty minutes after practicing qigong. Supposedly, this was because qi is stored in the bladder. I honestly don't understand this advice.

The explanation I can think of is that the bladder is located near the lower dantian. But that doesn't mean that qi is stored in the bladder. Urine is what's stored there!

Practicing qigong tends to get the juices flowing. This often makes people need to urinate. In my studio, I used to joke that you don't need a hall pass to go to the bathroom. If you need to pee, just go pee!

Now let's look at some non-crazy rules that you should be aware of. These are not commandments, but rather gentle guidelines. The first three rules should look familiar. That's because they are the Three Golden Rules in reverse order.

Twenty-Three Qigong Guidelines

1. Enjoy yourself!

If you only follow one rule, follow this one. The process of enjoying your qigong practice smooths out more kinks and solves more problems than any other rule I've found. Come back to this guideline often.

2. Repeatedly let go of thoughts.

This includes thoughts about crazy qigong rules! See the Three Golden Rules for more.

3. Repeatedly let go of worries.

Are you worried about breaking some crazy qigong rules? Let that go! See the Three Golden Rules for more.

4. Fall down seven times, get up eight.

This is a Japanese proverb, but it's perfect for qigong. I placed it near the top of the list because of its importance. What I love about this proverb is that it tells you, from the very first word, that you will struggle. You need to understand that everyone struggles. We all fall down. I've told you about my many falls and can assure you that my students have experienced the same. Instead of kvetching about your repeated falls, try to get better at picking yourself up.

5. Get results.

This should be obvious. Unfortunately, too many qigong students forget this rule. You should be getting measurable results with your practice. Use a Qi Diary and a Qi Chart to track your progress.

If one teacher's method isn't working for you, then go try something else! Give a method your best shot for six to twelve months and track your results. Qigong is about you, not your teacher or his lineage or his bank account. Go get the results that you deserve.

6. Butcher the form.

Don't try to do the form perfectly. Form is the least important thing in qigong, so worrying about it is just silly. Review the section about Mary the Butcher for more on this topic.

7. Don't breathe forcefully.

Gentle breathing is critical. Although there are some forceful breathing methods in qigong, these are more advanced. They are also unnecessary when it comes to health and happiness. Learn to breathe gently first. Learn to release all of the tension in your lungs and diaphragm. But gentle doesn't mean super slow or shallow. You should be enjoying your breath, not struggling for air.

8. Relax your jaw.

Relax your jaw so much that it hangs gently open. The lips can be either closed or open, but the jaw must remain soft. Try moving it around in all directions to check for tension. Relaxing the jaw relaxes the entire nervous system via the vagus nerve. Many modern humans have residual tension in their jaw and also in their nervous systems.

9. Less is more.

Some beginners are so enthusiastic about qigong that they practice for two hours every day. If you can sustain this and also keep the quality high, then great. But most people will burn out within a few weeks or months. Try focusing on high-quality sessions that last about ten to twenty minutes. This is doable and sustainable. Remember that we're trying to create a lifestyle with qigong. The goal is to practice daily for the rest of your life!

10. Practice somewhere safe.

We typically close our eyes halfway or all the way during practice, so make sure the space around you feels safe. There should be no coffee tables with sharp corners, for example. And please avoid practicing on balconies without railings!

I'm only half joking about the balconies. When we get into a meditative flow with qigong, especially during Flowing Breeze Swaying Willow, we tend to move around a bit. Students are often surprised to open their eyes and find that they wandered several feet during the session. That's normal with the Five-Phase Routine, but it doesn't mix well with balconies.

A safe space also means that you can practice without being disturbed. This isn't easy if you have young kids in the house, but it can be done. Get up earlier, set clearer boundaries, get a sign for your office door, or do whatever it takes. You need to carve out ten to twenty minutes for you. You deserve space to heal.

11. Avoid unclean spaces.

Some spaces are toxic to humans. For example, the energy in bathrooms, especially public restrooms, is not good for qigong. It's fine to do your business in these spaces, but it's not a good idea to do your qigong there. I understand that it can be convenient to sneak into a bathroom for a quick qigong session, but look for a hallway instead. Or go outside.

12. Avoid powerful storms.

The energy during thunderstorms and hurricanes is too yang for qigong. This is a traditional rule, but I learned it the hard way when I moved to North Florida in 2004. Florida is the lightning capital of the US. It's also the hurricane capital. When I first moved here, I had to wrestle with both. I experienced two major hurricanes during my first year in Florida, and thunderstorms are a daily occurrence in the summer.

The danger is not that you'll get struck by lightning, although that's conceivable if you practice outside holding an umbrella during a bad storm. No, the problem is that these storms screw with your energy. You'll feel agitated, your blood pressure may rise, and you may have trouble sleeping.

With thunderstorms, count the number of seconds between the flash and the thunder, then divide by five. That's how far away the storm is. So five seconds is one mile, thirty seconds is six miles, and so on. I've found that I can practice once the storm is about ten miles away, which is fifty seconds. Or you can look on the radar.

With hurricanes it's harder because they move slowly. But the energy is also weaker than a thunderstorm. If you are already stressed because a hurricane is approaching, then just practice. It's better to relieve some stress than to worry about the yang energy.

13. Avoid strong winds.

If the wind is too strong, it may disturb your energy. In Chinese Medicine, wind is considered a pathogenic force. This means that it can weaken the energy in your meridians. It turns out your grandmother was right—cover your neck to protect your Bladder Meridian from the wind!

A gentle breeze is fine; a tornado is not. How can you tell if the wind is too strong? It boils down to comfort. If you are bundled up in high-tech gear and the wind doesn't bother you, then you're fine. But if you feel like the wind is penetrating your body, then don't do qigong there.

14. Air circulation matters.

Traditionally, qigong was practiced outdoors. The qi outside is better than the qi indoors. When I lived in NYC, I would often go to city parks at dawn. They would be filled with Asians practicing qigong and tai chi. This same thing happens in parks all around the world because they understand this rule.

It's fine to practice indoors if you have good air circulation. Plants also help. In my studio, we had a bay window full of gorgeous plants, a ceiling fan, and an electric fountain with running water. We also had two French doors that opened onto a green area. The combination of all these things made the studio feel amazingly fresh and calming.

When I lived in NYC, I opened the windows up wide, and turned on a fan, even in winter. (In NYC, there is no thermostat for the heat. It's just a big boiler in the basement that sends hot steam to all the radiators in the building. So I wasn't wasting much energy by doing this.)

Practicing outdoors is ideal as long as you're comfortable. In NYC, I would bundle up and walk to a nearby park as long as the "feels like" temperature was above 35 degrees F (1.6 degrees C). In

Florida, you battle the heat and the bugs more than the cold, but I still practice outside whenever possible.

15. Practice in the morning.

The night owls will not like this one, but I would be remiss to exclude it. The morning energy is ideal for qigong. A morning session also sets the tone for the entire day. Plus, if you practice in the morning, then you can choose to practice again in the evening!

A compromise for those who struggle in the morning is to do the Two-Minute Drill first thing. I recommend that you do it immediately before or immediately after brushing your teeth. It's only two minutes, and then you can have your coffee or go about your morning.

16. Be patient.

Traditionally, qigong masters would tell you to wait three years before expecting any results. My method is much faster. I tell students they'll start seeing results after thirty days of using the Five-Phase Routine. That's thirty-six times faster!

But you know what? Students still get impatient and have unreasonable expectations. You can't expect to heal a chronic illness in thirty days with fifteen minutes of qigong.

You need to approach qigong more like a long-term investment. You are not day trading stocks and looking for immediate gains. Rather, you are doing the slow and steady work of contributing to a long-term investment portfolio, but one that has excellent compounding interest over time.

17. Keep the eyes closed or half-closed.

Humans are easily distracted by shiny objects. Even beautiful scenery can sometimes distract us from our meditation. Closing our eyes can help us to stay in the Zen state.

There's a big caveat for this rule, however. For those dealing with trapped trauma, I recommend that you do not close your eyes, because this can trigger your subconscious into feeling unsafe. That is the opposite of what we're trying to achieve.

Instead, try closing your eyes halfway. Let the eyes relax and lose focus. You remain aware of your surroundings, but in a relaxed way. Try both options and see which works better for you. Whether you have trapped trauma or not, the goal is to stay in a meditative state without getting distracted.

18. Be comfortable.

Everything should be comfortable when you practice qigong. Wear comfortable clothing. Try different shoes, and also try barefoot. Avoid extreme temperatures both indoors and out. Make the qigong exercises as comfortable as possible. Make sure to avoid the standard Western concept of "no pain, no gain." With qigong, it should be the opposite. Our motto is simply, "no pain!"

19. Wait twenty minutes before/after eating.

Traditional teachers will tell you to wait one to two hours before and after eating. This rule will make a morning session impossible for some people. Luckily, we can modify it.

Most people find that they can practice comfortably (see Rule #17) with a twenty-minute buffer. If you need to eat in the morning, then eat. Then go practice after about twenty minutes. Or if you practice first, then wait about twenty minutes before eating.

20. Wait twenty minutes before/after showering.

Two of my teachers warned against showering or bathing within thirty minutes of practicing qigong. I've experimented with this for years and have to admit that there's some truth to it. The water seems to affect the energy somehow.

This rule, combined with the rule about food, can make it tricky to create a morning routine with qigong. It's not easy to figure out when to shower, when to eat, and when to do some qigong, especially if you have kids in the house.

Do your best, but please don't worry about this rule. It's listed here because it can't be dismissed entirely, but it is a minor issue.

21. Aim for twice daily.

Practicing twice a day creates momentum in the flow of qi. Twice daily is more than twice as powerful. If your goal is deep healing, then aim to do the Five-Phase Routine for ten to twenty minutes twice a day.

Compared to some methods that ask you to practice qigong for hours every day, this sounds easy, but it's not. It is doable even if you are a working parent, but it is not easy.

Luckily, the Two-Minute Drill counts as a second session. It won't give you as much momentum as the Five-Phase Routine, but it will give you a significant boost. Considering that it only takes two minutes, this is a great deal!

Start with the Two-Minute Drill once a day. Gradually turn that into a fifteen-minute session using the Five-Phase Routine. Then try to add a Two-Minute session at the end of your day. Once you get to this point, you will have a ton of momentum with your qigong. From there, it will be easier to add another session of the Five-Phase Routine.

22. Experiment.

Students often ask if they should do qigong before or after yoga. I get similar questions for running, strength training, sitting meditation, and tai chi.

My advice is to experiment. Some students prefer to do qigong first, and then go for a run. Others prefer the exact opposite.

Despite decades of teaching, I cannot predict which group you will fall into.

There is one caveat: Practicing qigong immediately after a high-intensity workout will make it harder to Enter Zen. This is not a deal breaker, but it's worth noticing. If you do your qigong first, you may find it easier to relax your nervous system, which of course is critical for deep healing.

23. Be skeptical. But stay open.

Be skeptical of what qigong masters say, including me. But also stay open and be willing to experiment. For example, I promise my students that thirty days of the Five-Phase Routine will give them a glimpse of what qigong can do. It's fine to be skeptical of this statement, but before you dismiss it, you first need to try it.

I was skeptical of qigong in the beginning too, and I didn't believe it would work. I'm so grateful that I stayed open to the possibilities.

Note: If you want a handy PDF of these rules, you can find one in your book bonuses.

The Proper Dosage of Qigong

For thousands of years, qigong has been viewed as medicine in China. Today, Western research is gradually recognizing the same thing. Qigong, tai chi, meditation, yoga—all of these arts should be viewed as medicine in the twenty-first century.

As with any medicine, the dosage is critical. So what is the proper dosage with an art like qigong? Or rather, what is the minimum dosage needed for deep healing?

First, let me give you some perspective. Some masters will simply tell you to practice as much as possible. It's not uncommon for them to tell you to practice three hours a day. If this were necessary for deep healing, then I would not be writing a book about qigong, because I'd be dead. I never could have practiced three hours a day while also battling depression.

But even if I did manage to survive, I would not be so passionate about spreading the word about qigong. A medication regimen that requires three hours of daily practice isn't practical for modern humans. We need something more streamlined.

Luckily, you don't need to practice qigong for three hours a day. You don't even need to practice one hour a day. I can confidently say that the minimum viable dosage for deep healing is only thirty minutes per day.

There's a catch, of course. To get the best results, you need to split those thirty minutes into two sessions. In other words, you need to do about fifteen minutes in the morning and another fifteen minutes in the afternoon or evening.

Sound doable? It is, but it's not as easy as it sounds. Carving out fifteen minutes for moving meditation twice per day is fairly challenging for modern humans. We can address this problem with habit building, but it's good to know what we're shooting for.

Students often ask for specific exercises for their specific problem. That's a reasonable request, but in most cases, it's not really the issue. Dosage is the real issue.

I typically ask these students how many times they've practiced the Five-Phase Routine over the last 365 days. For example, I'm looking for answers like this:

a) 730 times (twice daily)
b) 365 times (once daily)
c) 156 times (thrice weekly)
d) 104 times (twice weekly)

Your answer will indicate whether you're getting the proper dosage. For example, if you are battling chronic pain or illness but your answer is C, then the problem is simple enough. You need to increase the dosage!

Don't get me wrong. If you're doing the Five-Phase Routine three times per week, and perhaps using the Two-Minute Drill on other days, then you're off to a good start. There's lots to celebrate here!

But let's also be realistic. If you're doing 156 sessions per year, then that's only 21 percent of the minimum dosage. In other words, it's not your choice of qigong exercises that is the problem; your dosage is too low.

If a student tells me they're doing about 700 sessions per year, then that's a different story. In this case, the dosage is 82 percent correct! So we might need to look elsewhere for a solution. We'll cover this in the troubleshooting section later.

Honestly, people who practice over 600 times per year tend to get great results. Tweaking a few things might help them get better results, or they might need to learn more advanced techniques. But because qigong is so holistic, they'll enjoy many benefits.

For example, one student was practicing qigong twice per day and getting solid results. But she still had a minor health issue that wasn't responding. Learning a more advanced technique solved it for her within a few months. If you're not practicing enough in the first place, then advanced techniques won't help. That's because the dosage is the problem, not the medication.

Remember that dosage is not just a total count. Some medications require you to take them twice a day, not just once. This is because the effect of the medicine wears off. The same is true of qigong. If you practice once a day, then there are twenty-four hours between each session. During those twenty-four hours, your energy flow will gradually diminish. By the time you practice again the next day, the qi flow has dropped considerably.

But if you practice twice a day, then there are fewer hours between sessions. Now the qi flow doesn't have as much time to diminish. When you do your second session, the qi is still flowing from the previous session.

In other words, your qi flow starts to build its own momentum. This momentum raises the effectiveness of practice. In fact, practicing twice daily is *more* than twice as effective.

I want you to be healthy and happy. If you aren't yet getting the results that you want, then the first place to look is at the dosage of your medication. This is something that you have full control over. You *can* do it. In fact, no one else can do it for you.

It might take you a year to fully develop a twice-daily qigong habit. Along the way, you'll fall down several times. That's okay. Don't shame yourself if you struggle with this. Everyone falls.

But not everyone commits to getting up after a fall. Remember the wonderful Japanese phrase I mentioned earlier? I share it often with my students because it is so useful:

七転び八起き

Fall down seven times, stand up eight.

One thing that can help you to get up more easily is ritual, which we'll discuss in the next section.

The Power of Ritual

Had I known about the power of ritual earlier in my training, I would have avoided a lot of suffering. I can almost guarantee that you are suffering unnecessarily right now. Some of that suffering can be alleviated by embracing the power of ritual.

Humans have embraced the power of ritual for tens of thousands of years. Rituals are not outdated in the twenty-first century. If anything, we need them now more than ever.

Rituals need not be religious or mystical. For many of us, it's better if rituals remain secular. But secular doesn't mean devoid of a certain kind of magic. Here's a quote from the playwright Somerset Maugham:

"I write only when inspiration strikes. Fortunately it strikes every morning at nine o'clock sharp."

In other words, he created a ritual for his writing. Every morning, he would sit down at 9:00 a.m. sharp to write. We should do the same with qigong.

Rituals work in alignment with human psychology rather than against it. If you had full control over your subconscious mind, then you wouldn't need ritual. But you do not have full control, or even half control. Your subconscious mind is a powerful beast that barely listens to you. And it rules much of your life.

Ritual gives us command over the beast. For example, the ritual of the Five-Phase Routine gives us a framework for practicing an esoteric art like qigong. Every time we practice, we know that we need to take certain steps. Once those steps are habitualized, they become a ritual.

This ritual is self-reinforcing. The more you perform the ritual of the Five-Phase Routine, the stronger it gets.

Here are some ways to add ritual to your qigong practice:

- If you drink coffee every morning, try merging that ritual with qigong. Either practice qigong beforehand and use coffee as a reward, or use coffee as your pre-qigong ritual.

- Create a beautiful, dedicated practice space for qigong. When you see this space inside or outside your house, it should inspire you to practice. In my one-bedroom apartment, the entire living room is dedicated to qigong.

- Try the Seinfeld Method and get a wall calendar. Every day that you practice qigong, put a line through the day with a sharpie. If you practice twice, add another line, making an X. If you do three sessions, perhaps using the Two-Minute Drill, then draw a circle around the X.

- Try sunrise and/or sunset. Matching your qigong rhythm to the rhythm of the day can be powerful. This isn't easy if you have a fixed schedule, since sunrise and sunset change each day. But if you can manage to do it, then you'll have a ritual for life!

Mixing with Other Arts

Roughly half of my students have previously learned qigong from another teacher. Some of them have been practicing for a decade or more. Even those who are new to qigong may have practiced similar arts like yoga or sitting meditation.

If you already know some qigong exercises, and if you enjoy them, then don't abandon them. It's easy to mix them into the Five-Phase Routine. Just plug them into Phase 2.

The same is true of tai chi. Put sections of your tai chi forms into Phase 2. I'm a fan of doing individual tai chi patterns, or a short sequence of 1–6. I rarely go through the entire form.

Yoga, on the other hand, doesn't work well in Phase 2. That's because it's based on different principles, as mentioned earlier. Because of this, it's best to separate your yoga practice from your qigong practice.

If you have a solid yoga practice already, leave it as is for now. Just add qigong elsewhere to your day. Try to put your qigong session as far away from your yoga session as possible. This will give you more momentum. Practicing yoga one time per day plus the Five-Phase Routine one time per day should give you excellent benefits.

If you have a sitting meditation routine, then you can follow the same advice. Try putting it at the opposite end of the day. If you want to do a few qigong exercises immediately before or after your sitting meditation, that's fine too.

Should you practice yoga in the morning and qigong in the evening, or vice versa? I recommend that you experiment, as there is no one-size-fits-all answer. The only way to find out what works for you is to try both.

You can, of course, do your qigong back-to-back with your yoga or sitting meditation, but you will lose the benefit of momentum. So if you're doing yoga first thing in the morning, immediately followed by qigong, but then you don't do anything in the evenings, you will not benefit from the momentum effect described earlier.

If you want to sneak in a little qigong around your Western exercise, like weight training or tennis or running, then the Two-Minute Drill can work wonders. You can even do it between sets!

How to Troubleshoot Your Practice

If you're not getting the results that you want with qigong, then something is wrong. In the final analysis, qigong is a formula, just like strength training. If you lift weights correctly and regularly, then you will get stronger. Simple.

The good news is that you can troubleshoot your qigong practice to identify the problem. Here are some tips:

1. Are you measuring progress with a Qi Diary and a Qi Chart? Do you even have a Qi Chart and a Qi Diary? You need to accurately measure your progress before you can reasonably determine that there's a lack of progress. In many cases, there's plenty of progress, but you just didn't see it because you weren't writing things down.

2. Are you following the Three Golden Rules? If you're following them, could you maybe do a better job? Over 70 percent of practice problems can be solved by committing to the Three Golden Rules every practice session.

3. Are you following the 10/30/60 Rule? Are you paying attention to what's important, i.e., the breathing and the Zen Mind? Or are you fretting over something that's not important, like picture-perfect form?

4. Are you getting the proper dosage? First determine if you are healthy, or if you are dealing with chronic pain or illness. If you're healthy, then you should be doing at least 365 sessions per year. If you are not healthy, then you will need to double that.

5. Are your expectations reasonable? Students who have been suffering from a chronic problem for years and have already tried to resolve it often expect qigong to magically fix everything in three months or less. This is unreasonable, especially if you are not tracking your progress. Although you should see good results in three months, it will take time for you to heal on a deeper level.

6. Are you being a Negative Nancy? Humans are hardwired to notice the negative, not the positive. If we do this with our qigong, then we will create a negative feedback loop. The more negative you are, the more you block the flow of qi in your body. Start to notice what's getting better, not what's still the same.

7. Do you have an awesome teacher? When it comes to learning the violin or tennis, everyone knows that you need a good teacher. But when it comes to qigong, people in the West get a little weird. For some reason, many people think that they can learn qigong without a teacher. Yes, a book can be a teacher, and so can YouTube. But also remember that books, DVDs, and YouTube are a one-way interaction. That's why a teacher is so important—so you can ask questions, get clarification, and most importantly, get inspiration. Some teachers get so well-known that they have too many students. If your teacher doesn't know your name, then they can only help you to go so far. It's up to *you* to go find a teacher with whom you can build a long-term relationship.

Which Qigong Exercise Should You Practice?

Which qigong exercise should you practice for chronic knee pain? What about irritable bowel syndrome? How about anxiety attacks? Or diabetes? Or Parkinson's Disease?

Look, I know you want to get results with your problem. To do that, to get results in the real world, we need to dig a little deeper. We can't just match a qigong exercise to a Western diagnosis and magically solve a longstanding health problem.

By this point in the book, you should have a better understanding of the subtle, invisible skills of qigong. You already know what matters in qigong and what doesn't. Choosing the appropriate qigong exercises matters, but it matters less than other factors, especially if you are already doing the Five-Phase Routine.

Years ago, I did a series of workshops in Orlando, Florida. A fifty-something woman, let's call her Martha, signed up for all of them. She had been doing qigong for years with other teachers, including some Chinese masters. But here's what you need to know about Martha's qigong: It was truly awful.

We're not talking about her form. A student from another school of qigong might have totally different techniques than mine. I might not even know the exercises, but I can still recognize the skill underneath.

With Martha, the skill wasn't there. Nada. She was practicing qigong purely on a physical level. She had zero awareness of the internal aspects of this art.

Because none of her other teachers had emphasized these aspects, Martha had trouble accepting what I was trying to teach her in the workshop. For example, I encouraged her to butcher the form, but she didn't listen. She opened her eyes during sessions, watched me like a hawk as I demonstrated the exercises, and asked irrelevant questions about the physical form. All of my teachings about the internal secrets of qigong were lost on her.

Later in the workshop, Martha asked if I knew a good exercise for back pain. It was at this moment that I realized she was what we call a "technique junkie." People like Martha can be found in many arts, from yoga to tai chi to qigong. They bounce from teacher to teacher collecting new exercises, yet they always remain on the surface of the art.

Here's where I often get into trouble with other teachers. If you're teaching Medical Qigong, then you're practicing a branch of Chinese Medicine. But if you're also telling students that X exercise will fix Y symptoms, then this doesn't mesh with Chinese Medicine theory.

The defining characteristic of Chinese Medicine is that it is holistic. This means that the treatments take the whole person into account, not just the most obvious symptoms. In fact, Western diagnoses like diabetes don't even exist in Chinese Medicine. If you are prescribing specific qigong exercises for symptoms like back pain but aren't treating the whole person and taking their mind and emotions into account—then it's not holistic. And if it's not holistic, it ain't Chinese Medicine.

I'm not saying anything radical here. Any professor from any acupuncture college would agree. But it still gets me into trouble with other qigong teachers and students, and here's why: This truth raises uncomfortable questions about a teacher's actual depth of understanding of Chinese Medicine.

Martha was aghast after I tried to explain that the specific exercise was not as important as the skill underneath. Her response was typical: "But my master said that . . ." I would have been happy to discuss her master's theories and compare them to the fundamental principles of Chinese Medicine, but that's not really what she was saying. What she was *really* saying was, "I refuse to believe that my master, who is Chinese and has a really cute accent, could possibly be wrong!"

This is a widespread phenomenon in the qigong and tai chi community. Far too many qigong teachers are brimming with ego and bravado. There's one qigong master who—as a matter of policy—never admits when he's wrong. He firmly believes that it's bad for the students' morale if they see that he's fallible. Yikes!

With attitudes like that, no wonder Martha was unable to accept that her teacher could be wrong! As you might expect, these teachers and their students don't really take kindly to someone raising uncomfortable questions about their methods. Sadly, the reaction from them always involves mudslinging.

Some teachers might argue that *all* qigong is holistic and that prescribing X exercise for Y condition still follows the principles of Chinese Medicine. Actually, I almost agree with this argument. Almost. If you're practicing Medical Qigong exercises but just doing the physical motions—then it's not an internal art. In other words, if you're just doing Phase 2 of the Five-Phase Routine and are completely ignoring the other phases, then your qigong is not holistic. It can barely even be called medicine.

An analogy may help you to understand better. Imagine two people practicing sitting meditation. One of them is sitting in a perfect double lotus meditation posture. The other is sitting on a chair.

Which one of them will get better results? Well, this depends on who is meditating! What if the person in the perfect lotus posture is constantly thinking about work? What if the person in the chair is consistently entering into a Zen state?

Just like in qigong, the physical aspect of sitting meditation is the least important thing for getting results. If you are not practicing sitting meditation as an internal art, then you won't get the results that you deserve. Simple.

Even if I had given Martha the absolute best qigong technique for her problem, it wasn't going to help. She would just take the technique and perform it on a physical level, ignoring the internal aspects of qigong. When it comes to back pain, the internal aspects are especially important.

Matching X exercise to Y problem ignores the elephant in the room. Skill is everything in qigong. But skill is also invisible and internal, making it harder to teach. Here's a great quotation:

"For the unskilled, the best technique won't help. For the skillful, even an inferior technique will suffice."

—Ke An Dao

Like that quote? I like it too. That's because I made it up. Ke An Dao is my Chinese name.

Even after this lengthy explanation, I know that people will still send me emails asking what exercise they should practice. In fact, I get them all the time. Want a simpler answer?

Let's pretend that you've just asked me which qigong exercises you should practice for _____ condition. Here's my answer, no matter what you put in that blank:

You should practice the following twelve exercises:

1. Entering Zen
2. Smiling from the Heart
3. Lifting the Sky
4. Pushing Mountains
5. Flowing Breeze Swaying Willow
6. Flowing Stillness
7. Consolidating Qi at Dantian
8. Washing the Face with Both Hands
9. Combing the Hair with the Fingers
10. Massaging the Vital Points
11. Rubbing Two Coins
12. Twenty-Four Heavenly Drums

If you've gone through your book bonuses, you will get the joke here. It's a trick answer. The exercises just described form the basis of the Five-Phase Routine. Except for Steps #3 and #4, we do all of these exercises during *every* practice session. As you learn additional exercises, you can swap them out for Lifting the Sky or Pushing Mountains.

Far too many qigong teachers are *only* concerned with #3 and #4. Sometimes they add #7 and #10. Rarely do they teach all the steps.

Looking at the exercises above, most of them focus on *internal* skills rather than external ones:

- Entering Zen and Smiling from the Heart get us into a meditative state.
- Lifting the Sky and Pushing Mountains are dynamic qigong exercises that help get our energy flowing.
- Flowing Breeze Swaying Willow circulates the qi through the meridians.
- Flowing Stillness and Consolidating Qi at Dantian help us store qi at our natural energy center.
- Steps #8–12 are part of what we call the Closing Sequence, a self-massage sequence that helps us transition back from a meditative state and also brings energy to the eyes and face.

Stop wondering which exercise you should practice for a specific problem. Instead, get good at the Five-Phase Routine. From there, you can start to tap into one of the most powerful forces in the universe: your intuition.

How to Plan Your Qigong Routine

Years ago, I frequently did private sessions with my students. In these sessions, I would ask a series of questions, and then select the best qigong routine for their situation. Back then, I didn't have any online courses, so I also had to teach them all of the exercises, as well as the Five-Phase Routine itself.

This process was effective, but expensive. A student could easily spend $500–$1000 on private lessons to get a customized prescription and learn all the exercises. This made it unaffordable to many people.

Luckily, I discovered a method that is more efficient and affordable. This method is simple, and you can start implementing it right now. Here it is:

1. Learn the Five-Phase Routine.
2. Learn at least twenty-five different qigong exercises.
3. Intuitively choose a handful of favorites and focus on those.

This approach is more sophisticated than it might seem. Your body has tremendous wisdom in it. When you tap into that hidden wisdom using intuition, your body knows what it needs. In fact, it often does a better job than if you saw me privately!

I like to compare this to a pregnant woman choosing food intuitively. She doesn't need to see a nutritionist or even read labels. If she just follows her cravings, she'll naturally get the nutrition that she and the baby require.

Choose your qigong exercises like a pregnant woman with cravings. These cravings may change from week to week, and that's fine too. Keep following those cravings and learn to listen to your intuition.

You need a working repertoire of roughly twenty-five exercises so that you have a sufficient pool from which to draw. In time, you will learn fifty or one hundred exercises. Along the way, you'll continue to find favorites. At the same time, you'll gradually let go of the exercises that you don't need.

By choosing your favorite qigong exercises, you'll be much more likely to practice. This will naturally increase your dosage of qigong. Remember that the dosage is critical and matters far more than the exercises that you choose! You'll also be more likely to *enjoy* your practice. This is Rule #3 of the Three Golden Rules. It is vital for getting results.

Gradually, you'll get better at following your intuition. You'll settle on exercises that are a perfect fit for your energy and your body right now. A year later, you may switch to a completely different routine.

I first started sharing this intuitive method before I was teaching online. Now that my students have an extensive online library of qigong exercises, they can review much more easily. This relieves the pressure of having to memorize every detail of every technique, allowing them to maintain an even bigger repertoire.

In the old days, you had to keep this library in your head. If you were literate, you could write down the names of the techniques, perhaps with a few crude drawings. This assumes that you could afford paper, which was not cheap.

I did something similar in the 1990s. Back then, you couldn't just go online to watch a video, and you were lucky to find books with pictures. Whenever I learned a new exercise, I wrote it down in what I jokingly referred to as The Sacred Scrolls. I wrote the name of the exercise and a short description to spur my memory.

Today, you can just log in to the Flowing Zen Academy and review whatever you have learned. There's no need for sacred scrolls, and you don't even need paper. This is a fantastic resource, and it will help you to gradually master the exercises you love the most.

I should mention that this method of choosing favorites will not work as well without the framework of the Five-Phase Routine. When you practice specific qigong exercises, you are moving the energy to and through certain organs and meridians. For example, when you practice Plucking Stars from the Eighteen Luohan Hands, then you are cultivating the energy in the Spleen and Stomach Meridians.

That might sound good, but Chinese Medicine is more complicated than that. Maybe the problem *seems* like it's in your digestive system, but it's actually in your Kidney Meridian instead. What happens if you move qi to the wrong meridian?

The Five-Phase Routine is the great equalizer. Even if you choose exercises that move qi to the wrong meridian, the qi will redirect to the proper destination during Flowing Breeze Swaying Willow. It's like an automatic guidance system.

Except for Phase 2, most of the Five-Phase remains the same from day to day. This gives us the best of both worlds. We get variation, the spice of life, in Phase 2. And we get consistency in the other three phases.

Remember that this is a lifelong journey. Even if you're seventy years old, there's plenty of time to learn new material! Five years from now, you may have a totally different repertoire of techniques—but you'll still be using them within the framework of the Five-Phase Routine.

Learn 100, Forget 75

I've explained why you should learn at least twenty-five different qigong exercises. Does that seem like a lot? If so, then fasten your seat belt because I actually think you should learn one hundred exercises in order to find your favorite twenty-five.

While at Columbia, I had to read dozens of books on a wide range of topics. This is known as the Core Curriculum, and it is the cornerstone of the educational mission at Columbia. Regardless of your major, you must read books on literature, philosophy, history, music, science, and art. I still have over one hundred of these books on my bookshelf.

I don't remember everything that I read, probably not even 25 percent of it. And if I'm honest, I probably won't read most of those books ever again. And yet, reading them was one of the best things I ever did.

Reading those books stretched and strengthened my mind. It offered a peek into the minds of the greatest artists and thinkers from Western Civilization and also taught me who my favorite authors are. In other words, Columbia accomplished its goal of providing me with a liberal arts education.

Today, there is tremendous value in bringing this liberal arts type of approach to qigong. Never before have students had the opportunity to peek into the minds (Zen minds, in this case) of past qigong masters. By learning a variety of techniques, you will stretch and strengthen your own Zen mind.

My school of qigong is a lot like a university. I aim to give students a liberal arts education in qigong. In the end, I want you to figure out not which types of qigong are best, but which types are best for *you*.

I think every qigong student should take this approach. Today, you can learn from a dozen qigong masters without ever leaving your home. I'm not suggesting that you overwhelm yourself with tons of techniques. Fortunately, with the ability to review the exercises and teachings on the internet, you won't be overwhelmed with having to memorize everything.

There are literally thousands of qigong exercises out there. If you learn twenty-five of them per year for four years (a reasonable goal), then you'll have learned one hundred total. But you probably won't remember them all just like I don't remember all the books I read in college.

I want you to understand that it's okay to forget qigong exercises. This is all part of your liberal arts education in qigong. After learning one hundred exercises, you will probably only remember twenty-five. But those twenty-five will be the absolute best ones for *you*. Through your own experience, will have come up with the perfectly customized set of exercises.

For example, Sinew Metamorphosis, one of the traditional qigong sets that I teach, is unusual. It uses subtle contractions of the muscles and fascia to stimulate the flow of energy. If you've only ever done gentle qigong exercises, then this set will be an eye-opener.

Some people absolutely love Sinew Metamorphosis. For others, it's just not their cup of tea. Either way, it's valuable to learn Sinew Metamorphosis so that you get exposed to other types of qigong. How can you know which foods you like if you always eat the same thing?

I call this liberal arts method "Learn 100, Forget 75." Learn one hundred exercises, forget seventy-five of them, and settle on twenty-five of your absolute favorites. In the twenty-first century, this is the best way to develop the ultimate qigong routine.

Success Story: Jim

In 2018, Jim was diagnosed with glaucoma by an ophthalmologist in Washington, D.C. The doctor prescribed eye drops, one in each eye every night. Around the same time, Jim's wife found Flowing Zen online.

Jim started practicing qigong the same week and faithfully did his exercises for six months. When he went back for a semi-annual exam, his doctor was shocked. He had never seen such a profound improvement in a case of glaucoma. The doctor's use of the word "profound" made a powerful impression on Jim and bolstered his faith in qigong.

Of course, Jim used both the prescribed eye drops as well as qigong. Nevertheless, the shock on the doctor's face convinced him that qigong had contributed greatly to his recovery. Otherwise, all the doctor's patients would get similar results just with medication, which wasn't the case. The combination of qigong plus the drops resulted in profound results.

Since then, Jim's glaucoma has not progressed. In fact, a recent exam showed a slight improvement. Jim told me that he's "sticking with qigong." He's sold on the benefits!

CHAPTER 8
Qigong without All the Bull$h!t

Many of my newer students, after falling in love with qigong, ask the following question: Why isn't qigong more popular? It's an important question. If qigong is such an amazing art, then why aren't billions of people practicing it?

In my opinion, there is one thing that is holding qigong back from its rightful place in the modern healthcare landscape; that thing is called bullshit. Pardon my French, but there really is no other word for it. Not all qigong teachers are shoveling bullshit, but far too many of them are. This frustrates me to no end because these teachers are holding the art back. Meanwhile, people are suffering and in desperate need of qigong like I was.

For years, I have worked hard to present qigong to my students free from bullshit. In fact, a student once suggested that I change my logo to the following:

Flowing Zen—Qigong without All the Bullshit

That pretty much sums up my approach to teaching qigong. It also explains why students from all over the world are attracted to my website. People are searching for a no-BS approach. That's how they ended up on my blog.

Here are some common examples of bullshit in the qigong community:

- Teachers who irresponsibly sell qigong as a panacea or cure-all
- Teachers who directly or indirectly condone sexual, emotional, verbal, or physical abuse
- Teachers who do not practice what they preach
- Teachers who do not embody what they teach
- Teachers who embrace hierarchical structures that promote corruption
- Teachers who embrace dogma in the name of tradition
- Teachers who use outdated, ineffective teaching methodologies
- Teachers who intentionally mystify the art
- Teachers who tell you that your form must be perfect
- Teachers who overly complicate qigong theory
- Teachers who create a cult of personality
- Teachers who refuse to use modern marketing tools (ahem, like the internet)
- Teachers who defend the tradition of secrecy
- Teachers who disempower students

For example, I once saw my primary teacher, Grandmaster Liu, encourage a student to discard her antipsychotic medications. "Just throw them away," he said enthusiastically. "Qigong can cure you!" She was a dutiful student, so she literally threw her meds in the garbage. A few days later, she had a psychotic break and had to be taken to the hospital. (She was fine once she got back on her antipsychotic meds.)

This woman was not to blame—she trusted her teacher. He was to blame. But the disciples who turned a blind eye to Grandmaster Liu's irresponsible advice were and still are complicit. I include myself in that category.

Grandmaster Liu's mantra is that qigong can cure anything and everything. This is a half-truth that is just an unethical marketing technique. Qigong is powerful, but it is irresponsible to oversell it to people who are desperate for healing. I know because I was one of them. (Read chapter 5 for the full truth on what can and cannot be healed with qigong.)

For too long, I deferred to Grandmaster Liu even though I should have known better. I should have spoken up. He is to blame, but so am I. If you've been in the qigong community for a while, then you've already seen your share of bullshit. You've probably seen things that made you cringe. Did you speak up?

A student told me that one of her teachers forced her to continue doing qigong for hours despite crippling shoulder pain. This poor woman was literally crying from the pain, tears rolling down her cheeks, but the teacher just told her to continue. Her fellow classmates, many of them long-term disciples, did the same. Peer pressure is a powerful thing.

And so this woman suffered terribly and unnecessarily. By the time she found me, she was traumatized. Thank God she didn't give up on qigong! (You'll be glad to hear that she now loves qigong and has fixed her shoulder.)

Another woman told me that her teacher threw her to the ground during class under the pretense of helping her clear emotional blockages. Let me be clear that this was a Medical Qigong class, not a martial arts class. What the actual f#$k? This is abuse, plain and simple.

Another student told me about a qigong master who still claims that qigong can cure cancer even after several of his disciples died of cancer. His explanation is that it was karma. In other words, qigong can cure cancer—except when it can't. Always read the fine print folks!

The stories are endless. I receive them in my inbox every week, and they are always heartbreaking. And I have my own heartbreaking story too.

Why I Left My Master after Seventeen Years

I've been working up the courage to tell you my own heartbreaking story. I left Grandmaster Liu in late 2014 because of a sexual abuse scandal. The abuse was perpetrated by one of his certified instructors, not by Grandmaster Liu himself. Nevertheless, the way that he handled the scandal was unethical and just plain wrong. The scandal showed me, without a shadow of a doubt, that despite his skill in qigong, he lacked integrity.

I won't go into the gory details. I have a lengthy blog post where I blew the whistle on the scandal, presenting all my evidence (which took me over a year to compile). Read it if you must. Either way, you should know that I received death threats for publishing that article, as well as threats of legal action. Empty threats, yes, but threats nonetheless. I also lost dozens of friends, including some close ones.

The thing to understand is that international organizations like Grandmaster Liu's school are rife with abuse, whether it is sexual, emotional, verbal, or physical. This pattern is common in yoga schools, tai chi schools, and Zen schools. The sad truth is that teachers often abuse their power and take advantage of their students.

And then, as happened with my ex-teacher, people in power try to sweep the abuse under the carpet to protect the organization. I left the organization and left him, because it was the right thing to do. I left because I wanted to keep the trust of my students, especially my female students. If I tacitly condoned abuse by allowing my teacher to sweep it under the rug, how could they ever trust me again? How could they ever feel safe in my classes?

And so I blew the whistle on the scandal. The zealots from Grandmaster Liu's organization attacked me for "betraying" the master. How ironic that they chose that word. If anything, it was Grandmaster Liu who betrayed his students.

To make things worse, Grandmaster Liu literally said that my betrayal was worse than rape. In other words, blowing the whistle on the scandal was worse than the actual scandal. You can't make this stuff up!

I originally chose Grandmaster Liu because I thought that he had integrity. Unfortunately, it took me seventeen years to figure out that I was wrong about him. I don't want you to make the same mistake that I did.

I've forgiven him and moved on. I should point out that forgiveness here does not mean that I condone what he did. It simply means that I have stopped drinking poison and expecting the other person to die. I sleep well at night knowing that I did the right thing, that I acted with courage to protect the victims, that I stood against my teacher, and that I worked to keep the respect of my students.

Stories like this are not uncommon in the world of qigong. Since I blew the whistle in 2014, countless women have come to me, discreetly, to tell me their horror stories. I not only met two more victims from Grandmaster Liu's organization, but victims from other schools and from other arts.

I don't want to dissuade you from learning qigong. I have tried to inspire you through this book. I hope you can see how much I love this art. I love it so much that I want to reclaim it from hierarchical organizations that are rife with abuse. I want you to discover qigong without all this bullshit.

Don't be afraid as you navigate the world of qigong teachers. Simply keep an eye out for potential abuse, from both male and female teachers. The sad truth is that hurt people hurt people; and many people have been hurt. Hopefully, they will rise above their trauma but there's still the possibility of passing it on to the next generation.

The Guru Trap

The guru tradition is an Indian one, not a Chinese one. But the word has become ubiquitous. For Westerners, all the various master/disciple relationships blend together into what I call the Guru Trap.

You want to avoid this trap. Let me be absolutely clear: it is dangerous. If you are battling a serious health issue, then it can even be deadly.

One of the best compliments I've ever received came from a well-respected, progressive Rabbi from NYC. We had met in Costa Rica, and he later invited me to teach qigong at his synagogue. Over dinner, he said that he was pleasantly surprised by my teaching. "You're like an un-guru," he said, smiling.

I love this. I don't want to be anyone's guru. I want to be my own guru. And I want you to do the same.

I am not criticizing the guru-disciple tradition of India. It seems to have worked for them for centuries. In rare cases, Westerners have developed healthy guru/disciple relationships with Indian masters. The same is true of Chinese masters. There are some success stories.

But the number of horror stories is far too high to ignore. The guru/disciple tradition—whether it is of the Indian, Chinese, Korean, or Japanese variety—does not function smoothly in the West. You have been warned.

After I left Grandmaster Liu, I began to dig into this topic. I scoured the internet for articles and blogs and bought every book on the topic. I talked to colleagues in and out of the qigong community. And I meditated deeply on my own journey as both a disciple and a teacher.

My research showed me that my negative experience with the Guru Trap is not uncommon. In fact, it is the norm for Westerners. Scott Edelstein catalogs abusive behavior of a variety of Eastern spiritual teachers in his book, *Sex and the Spiritual Teacher: Why It Happens, When It's a Problem, and What We All Can Do.* It's worth reading, and Edelstein also offers some practical solutions, many of which I immediately implemented in my teachings.

The book points to a larger problem in the meeting of East and West. It's not just about sex. What if the entire master-disciple relationship is flawed? In my opinion, the tradition needs to be overhauled if it is going to thrive in the West. We need something fresh, something modern. We need to find a way to show respect to a teacher without it turning it into worship.

When I left Grandmaster Liu, many of my friends and colleagues couldn't bring themselves to leave the organization. I know in my heart that these people don't condone sexual abuse. And even if they do believe that I betrayed Grandmaster Liu, I still don't believe they really think that my betrayal is worse than rape.

And yet they stayed. These otherwise good people are stuck in the Guru Trap. They may never escape, even after Grandmaster Liu dies. Or worse, they may perpetuate the tradition by unwittingly trapping their own students.

I'm grateful to Grandmaster Liu for giving me such a powerful, if painful, lesson. It was a wake-up call. As a result, my entire approach to teaching has changed for the better.

Why I Still Use the Sifu Title

Despite all of this, I still use the *Sifu* title for myself. It's an honorific title that simply means "teacher," with subtle connotations of mastery. Although it sounds a bit like the word "guru," it doesn't have the same meaning. Specifically, it does not imply that a sifu is a spiritual teacher.

I don't think anyone out there, even my worst critics, would argue that I haven't earned the title of sifu. In fact, I earned it the traditional way—which is to have *other* people call you sifu for years before you even start teaching. People called me sifu and asked me to teach for a long time before I relented.

But should I still use the title? After I left Grandmaster Liu, I polled my students to get their thoughts. The result was an almost perfect 50/50 split. Keep in mind that all these students had sided with me in the scandal, so they were not stuck in the Guru Trap. Nevertheless, I listened intently to their opinions.

Half of the students said that the title was helpful. It helped to clearly draw the lines of the relationship. This makes sense to me. I called my college professors by their title and it felt right. However, one of my professors was a famous writer who held his office hours at the local bar (I kid you not). He didn't like this title, so we called him by his first name, and it always felt weird to me. Or perhaps it was the bourbon and cigarettes?

I am younger than many of my students. For them, the sifu title is especially helpful because it clarifies the nature of our relationship. I am their teacher, their coach, their mentor, their advisor, their advocate. Yes, we can go grab a coffee together and we can be friendly. But when a student uses the sifu title, it instantly clarifies the nature of our relationship. It tells me, in a word, that I'm on duty.

On the other hand, half of my students disliked the title. After the scandal, it left a bad taste in their mouth. For seventeen years, I called Grandmaster Liu "Sifu," so I know that taste all too well.

When I asked these students what they would prefer to call me, I got several answers. Some preferred to call me by my first name. Others preferred to call me Mr. Korahais. A few wanted to call me "coach" or "teech." And one student suggested that we come up with a nickname, offering "Big Tony" as a humorous option.

The nickname stuck. In case you don't get the joke, I'm 5'7" and weigh about 155 pounds. I have a big personality perhaps, but I'm not a large man. The nickname made people smile, including me. It still does.

Today, students call me many things, from Sifu to Big Tony to Anthony. Ironically, a few Indian students call me "sifu-ji," which is a combination of Chinese and Indian honorifics. Whatever a student wants to call me is fine.

The key for Westerners is to feel sufficient respect for the teacher without veering into worship. Feeling that respect is the important part. Someone can use respectful words without actually feeling any respect. Meanwhile, a student can call me Big Tony and still feel deep respect for me and my teachings.

This respect is for your benefit, not mine. It's the same respect that you should show a college professor or a violin teacher. Respect puts the student in the proper learning mindset, what Zen master Shunryu Suzuki called the Beginner's Mind.

Sifu is my traditional title, and I'll keep it. Believe it or not, this is my way of showing respect to all the great masters who came before me. I won't let Grandmaster Liu ruin that tradition for me or my students.

Call me whatever feels right. I promise that you will not offend me. Don't ever feel pressured to call me Sifu. When in doubt, just call me Big Tony, and we'll all have a chuckle.

How to Spot Bullshit in Teachers

Let's talk about practical ways to avoid BS in qigong teachers. The truth is that you may not be able to avoid it 100 percent. If you have an otherwise good teacher who shovels, say, 20 percent bullshit, then focus on the 80 percent that is not. Here are some tips:

1. How does the teacher look?

It amazes me how many teachers look absolutely terrible. Their skin is pale, their eyes are dull, their posture is awful, their voice is weak, and they have no pep in their step. Or worse, they have a beer belly but try to pass it off as a "qi belly." Puhleeese!

Look at your teacher objectively. Do they look healthy? Be honest with yourself. Don't make excuses for him or her. It doesn't matter what certifications or titles they might have. It doesn't even matter who their teacher was. If they look unhealthy, then they aren't a good role model for self-healing. They either aren't practicing what they preach, or what they preach doesn't work. Either way, it means that they are shoveling big piles of manure.

2. What kind of students do they produce?

If a teacher is repeatedly producing students who get great results, then this is a good sign. In other words, you're not just looking at the teacher, but also looking at her students. There's a well-known phrase in Chinese:

名師出高徒
Ming shi chu gao tu
Great masters generate excellent disciples.

Look for multiple success stories. I once met a qigong teacher who constantly referred to the same success story over and over. No other success stories were ever mentioned. Considering how many students this teacher had, I found it odd. Even if the one success story was genuine, it didn't speak well for the average student's chances in his qigong school.

If your teacher is local, then you should be able to talk with other students and hear their stories directly. If your teacher is online, then you should be able to find lots of heartfelt testimonials on their website. Hopefully, there is also a way for you to interact with other students online and get their stories.

3. Can they teach?

Back in my violin days, I studied with a world-class violinist for a few months. He was, without a doubt, the best violin player I have ever studied with. But he was also, without a doubt, the worst violin teacher I ever had.

There are people out there who are highly skillful in their art, but they can't teach worth a damn. If you're an advanced student, like I was with the violin, then you may still be able to learn from this kind of teacher. You'll need to be strategic in your learning, but it's possible.

If you are not advanced, however, then run the other way. This kind of teacher, despite their skill, can be a disaster for an intermediate or beginning student. Avoid them until you are more advanced.

And if a teacher is both unskillful and also a bad teacher, then what the hell are you doing? Get out of there, pronto! This is precisely the kind of BS we're trying to avoid.

4. Do they hurt people?

As with any art, bad teachers can be dangerous. Whether it's yoga, karate, or qigong, a bad teacher can hurt you physically, mentally, and emotionally. Don't let this scare you away from qigong, but do let it scare you away from bad teachers!

Make sure to account for what we call "growing pains." In the early stages of practicing qigong, even within the first few hours, students often experience various growing pains, like a burning sensation in their feet, or a dull ache in an old injury, or even mild nausea. These are good signs, and they are temporary. They show that the energy is flowing, and the healing is starting. A good teacher will address these growing pains and explain them in a way that makes sense.

But if students are constantly getting dizzy, having palpitations, or feeling severe nausea in class, and if the teacher typically dismisses or ignores these problems—then you've got a problem. Either the teacher doesn't know how to handle these problems, or the qigong is inappropriate for beginners, or both.

Obviously, if the teacher verbally, physically, or sexually abuses students—run like hell. Believe me, I know how hard it can be to leave a teacher like this. But if I could leave my abusive teacher, so can you.

5. Can they answer questions?

A modern teacher needs to be able to intelligently answer a wide variety of questions. The answers should leave you satisfied, like a good meal. If the answers leave you hungry, or nauseous, then you've probably spotted some BS.

Question your teachers. Do it respectfully but do it often. Some teachers will be fluent in both Eastern and Western terminology, and some won't. But regardless of terminology, they should offer intelligent answers.

Be honest about your own experiences. For example, if you are feeling some discomfort while doing a particular qigong exercise, then talk to your teacher about it. Don't try to hide it or push through. This is an opportunity to see whether your teacher can give you a good answer. If not, then it's time to search for another teacher.

6. How much training do they have?

Forget about certifications. Forget about shiny suits. Forget about titles. The first thing you need to look at is how much training a teacher has.

Teachers will have varying amounts of training in qigong and other arts. For example, a teacher might have three years of qigong training, but twelve years of additional sitting meditation training. Or a teacher might have three years of qigong training, but seven years of Shiatsu training, which uses many of the principles of Chinese Medicine. Both teachers might have something valuable to offer you.

If you want a high-level teacher, then choose someone with over a decade of total experience. The two teachers described above, for example, have fifteen and ten years of total experience respectively.

A teacher with ten to fifteen years of experience entirely in qigong would probably be an even better choice.

Personally, I think that some of their training should be teacher-specific. In other words, if your teacher has only ever trained as a student and has zero hours of teacher training, then it might be a problem. You'll spot the problem because they will not be good teachers. They may also lack proper ethical behavior because they were never taught.

Ask questions. For example, if you were to ask me about my training, I would say something like this: I've been practicing qigong since 1997; I did a seventeen-year discipleship with a Chinese master; I was his chief instructor in the US for years; I've been teaching professionally since 2005; I have certified forty instructors; I was on the board of directors for the National Qigong Association; I did over fifteen hundred hours of Chinese Medicine training at an accredited acupuncture college; and I also did teacher training in the Suzuki Violin Method, which is unrelated but definitely made me a better teacher.

Not all teachers will have as much training as I do; some teachers will have more. Their total experience should not be the only criterion, but it should be included in your assessment.

7. Do they understand Chinese Medicine?

Qigong is a major branch of Chinese Medicine. Many qigong teachers are also acupuncturists and thus have plenty of training in Chinese Medicine. Don't expect all teachers to have this much training, but it can be a nice bonus. If a qigong teacher doesn't know a thing about Chinese Medicine, or if they reject it outright, that's a bad sign.

8. Do they inspire you?

Do you feel uplifted when you interact with your teacher? Do they inspire you with their experience, their results, their energy, and their confidence? Do they always know the perfect thing to say to help get you back on track? If so, then you probably have a good teacher.

Bad teachers have trouble inspiring their students because they aren't inspired themselves. They can't lead by example. If you aren't healthy, how can you inspire students to become healthy? If you haven't practiced daily for years, then how can you inspire students to practice regularly?

Watch out for bravado. Some teachers puff themselves up to seem inspiring. This false bravado is easy to spot in teachers (and also politicians).

9. Do they have integrity?

A teacher should have high moral standards. There should be tell-tale signs of integrity, kindness, courage, sincerity, and honesty. Basically, they should be a good person.

If you suspect that the teacher lacks integrity, then get the hell out of there, no matter what their skill level. As I mentioned earlier, it took me years to acknowledge that my own master lacked integrity. Perhaps he had changed over the years, or perhaps I was looking the other way for too long. But when I finally saw how things were, I left, even though it was incredibly painful to do so.

10. Do they talk about qigong as a panacea?

Too many qigong teachers present the art as a panacea. As discussed, this is a half-truth. According to qigong theory, it can heal an incredibly wide range of ailments. But to say that it will cure anything and everything is just irresponsible. Qigong can bring benefits, but it is not a panacea.

Modern teachers, whether they are Asian or Western, should be responsible with their words and honest about their results. They should clearly explain what qigong can and cannot heal. See chapter 5 for more on this.

11. Is there a hierarchy?

The traditional hierarchy in qigong and kung fu is modeled after a large family. The word *sifu* actually means "teacher-father." In this tradition, there are titles for every person in your larger family, from your classmates to your teacher's classmates. It's a dizzying list of Chinese words to memorize.

Problems arise when this familial model becomes a military hierarchy, with more senior family members giving orders to junior ones. It's especially problematic when you have a Grandmaster at the top of the hierarchy who likes to play pharaoh.

It's not always easy to sift out the BS from Chinese tradition. My best advice is to trust your gut. Does the hierarchy make you feel uncomfortable? Does your teacher act more like a celebrity or royalty than a human being?

12. Is there a method?

A good methodology will save you years if not decades of time. Although Grandmaster Liu was a decent teacher, he did not have a good methodology, and my learning was haphazard. For example, it took me a decade to learn all eighteen Luohan Hands, a qigong set that I now teach in less than one year online.

If there had been a better methodology, I could have gone much faster. In the twenty-first century, it's entirely reasonable to expect a qigong teacher to have a curriculum. If the teaching is too haphazard, you will probably get faster results from someone with a clearer methodology.

15. Is there too much emphasis on the physical form?

Many qigong teachers are so focused on the physical form that they don't know what else to teach. If you want to continue learning from a form-based instructor, perhaps because she is local and there is a good community with the classes, that's fine. Be polite in class, but in your own mind, it's important to remember that the physical aspect is the least important thing in qigong.

The Bottom Line

Spotting bullshit in a teacher will save you time, money, and frustration. If you are in desperate need of healing, like I was when I started qigong, then spotting a bad teacher might even save your life. Take the time and put in the energy to find a good one.

These days, you can sample many different teachers online, which is simply amazing. I traveled all over the US and eventually to Asia to find a good teacher. Take advantage of online learning and find a teacher who you connect with.

A good rule of thumb is to give a teacher six to twelve months before moving on. If you give it your best shot for six to twelve months but don't get good results, then look for another teacher. Of course, if you don't practice or don't follow the method, then you can't blame the teacher. On the other hand, a good teacher can help you to develop a daily qigong habit.

Some traditional teachers will tell you that you can only learn one style of qigong at a time. This is rarely true. Different types of qigong are usually complementary even when they offer conflicting advice. Problems only arise when one of those teachers is bad. In that case, learning from multiple teachers will help you to quickly identify the inferior teacher!

My final advice when it comes to choosing a teacher is this: beware of teachers who talk endlessly about "lineage." Since lineage is such a big topic in the world of qigong, let's take a closer look at it.

Lineage Schmineage

Let me begin by saying that I am a fifth-generation disciple with lineage tracing directly back to the Shaolin Temple in China. Had

I not left my teacher, I would have been an official lineage-holder. As lineages go, mine is impressive, but only if you are impressed by such things.

Lineage is a concept that is bandied about in the qigong community. Many teachers use it as proof that their school is superior. Their logic is that a school with a strong lineage *must* be a good one. This idea is simply not true, and everyone knows it. There are many teachers with strong lineages who you don't want to touch with a ten-foot pole. Despite their lineage, they are terrible teachers, and they produce subpar students.

This shouldn't be surprising. Imagine a skillful lineage holder who is nonetheless a bad teacher. Then imagine his successor. All the teacher's skills could easily be lost in just one generation. It's not unlike the son of a good king who, despite his lineage, is a pathetic ruler.

Meanwhile, there are other teachers who are skillful despite the lack of a strong lineage. They have no titles or certifications and yet their students get remarkable results. Maybe they learned from several teachers over the years. Maybe they also read a lot of books and blogs. And maybe they practiced more efficiently than other people.

Which would you prefer? An official lineage, or remarkable results? Obviously, most of us would choose the latter.

And yet, some people still choose lineage! People get really illogical when they talk about this stuff. For example, a few of my ex-classmates argue that I somehow lost my lineage when I left Grandmaster Liu. They believe that seventeen years of discipleship just vanished into thin air. All my skills just magically disappeared the moment I left my teacher, like Superman suddenly losing his powers. Poof!

This is the politics of lineage. I'm glad to be done with it. I will not subject my students to this kind of drama.

The truth is that lineage is quickly becoming outdated in the twenty-first century. This is a good thing because lineage is mainly there to benefit the teacher, not the student. It's a way to hoard information and keep secrets.

I don't hoard my qigong secrets. Instead, they are shared openly. In fact, a well-known qigong teacher once learned the secret of Flowing Breeze Swaying Willow from my online programs. He then rebranded it with a new name and started teaching it himself!

In the old days, this would have been considered theft. But in the twenty-first century, I say, good for him! Today, you can "steal" a dozen techniques without leaving your home. I know because I continue to learn from other teachers online and integrate their materials and wisdom. Why would I stop learning when there is a veritable buffet of qigong techniques and skills out there?

Don't get me wrong. I'm not saying that someone can just learn qigong from YouTube videos and become a master. Nor am I saying that you can just dabble with different teachers and learn everything you need. That is not my vision of twenty-first century qigong. You need to spend quality time with quality teachers, just like with any art.

But the big question for the twenty-first century is—how much time do you need to devote to each teacher? In the old days, you were expected to devote at least a decade. Often, you were expected to commit for life.

Today, that is not only unreasonable but also unnecessary. For example, I learned from one of my teachers for only twelve hours. It was a weekend workshop, about six hours on Saturday and again on Sunday. Although the master was very happy with my development during the workshop, I'm quite sure that he doesn't remember my name. Why would he? It was just one weekend.

To be fair, I also learned the same style of qigong from one of his disciples for over two years and had purchased several of the master's DVDs (remember those?). Most importantly, I practiced diligently. After ten years of practicing this type of qigong, I began to incorporate it into my teachings. Keep in mind that I was teaching Grandmaster Liu's qigong during this entire time.

I am not a lineaged disciple in this other teacher's tradition. And yet, what I learned from him is powerful, specifically a qigong set called the Twelve Qigong Treasures. Anyone who has learned this set at our school can attest to how amazing it is. It is a wonderful addition to the other types of qigong that we teach.

This is a perfect example of what the twenty-first century can look like if we move past the idea of lineage. When information is shared freely, amazing things can happen.

What's in a Style Anyway?

This brings us to the topic of various qigong styles, of which there are literally thousands. What is a style? Who gets to create one? To understand this, let's first look at the basic building blocks for all styles of qigong. The structure is as follows:

pattern → set → style

A **pattern** is a single, distinct qigong move. Usually, a pattern will have a poetic name, like Lifting the Sky or Pushing Mountains.

A **set** is an intelligent combination of patterns. Some people refer to a "set" as a "form." I think the word "form" muddles the distinction between a set and a pattern. In fact, some people refer to a pattern like Lifting the Sky as a form. Confusing, right? The word "set" is better. Here are a few examples of qigong sets: The Eight Brocades (Ba Duan Jin); Sinew Metamorphosis (Yi Jin Jing); The Eighteen Luohan Hands (Shiba Luohan Shou).

A **style** is a comprehensive methodology that includes several different sets, as well as specific training theories. Think of a style as a curriculum. For example, Shaolin Hunyuan Yi Qigong, the style that I originally learned from Grandmaster Liu, includes the sets: the Eighteen Luohan Hands, Sinew Metamorphosis (Yi Jin Jing), One Finger Zen, Golden Bridge, Cosmos Palm, Small Universe, and Big Universe. Some of the training concepts included entering a qigong state of mind, letting the qi flow spontaneously, tapping cosmic energy, and consolidating qi at the lower dantian.

If you can understand this basic structure of pattern, set, and style, then you will find it much easier to navigate the confusing world of qigong. For example, one of the reasons why it's hard to count the total number of qigong styles is because many people don't understand the hierarchy of pattern, style, and set described above. Some people think that the Eight Brocades (Ba Duan Jin) is a style of qigong, but it isn't. It's a set.

Another problem is that the Chinese tradition of secrecy makes historical study more difficult. How do we count the styles that were lost to secrecy, or that are still secret even to this day? We can't.

It's hard to count the number of qigong styles out there, but it's easy to count the ones that I myself have learned! As of this writing, I've studied and practiced the following styles of qigong:

1. Shaolin Hunyuan Yi Qigong
2. Chu Style Nei Kung
3. Yi Quan
4. Cosmic Freedom Qigong
5. Wild Goose Qigong
6. Primordial Qigong
7. Bagua Zhang
8. Dragon and Tiger Qigong
9. Zhineng Qigong
10. Wisdom Healing Qigong
11. Healing Tao Qigong
12. Spring Forest Qigong

Please understand that I did not study all these styles as deeply as #1. Shaolin Hunyuan Yi Qigong is the only style I can claim lineage to.

I did, however, practice a lot. And practicing these different styles influences me greatly, not unlike a rock musician influenced by, say, the Beatles. This kind of influence leads to innovation and discovery. In my case, everything I learned influenced the creation of what we now call Flowing Zen Qigong.

In the twenty-first century, there is resistance to innovation when it is done by a Westerner like me. People don't blink when a Chinese master makes changes to a qigong style—but when someone like me does the exact same thing, some people get their panties in a twist. For example, I once received this hilarious message in response to a blog post about qigong styles:

"I find it outrageous and disrespectful that you invented your own style of qigong. Only an arrogant American would do such a thing. No thank you! I'll stick to traditional styles like Chilel and Shibashi."

If you don't get the irony, here's why this message is so funny:

- Chilel Qigong was invented in 1995.
- Shibashi Qigong was invented in 1979.

Both are modern styles that were influenced by traditional lineages, just like Flowing Zen Qigong! The difference is that the founders of these arts are Asian. In other words, people are not really upset that I invented my own style of qigong; they're upset that I'm not Asian.

The truth is that Grandmaster Liu heavily modified the qigong that he learned from his four teachers. His teachers did the same thing. Considering how many styles of qigong there are today, this practice seems to have been common throughout history. In other words, it's likely that there is no such thing as a traditional style of qigong.

A New Era of Qigong

Today, qigong is much more widely recognized than when I first started teaching. I wouldn't go so far as to say that it's a household word like yoga yet, but awareness is growing, and that's a wonderful thing. Change takes time. It took time for yoga to become a billion-dollar, global industry. I believe that if you give qigong a little more time, it will become huge. In fact, qigong may become more popular than yoga one day.

Yoga is wonderful. I wish more people would do it. But it's not for everyone. It certainly wasn't for me. I discovered yoga before discovering qigong. My first karate teacher, Sensei Bonnie, was also a yoga teacher, so I was exposed to it as far back as 1993.

When I found qigong a few years later, I felt like I was coming home. Many students have said the same thing. There's just something about qigong that fits for us.

In the US, less than 10 percent of the population practices yoga. This is why qigong is desperately needed. The people who failed with yoga may succeed with qigong. In fact, I hear this over and over from my students: "I tried yoga, but I fell in love with qigong."

People all over the world are turning to qigong as a practical and affordable solution to the stress of modern life. As of this writing, students from forty-eight countries attend my online programs even though they are only taught in English. Imagine how many people will practice qigong when good instruction is available in their native tongue!

The future of qigong is bright. I believe that qigong will explode in popularity over the next decade. This renaissance will be driven by a growing number of forward-thinking teachers who are working hard to make qigong accessible to a larger audience. These teachers are bringing qigong out of the fog of secrecy. The twenty-first century is a chance for humanity to breathe new life into the art of qigong.

And it's not just qigong. A mindfulness revolution is sweeping the world. Qigong is part of this revolution, along with yoga, tai chi, sitting meditation, and other forms of mindfulness. This is just what the doctor ordered. I often wonder if humanity can survive another one hundred years *without* mass adoption of mindfulness. We desperately need this revolution.

We often forget that revolutions involve individuals like you and me. Inside the larger mindfulness revolution are millions of personal revolutions. My revolution started decades ago. Perhaps it started years ago in you as well. Or perhaps that revolution is new in you. Either way, here's a fantastic quotation:

> "I am inviting you to go deeper, to learn and to practice so that you become someone who has a great capacity for being solid, calm, and without fear, because our society needs people like you who have these qualities, and your children, our children, need people like you, in order to go on, in order to become solid, and calm, and without fear."
>
> —Zen Master Thich Nhat Hanh

Thich Nhat Hanh is a Vietnamese Zen monk, a global spiritual leader, and activist. He is respected around the world for his teachings on mindfulness, global ethics, and peace. Martin Luther King Jr. even nominated him for a Nobel prize! He's the real deal, folks. I encourage you to read his books, especially *Peace Is Every Step*.

I also encourage you to accept his invitation. My invitation is the same. I'm inviting you to learn and to practice because our society needs people like that. People like you.

Take a moment to imagine a lighthouse. Imagine a tall, solid structure standing on the shore. Imagine waves crashing onto the base of the lighthouse, foam spraying into the air. Imagine the lighthouse staying totally calm and centered during the darkest hour of the night, even during the most turbulent storm.

And now imagine beams of light shooting out from that lighthouse, cutting through the darkness, the rain, the wind. That is you. You are that lighthouse.

Now imagine a ship approaching during a storm. Imagine the tremendous danger it faces. Imagine the people on that ship, desperately looking for guidance, for a beam of light through the darkness. And then they see it, the light from the lighthouse sweeping through the darkness. They see you. Your light leads them out of the darkness and to safety.

I'm inviting you to become a lighthouse in the world. Do it with qigong. Do it with other mindfulness practices too. Do it with art, poetry, and music. Do it with your work and with your family. Any activity, when practiced in a way that makes you fully present, brings you closer to peace and enlightenment.

When other people are suffering, it may seem selfish or unimportant to focus on your own practice, to focus on your inner self. But it's not. It's the opposite of selfishness, and it's exactly what the world needs. It's the steady grounded calmness of the lighthouse that is so powerful. If you were to try to sail out to meet the ships during a storm, you might end up in danger yourself. Those ships don't need you to join them in the storm. They need your light on the shore, and this is what will elevate them and what will show them the way to safety.

Maybe another analogy will help. When I was sixteen, I trained to become a certified lifeguard. Many people think that lifeguards learn to dive into the pool or the ocean to rescue someone who's drowning. That works on TV, but it's not how we do it in real life. In real life, the absolute *last* resort is to get in the water.

First, we try to reach them with a floatation device, or a pole. If that doesn't work, then we bring a floatation device into the water with us. We keep it between us and the person who is drowning, and we do this because people who are drowning are dangerous. They flail and kick and scream and they will grab on to anything that comes near them—especially you. If you are not skillful, both of you will drown.

The point is this—rushing out to save people, or to save the world, isn't a good strategy. Whether you prefer the lighthouse analogy or the lifeguard analogy or a combination of both—I hope that the message is clear. If you want to help heal the world, then start with yourself.

Heal yourself first, and then you can start to make a difference in the world. The old airline analogy of putting the oxygen mask on yourself first before placing it on another is apt here. That's exactly what we are doing when we practice qigong.

A World with Better Qi Flow

After practicing qigong for a few weeks, you'll start to feel the qi flowing in your hands and arms. With more practice, you'll feel rivers of qi flowing through other parts of your body—your legs, your torso, your head. Eventually, swirls of concentrated qi— almost like tiny, spinning galaxies—will begin to consolidate in the energy centers of your body, especially the lower dantian.

But this is not the end goal of qigong. The end goal is to let the qi flow not just through your own body, but out into the world. You become a locus of good energy. The energy of the cosmos flows not just into you, but *through* you. It manifests in your thoughts and actions, and thus moves back out into the world.

I want you to be happier and healthier, and qigong is a powerful tool to realize that. But I also want something else. After you've healed yourself to a certain degree, I want your vibrant qi to flow out into the world and help others.

I'm not talking about you walking around projecting qi to everyone you meet. Please don't do that until you are a master of qigong, and even then, do it selectively or else you will drain your reserves. Rather, I'm talking about projecting your qi through your daily actions.

Project your qi by smiling at the cashier. Smile from the heart and connect with this other human in front of you. Look them in the eye, be gentle, and wish them well.

Project your qi by listening deeply to a friend in need. This ain't easy. You'll need steady mindfulness to simply listen without judgment, to be fully present, and to empathize with this person's suffering.

Project your qi into your work. Whatever you do, whether you are a nurse, a teacher, a programmer, an administrator, or a stay-at-home mom or dad, put your heart and your energy into your work. Do the same with your creative work.

And finally, go out and do some good. Use your extra energy to do something out of your normal routine. Volunteer. Donate money to a charity. Pet a dog. Be kind to a stranger.

I started my qigong journey as someone who could barely take care of himself. I was suffering so deeply that I wanted to escape through suicide. Today, I'm privileged to help thousands of students from all over the globe. I give to several charities, offer scholarships to my programs, and of course, pet dogs as often as I can.

This is the path that I encourage you to take with qigong. Start with yourself, then gradually widen your influence. Go from the personal level, to the local level, to the national level, and eventually to the global level. Be patient and eventually your good vibrations will ripple out into the world.

Maybe you have an idea for a business or an activity that could really help your fellow humans. Maybe you've had this idea for years, but you've been afraid to implement it. Once your qi is flowing better, you'll have the impetus and strength to go out there and make it happen.

Maybe your new energy levels will spark an amazing idea. You suddenly envision an invention, a community project, a restaurant, or a book that will help people. As the saying goes, talk is cheap. What matters is following through and turning an idea into reality. To do this, you'll need lots of qi.

Are you starting to see how healing yourself is the best way to heal the world? Start with yourself, with your own energy, and make it healthy and vibrant. Then take your beautiful energy and share it with the world.

Let's return to that Wang Fu quote from the beginning of the book:

> "If you want to awaken all of humanity, then awaken all of yourself. If you want to eliminate the suffering in the world, then eliminate all that is dark and negative in yourself. Truly, the greatest gift you have to give is that of your own self-transformation."

Qigong is not the only path of self-transformation, but it can be a magical one. For me and thousands of my students, qigong is a beautiful way to transform our lives and our world. I invite you to take this path. I hope that this book has given you a map of the terrain, and also inspired you to act. Whether that means starting fresh with qigong, or taking your existing qigong to a new level, keep qigonging on!

Inaction and Self-Help

S elf-help books are awesome. Maybe you've read a bunch of them. I know I have. I love reading and wish more people would make it a habit. I applaud you for finishing this book. High five!

But I also know what happens when folks get to the end of a self-help book. Even if the book is amazing, even if it inspired them to make big changes in their life, what usually happens is . . . very little. They don't take action and frequently don't implement the wisdom offered in the book. A few ideas may circulate in their head and their heart for a few weeks, but after that, they just move on to the next book.

If you want to transform your life, then you must avoid this trap. For example, if you simply read through a healthy cookbook, but never actually cook even a single meal, then you won't get any healthier. The trick—and it's a hard one—is to cook something. Get yourself into the kitchen and make something. Even if you botch the recipe and the food tastes awful, you still took action. And that, my dear reader, is what really matters.

Before you set this book down and forget about it, I'm encouraging you to act. If this book resonated with you, if you think that my teaching might be a good fit for you, then go get your book bonuses already: www.flowingzen.com/bookbonus

Or if you've already gotten your bonuses, then good for you. I hope you're starting with two minutes a day. If that's all that happens, if all you do is practice qigong for two minutes a day, then that's wonderful. Maybe you're the type who will need to put this book down for a while, practice your two minutes a day, and let things simmer.

It starts with two minutes. You can do that. You can do two minutes a day. And then, a few months or even a few years from now, I hope you'll pick this book up again. And perhaps then, you will upgrade from two minutes to the Five-Phase Routine.

Qigong is a gateway habit. When you start practicing qigong, other healthy habits start to fall into place as if by magic. This happens over and over with my students. After beginning their qigong journey, they suddenly start making healthier food choices, they exercise more, they drink less, and they sleep better. All of this happens without much effort. Many of these people made these changes simply by practicing two minutes of qigong per day. So don't think for a moment that two minutes can't change your life.

Don't forget this is precisely how I started. I began with two minutes a day and built from there. Along the way, I also built other good habits like starting to go to bed earlier and eating better, and I eventually used qigong to quit smoking.

I love Lao Tzu, so let's end with his most famous quotation.

"The journey of a thousand miles begins beneath your feet."

Your qigong journey begins right beneath your feet.
Bon voyage!

ACKNOWLEDGMENTS

A book is not created by one person. I'm grateful to everyone who helped, directly or indirectly, to bring this project to completion.

I'm grateful to my parents for always supporting me, especially by investing in training and education, even when money was tight. I don't play the violin or tennis these days, but years of lessons taught me the art of practicing. Whatever level of mastery I have achieved in qigong really began at age five with my parents' decision to pay for violin lessons.

I'm grateful to three of my high school teachers: Cliff Cobb, Carolee Kamin, and Bill Reilly. I've never had better writing teachers, not even at Columbia.

I'm grateful to Professor Ted Tayler for teaching me why we really read books.

I'm grateful to Azul and Kim and the entire publishing team at Authors Who Lead. They were patient beyond reason and helped to create a book that I'm proud of.

I'm grateful to Rama and Adelaida for building and growing such an amazing retreat center in Costa Rica. La Montaña Azul is not only paradise on Earth, it's also the perfect place for true healing.

I'm grateful to Sensei Bonnie Baker for introducing me to the martial arts. She taught me more than just the fundamentals of karate; she also taught me the fundamentals of teaching.

I'm grateful to Grandmaster Liu for teaching me, in an unexpected way, what integrity really is.

I'm grateful to Dr. Eric Robins for his foreword, his edits, and his encouragement.

I'm grateful to Sensei Teruo Chinen for giving me my first glimpse into the world of internal martial arts.

I'm grateful to Sifus Yang Jwing Ming, C. K. Chu, Bruce Frantzis, Bingkun Hu, William C. C. Chen, Park Bok Nam, and Yap Soon-Yeong, all of whom influenced me even though they probably wouldn't remember me.

I'm grateful to Melissa Coast, who is not only a good friend but also the world's best assistant. I truly do not know how I managed for so long without her help.

And finally, I'm grateful for my doggo, Sgt. Pepper, for snuggling with me through the worst of times.

ABOUT THE AUTHOR
Anthony Korahais

Anthony Korahais is a master qigong teacher and a healing success story. He has been practicing qigong since 1996 and teaching full time since 2005. His website, flowingzen.com, hosts one of the most popular qigong blogs on the internet. Anthony has thousands of students worldwide and has certified over forty qigong instructors.

Fed up with his low back pain, depression, anxiety, and chronic fatigue, Anthony began searching for a long-term solution. In his twenties, he discovered a book about an ancient Chinese self-healing art called qigong (pronounced "chee gung"). Convinced that this art was exactly what he needed in order to heal, he travelled the world in search of teachers, eventually completing a seventeen-year discipleship under a Chinese grandmaster.

After nearly a decade in business, Anthony closed his brick-and-mortar qigong studio in order to focus on sharing this art with the entire world. Today, his online programs have over ten thousand students from forty-eight countries.

Originally from New York City and a graduate of Columbia University, he now lives in Florida with his miniature schnauzer, Sgt. Pepper.

I would appreciate your feedback on what chapters helped you most and what you would like to see in future books.

If you enjoyed this book and found it helpful, please leave a REVIEW on Amazon.

Visit me at

WWW.FLOWINGZEN.COM

where you can sign up for email updates.

And remember to get your book bonuses at

WWW.FLOWINGZEN.COM/BOOKBONUS

or scan the QR code below:

THANK YOU!